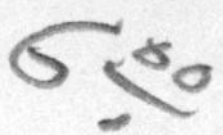

AN INTRODUCTION TO LEGAL SYSTEMS

AUSTRALIA
The Law Book Company Ltd.
Sydney Melbourne Brisbane

GREAT BRITAIN
Sweet & Maxwell Ltd.
London

INDIA
N. M. Tripathi Private Ltd.
Bombay

ISRAEL
Steimatzky's Agency Ltd.
Jerusalem Tel Aviv Haifa

NEW ZEALAND
Sweet & Maxwell (N.Z.) Ltd.
Wellington

PAKISTAN
Pakistan Law House
Karachi

U.S.A. AND CANADA
Frederick A. Praeger Inc.
New York Washington

AN INTRODUCTION TO LEGAL SYSTEMS

Edited by

J. DUNCAN M. DERRETT

FREDERICK A. PRAEGER, *Publishers*
New York · Washington

BOOKS THAT MATTER

Published in the United States of America in 1968
by Frederick A. Praeger, Inc., Publishers
111 Fourth Avenue, New York, N.Y. 10003

Library of Congress Catalog Card Number 68–31830

Printed in Great Britain

CONTENTS

PREFACE

PROFESSIONALLY the law student seldom has any need to know foreign systems of law. Conflicts of law arise (a topic in which he usually interests himself readily), but in practice, as often as not, a specialist in that class of work is consulted. But while the student is a student he participates in education. Much of that process, inevitably, consists in memorising rules and learning how to apply them. But what is it all about? The answer must be much the same in principle whether one asks in London, in Buenos Aires, in Cairo, or Sydney. To elicit the answer doubtless one must find the wavelength, as it were, on which one's informant communicates; but what he attempts to tell relates broadly to the same complex of factors against which litigation has to be seen. A law exists in relation to litigation (actual or hypothetical), just as answers must be taken to operate in relation to their questions.

A very common starting-point is that of the Roman jurist Gaius, whose initial proposition expresses not only the Roman outlook but one very frequently found among us too:

> 'The laws of every people governed by statutes and customs are partly peculiar to itself, partly common to all mankind. The rules established by a given state for its own members are peculiar to itself, and are called *ius civile* (civil law); the rules constituted by natural reason for all human beings are observed amongst all nations equally, and are called *ius gentium* (the law of peoples), for this law applies to all peoples. So the laws of the people of Rome are partly peculiar to itself and partly common to all mankind. . . .'

But, when we do look into the laws of peoples removed from the Mediterranean in space and from the Roman epoch in time do we really find this proposition justified, beyond trivialities? Professor R. Dekkers' *Le Droit Privé des Peuples* (Brussels, 1953) was an attempt to test Gaius' principle, and of course it left very little substance in the idea, which in fact is illusory. What law is *about* is much the same the world over. How it does its work, both in principle and in detail, is an unexpectedly diversified story.

Some of the systems of law dealt with in this book are usually called 'religious.' Since a misunderstanding is very likely, a careful preliminary enquiry is called for into the relations between religion and law. The subject is deep and cannot be handled in a Preface,[1] but at least a warning can be given. It is one thing to talk about 'religious laws' when what we

[1] In 1951 a colloquium was held at Cologne on the theme, 'The religious elements in the laws of oriental and primitive peoples.' The papers covering early cultures (including Micronesia and pre-Columbian Mexico) and oriental laws (Islamic law, the

mean is a situation in which a system of law is chosen to apply to an individual because of the social community to which he belongs, identified by its common religious designation: it is another to say that the law applied to him is derived from his, or anyone else's religion. It has proved easy for the Anglo-Saxon mind to comprehend the notion that laws are applied to people because of their religion, but the essential difference between the nominal religion for the purpose of selection of the rule and the actual religion as a matter of the individual conscience seems often to elude us.

One must avoid the error of supposing that any true law is based on religion or philosophy as such. This cannot be, any more than the size of my feet is based on the size of my shoes. Religious impulses do not operate in a vacuum, nor indeed do anti-religious impulses. They are expressed through psychological patterns which are themselves called up by hereditary and environmental factors. In practice, indeed, injunctions which are religious (or superstitious—we shall not distinguish between the two terms) are found side by side with legal provisions in many an old law book: this is not because the author could not distinguish between the two, but because in his society the binding nature of the two classes of injunction was nearly indistinguishable, so that for practical purposes both had to be taken into account. One may test the matter best by asking whether any act which is legally exacted ceases to be so when those who exact it or those from whom it is exacted (but not both of them) cease to have the relevant philosophical or religious belief. What is exacted in the name of religion is usually required for other purposes than the religious,[2] and it is small wonder that the progress of civilisation which has loosened the bonds of

[2] The ancient Indian jurist Brihaspati says: 'The cultivator who pays a sixth part to the king, a twentieth to the gods and a thirtieth to Brahmins is guiltless,' *i.e.*, he is freed from the sin of injuring living beings in the course of agriculture. Is this spiritual blackmail? The cultivator did not share the squeamishness of his Brahmin preceptors. The king was entitled to his sixth for 'protection' (see below, p. 96); and temples and charitable endowments were essential social services. For a law to be religious in the sense that law is founded upon religion both those who enforce and those from whom it is enforced must share the religious belief; but the notion of enforcing that which is a religious belief (though our more socially minded ancestors once accepted it) is really an absurdity. When William Lambard, in his *Eirenarcha* (London, 1582), compiled the law as it then fell to be administered by the Justices of the Peace within a scheme based on the Ten Commandments, he was not asserting that the law of England was founded on the positive law of God (though he believed it was consistent with it), but relying upon the Elizabethan anxiety to re-create, without papal supremacy, the medieval belief that society was one, and that the spiritual and temporal powers were mutually supporting and indispensable. We may compare the curious maxim *cuius regio eius religio*, which, if it made a mockery of religion in Europe, was at least practical. How the social need for religious conformity has declined in purely legal terms can be observed in, for example, G. D. Nokes' *A History of the Crime of Blasphemy* (London, 1928).

customs of the Beduin, and Chinese law) were published by K. Bünger and H. Trimborn under the title *Religiöse Bindungen in frühen und in orientalischen Rechten* (Weisbaden, Harrassowitz, 1952). This was a pioneering enterprise in comparative law. It is unfortunate that Julius Stone's *Human Law and Human Justice* (London, Stevens, 1965), which bears so comprehensive a title, makes no significant mention of Hindu, Chinese, or Islamic contributions to the search for justice (a reference to Indian traditions at p. 284 is unfortunate). Copious references to Hebrew notions of law and justice appear in such a guise as to suggest to a hasty reader that Jewish law was 'western'!

society and correspondingly increased the initiative and independence of the individual (who alone is the focus of religion) has at the same time diminished the scope of compulsion in religious contexts.

Religion may support a prudent expedient (and for this there are good examples both in Islamic and Hindu jurisprudence)—but that is a very different matter. The harnessing of a legal concept to the powerful machine of religious aspiration is a shrewd, though one would hardly say invariably a spontaneous, move. It is the work of the juridical mind. To utilise the appeal of the religious motive, to base reforms or restatements of law upon superstitious fears, cannot be dismissed as disingenuous or fraudulent: it was a question of finding the key to a lock which a great many people wanted opened.

In general, people's arguments and ideas suit and usually betray their temperaments and their desires. Have we ever heard a man preaching a doctrine which did not suit his personal interests? A man's image of the Divinity tends to accord with his own personality, sometimes with anomalous results. An objective judgment is possible, but its author must mentally step aside from his creed. Many grasp these facts, but it is necessary to bear them in mind when thinking about legal systems, which, though they are dry and sometimes repel, have personalities and colours like any other thing which human beings have created.

The philosophy or philosophies connected with a legal system, and indeed the religion itself, represent or voice the customs, usages, and aspirations of the people or peoples, not vice versa. This is why there are territorial and/or social branches or schools both of religion and law, a curiosity which it would otherwise be difficult to account for. Thus law as law students know it is indeed often coloured by and informed by the motives, ideals, ethics, categories, and still more the self-conscious learned tradition of the society; and to that extent the formal language and detailed reasonings of the law reflect and derive from the spirit of the age or, more often, of its immediate predecessor, and from their philosophical conclusions and spiritual convictions (if any)—but all law is based upon what people accept, acquiesce in, or want, and upon what they collectively find, by experience, works.

The notion that in oriental societies relatively immune from western influence law is derived from religion is deeply ingrained. It is difficult to shake off the mistaken notions of our former teachers on this subject. Even if one takes, for example, the rules against usury in Jewish and Islamic law, or the rule in Islamic law that a gift is not completed without a transfer of possession, and even if one is convinced that these rules are not due to religion but, on the contrary, in the first place to a primitive view of the need for reciprocity in a compact society, and, in the second place, to somewhat primitive canons of evidence, the suspicion still remains that adherence to such rules may be traced to (as distinct from 'enjoined by') the religion. The improbability of this we have already stated: it is rather the case that religion suits society than that society has to suit the religion. But there is an indication that this very point was observed in very ancient times in one oriental society in which religion certainly played some role in the development of law, and the indication should be illuminating. The Hindus, whose legal system was always a 'prestige-symbol' among the numerous social groups which had different levels of civilisation and a wide variety of religious beliefs and practices, naturally gave earnest thought to this matter.

As will be found repeated below, injunctions were conceived by the Hindus as of two main types, the *drishtārtha* and the *a-drishtārtha*. The first was a class of commands the purposes of which were obvious, 'seen,' usually matters of prudence and common sense. The reason for the injunction was practical. The second class comprised those commands the reason for which was not evident. For example, rules regarding diplomacy and home politics would be *drishtārtha*, whereas the more elaborate rules of prohibited degrees for marriage, the dietary laws, and rules regarding worship would be *adrishtārtha*: they *had* their reasons, but these were esoteric, arcane, and not strictly practical. There was also a third class, having both characteristics: the rule that a student must carry a staff of a particular length and wood subserved both purposes, a ritual one, and a practical one (he might, after he had finished begging for his teacher and fellow-students, be an object of interest to bandits). Again the rules relating to adoptions were *drishtādrishtārtha*, belonging to both categories, since the adopted son performed spiritual *and* secular functions in his new family. Furthermore, there were injunctions of a purely logical character, going back ultimately to natural reason; and there were those which repeated something already known from the Vedic literature (for example, what might be the reward for meritorious actions).

Now the interesting point is that the leading text on the subject assures us that all five categories are 'rooted in the Veda,' that is to say, they are authorised ultimately by the Veda, the final corpus of transcendental knowledge and authority for the Hindu, *except* the first category: the injunctions which have a 'seen,' practical purpose or reason behind them, though found in the *dharmaśāstra*, the sacred law, do not have Vedic authority. The social norm requires obedience to all the rules (if possible), but religion as such does not purport to be the source of all the vast array of practical injunctions, among which almost all the civil and criminal law will be found as well as the rules relating to home government and international relations.

The reader will appreciate that this was a shrewd idea. Orthodox tradition tells us that the Veda does not *enjoin* anything which human nature and normal appetites in any case suggest. If the *drishtārtha* injunctions are not founded in religion the general requirements of moral rectitude, though not forgotten, are somewhat relaxed—questions of expediency have greater scope. In 'unseen' matters such flexibility is not tolerated. If an 'unseen' rule is broken—even for good reasons—a penance must be performed. Ancient Indian learning thus confirms that the greater part of law as we know it was not founded in religion. There was, however, a strong suasive force in all elements of the *dharmaśāstra*, which every Hindu was expected to reverence, whether or not he was able to carry out its precepts to the letter.

We are, meanwhile, unable to account for the cleavage (and it is a cleavage transcending individual psychologies) between the western, secular legal systems, in which even fundamentals are empirical and which make not even a pretence of attributing law to a superhuman force, and the oriental systems, which (if one makes the appropriate, limited reservations in the case of China) deny the competence of a human legislature. Western ideas of business cannot cope with the notion that 'usury' is morally abhorrent—and the tricks which modern Islamic and orthodox Jewish (as also medieval Italian) lawyers used in order to evade the issue disgust rather than amuse us. Perhaps we have a little more sympathy with the religious rejection of birth-control and abortion as methods of regulating population; but our premise is a belief in individual freedom, whereas with them it is a holy horror. As our own ideas penetrate and begin to permeate their world they suffer distress, and conflicts arise for which we are paying (the closure of the Suez Canal in 1967 may well be an example, and it could be argued that the long story of 'Vietnam' could be read in this way). It would be agreeable to be able to account for this division between the two main systems of ethics and law, if only to assess how soon, and at what cost, a balance can be achieved, and incidentally to discover at what risk we ourselves can begin to sympathise with their ideas.

But no explanation is forthcoming, and we are thrown back on speculation. Perhaps geography and history will supply the key. It is, after all, not unlikely that the stable societies living in predictable climatic and agricultural environments will suppose that behaviour and law must conform to patterns which the Creator himself pre-determined. Babylonia and Assyria, which unquestionably influenced the Jewish civilisation and through it Islam, may have had this in common with ancient Egypt and the ancient Ganges Valley: whereas the forests, the swamps, and seas of northern Europe, the unpredictable weather and harsh habitat placed nothing but a man's family, blood-kin, and tribe between him and disaster. A more democratic and empirical approach to behaviour, and a greater inclination to experiment would be only natural under such conditions.

After centuries of battling with the elements, after literally the survival of the fittest, our formerly barbarous ancestors received Christianity as in some senses a recall to a more spiritual past. The notion that righteousness transcended customs, that there was a law above warriors and chieftains, was accepted at the spiritual level. On the political level it did not sink deep, and, whatever lip service may be paid to Law as something transcending day-to-day business, in fact Europe and the parts of the world colonised from Europe do not believe[3] that conscience and law are the same thing: quite the contrary. That in England a system of law could grow up which frankly needed a separate jurisdiction to enforce the requirements of

[3] It is said that the individualist concept of law arose in Europe in the fourteenth century (M. Villey, *Cours d'histoire de la philosophie du droit*, fasc. 2, Paris, 1963); that which preceded it possessed features allowing more ground common to eastern and western systems. It is arguable that what we conceive as 'individualist' is fundamentally egalitarian as opposed to authoritarian, and in this the ancient Romans (as opposed to those of the Principate) and the northern tribal peoples may have had more in common than is usually supposed.

conscience tells its own story. But we cannot pursue this theme. It is enough to realise that the differences between secular and religious concepts of law go far deeper than intellectual conviction, and if we are to grasp them we have to be concerned with much more than rules and what can be found set out in law-books.

It is doubtful whether anything is gained by concentrating on law as a technique divorced from righteousness. There is, on the contrary, a certain maturity in treating law only as one method of achieving the latter. This enables the ancient Indian jurist Yājñavalkya to say, somewhat tartly, that all *dharma* (which kings must uphold) amounts to nothing but the sum total of 'truthfulness, abstention from stealing, abstention from anger, modesty, purity, discrimination, courage, tranquillity, subjugation of the sense-organs, and right knowledge'—and that any search for esteem or status which neglects this is fruitless.

Meanwhile the notion that the various legal systems are riveted in watertight compartments capable of being visited only by adepts in their respective mysteries dates from the early nineteenth century. Sir Thomas More's *Utopia* (1516) shows how flexible the English practitioner's mind could be in the Renaissance. By 1800 the case-hardened oddities of the common-law system were ripe for Benthamite sarcasms. The French had indeed cleared their decks, and might enact new laws at their pleasure (turning to an international jurisprudence for the purpose), and English jurists could effectively discuss reforms for adventurous France or for rebel America; but the prestige of the law relating to descent of land and settlements of property only emphasised the seeming impossibility of a two-way traffic in ideas, or at least the impractibility of opening English doors to successful pioneering achievements. None but the aristocracy could entertain thoughts of reform, and no reforms were taken up which could, in any way, however indirect, threaten the security of the aristocracy. An *apparent* exception to post-Revolutionary inhibitions would be the mid-century reforms which still further reduced the scope in England of the ecclesiastical law; but the latter was, in fact, basically foreign in origin.

This relatively recent insularity hindered the continuance of what had been a long tradition of comparative legal study. Formerly Englishmen, too, had been willing to learn the civil law, the common Romano-Canonical system of western Europe, the only language in which international negotiations could for long be conducted. That system gave them, apart from the courts of the Church, a great part of their Admiralty law (some of which survives) and the minute, but still interesting, law of Chivalry.[4] The civil-law system, strengthened by theoretical adventures into Natural Law, had made its contributions in turn to equity, especially during the first half of the eighteenth century. Chancery lawyers then talked a language more civilised than that spoken in the courts of King's Bench or the Common Pleas. In the age of Blackstone and of the later popularisers of civil law an education through law irrespective of any apprenticeship at law began to be sought after—as in some measure it still is. English transla-

[4] G. D. Squibb, *The High Court of Chivalry* (Oxford, 1959). The Court sat as recently as 1955.

tions of the works of the French Jurist Domat and the German Puffendorf went through many editions, and lawyers bought them. Colquhoun's four-volume *Summary of the Roman Civil Law* (London, 1849), a work which incidentally deplored the abolition of the slave-trade, and Bowyer's *Commentaries on the Modern Civil Law* (London, 1848) testify to the survival in some measure of a belief that all law was not common law and statute, and to the emergence, with the then recently improved jurisdiction of the Judicial Committee of the Privy Council, of responsibility towards the complex legal heritage of the nuclei of the future Commonwealth.

One may wonder whether now a man can call himself educated who, having studied, for example, English law for three years goes into the world as a 'lawyer' and has never heard of other systems of law. The present editor once asked a London law graduate what he thought of Indian law, and this was the answer: 'I really don't know anything about it, but I presume they mostly follow English law. I suppose the natives may stick to some bits of their ancient systems where their religions are involved.... You know, like not eating cows...?' In other words those parts that matter are likely to be as similar to ours as makes little significant difference, and those that are 'religious' are unlike ours, and so fit to be ignored. But, provided the target for the unexpected question is young enough, ignorance rather presages than repudiates a readiness to learn, and this book is intended to help.

The conflicts between the outlooks induced by different systems of law and morality can come home to us unexpectedly. India and England share the legal remedy known as 'restitution of conjugal rights.' There is some doubt whether it has any useful function to perform in England. Among Hindus in India it is still a real remedy. Hindus in England must understand it as it is understood here. A Hindu wife coming straight to England to enforce her rights against her erring husband who has become domiciled there will run up against the, to her, incredible fact that a deserted wife, with a decree for restitution in her hand, has no right to her husband's society against his will, and may be restrained by injunction from disturbing his peace and quiet. English law protects his 'concubine' in a way that Indian law would hardly do, and Indian customs of our day would not. The learned judge in *Nanda* v. *Nanda*[5] recognised that Indian ideas explained the wife's behaviour: it is doubtful whether anyone could explain to her why English law could not give her back a husband whom she had lost through no fault of her own. Such contrasts in outlook cannot but multiply, and it is time that basic information on such matters was more readily available to practitioners as well as to students.

The systems of jurisprudence chosen for treatment in this book were chosen because they are historic. 'Historic' does not mean 'dead.' Even the Roman law, as we shall see, whose roots lie in a civilisation which has passed away, is in very real senses alive, even if the life it now enjoys could more appropriately be called a reincarnation. These systems are coherent, possess a unity, and have made their marks on the world. They have passed the test of time. Yet it happens that citizens of countries which are governed

[5] [1967] 3 All E.R. 401.

largely in consonance with traditional, ageless juridical principles are tempted to adopt methods and accept standards developed relatively recently where the bond between what ought to be done and what must be done has long been broken (if it ever existed). Here it is reasonably easy to get away with behaviour which the older civilisations do not tolerate, greater burdens being forced thereby upon the law itself. An awareness of the broad features of the competing systems is obviously desirable, and it is high time we knew more of them, especially in their confrontation with our own ideas.

The common law, itself of great age, has spread throughout the English-speaking world. Its effects in non-western jurisdictions, such as Burma and Mauritius, have been deep. Its effectiveness in Malta has recently provoked judicial animadversions in London. But in Africa the present movement to combine or reconcile western-type law and indigenous laws is being led by the French, Portuguese, and English modes of legislation, and there are no signs that one of the latter gives way to another. Similarly, in Louisiana and Quebec the modern representative of Roman law fully holds its own with the common law. And what of Scotland? Her long integral association with England has hardly weaned her from her civilian jurisprudence, and one wonders whether the latter can ever be eroded by the growth of statute and other law common to both England and Scotland. The real virtues of the common law make themselves felt more subtly, as we shall see.[6]

In choosing the systems that have contributed most to experience and education we have had to leave aside laws of great age and academic importance, those of the Ancient Near East, for example, and laws peculiar to countries of very involved juridical history, such as those of Japan and Turkey. Customary laws of antiquity which have not survived in any prominence and have made no contribution to the central systems must also be passed over. The juridical doctrines of the Soviet Union and other communist countries depart in many respects from the post-classical Romanic tradition, which (in contrast with the common law) has in any case favoured absolutist or totalitarian tendencies. These have hardly been given scope here, not because we have evaluated the theories or their effects, but because they lack the depth given by undisputed maturity.

After settling which systems should be explored, and at what level of generalisation, the next question—a more delicate one—was how to explore them.

An English-speaking student of average curiosity might be interested to meet in turn, as fellow lawyers, a jurisconsult (if one could be resurrected for the purpose), a *mufti*, a rabbi, a pandit, or indeed a representative of any one of our legal systems. He would have questions to ask them: whether in their view the state ought to be liable for the torts of its servants,

[6] It is argued, for example, by Dr. R. A. Marchant, that the common lawyers exaggerated in the seventeenth century and onwards the failings of the administration of justice in the English ecclesiastical courts, which applied canon law with the Romano-Canonical style of procedure, pleading, and proof. Yet the actual working of the formerly international system within England never gained Englishmen's entire confidence. A process which contemplated a man's being obliged to incriminate himself was only one of many possible points of attack. The victory of the common law, though conceivably won by interested and disingenuous critics of the civil law, unquestionably met the needs of the people.

whether it should compensate the victims of crime, whether capital punishment should be retained, whether divorce should be allowed by mutual consent of the spouses. But such questions might have little meaning for his new friends, whose concepts of the 'state' (to go no further) would not necessarily agree with his, nor with each other. Our imaginary enquirer would soon be equipped to foresee misunderstandings, and he might indeed be able to undergo re-education in law at the hands of these informants. He might be disappointed to find few of them as curious about his system as he is about theirs, but he would soon find points of contact and comparison and teach himself how to learn from them. Now no doubt he would prefer to hear about a foreign system of law in the terms used by that system itself. But this involves the hearer in an effort of translation, and that too of much more than words. The nuances of each legal literature, and its presuppositions, are seldom set forth for the foreigner's assistance. No system appears to have a built-in cultural dictionary and guide. Whatever difficulties the qualified man would have, those of the beginner are bound to be daunting.

And yet it is the beginner who needs to know where his own national system of law fits into the pattern created by the seven systems as a consortium. There is little point in exploring the minutiae of one's own system if one has hardly grasped that it is itself only one of a group of intensely developed attempts to effectuate justice amongst human beings. It is only one method, agreeing perhaps with others in many places (as one would expect), yet disagreeing in many ways, ways of varying significance and importance—some apparently fundamental.

This book attempts to show the beginner what the specialists would say to him if they spoke his language, knowing his limitations and anticipating his curiosity. The common law, under its historically accurate title 'English law,' has been redescribed for him in rather greater detail and reappraised. If the result interests him he can move on to other treatments, more full and perhaps unashamedly professional. To help him, short reading lists have been given, the contents of which have been so chosen as to enable him to meet experts writing about aspects of law which matter.

Many teachers will be reminded of Rabbi K. Kahana Kagan's *Three Great Systems of Jurisprudence* (London, Stevens, 1955), in which salient features of the Roman, English and Jewish law were compared, at times to the disadvantage of the first two. The learned rabbi's work was more elaborate, and yet its scope was somewhat narrower. He did not seek to further our acquaintance with other systems, one of which (the African) he might not, on his premises, have recognised as a system at all. The contributors in this present volume have not as a matter of policy eschewed evaluation, especially in relation to social change; but it was thought undesirable to use the word 'great,' which might imply that other ancient and effective systems were in some way less than great.

Perhaps the best-known introduction to comparative jurisprudence is the range of works of Sir Henry S. Maine, especially his celebrated *Ancient Law* (written in 1858). Maine was a man with a brilliant flair.[7] Well

[7] See *The Juridical Review*, April 1959, pp. 40–55.

acquainted with the claims of the common law and equity, he asserted with vigour the educational as well as practical value of exploring the spirit and rules of other legal systems. An unintended by-product of his technique was that after him English lawyers, at any rate, doubted whether deeper research could be helpful to the general reader. Maine's ideas about Indian law, which play an ever-increasing role in his books, were, until almost the end of his writing, naïve. The plausible picture which he paints fits, perhaps not altogether unconsciously, the growing imperialistic and missionary quality of English public life. It is high time that while we admit his status as a pioneer, and admire his mellifluous style, we substitute for his bland suggestions information such as is demanded both by more recent discoveries and by the concerns of our own day.

Our book should end with a question-mark. Does the future offer us more and better law, more or fewer divergencies between the systems, or even a deliberate rejection of law and all that it implies? This book will come into the hands of future members of the 'Establishment,' and also of those who will eschew it. Both will agree, we may confidently suppose, that the Rule of Law, the concept that the individual must not be at the mercy of his society or any part in it, and that honesty and fair play must at all times protect him, in the last resort through the judicial process, is not yet firmly established in all parts of the world.[8] In times of stress even mature nations, and otherwise respectable persons, are tempted into misbehaviour. This kind of mischief, though (as yet) not all others, is gradually being seen as potentially, if not also actually, *unlawful*: a considerable advance. The capacity to sympathise with the other man, a quality of civilisation as it is distinguished from barbarism, must with ever-increasing efficiency turn itself from a mere benevolence into a practical and systematic implementation. The basic question is whether that recognisably human creature, not our friend at the material moment, comes within the principle conveyed by the words 'Love thy neighbour as thyself.'[9]

If this prudent principle is applied most problems dissolve. If *my* rights are no greater than *his*, except by that margin (if any) which he himself has properly created in my favour, many, if not most, causes of conflict vanish. The trouble must arise from my failure to esteem his needs equal to my own. The working out of that equality still requires the judicial process with all its trappings. In reality, it requires something more.

It was not from London, nor from New York or Moscow, that the principle derived, this articulation of the dumb knowledge possessed by every individual in normal balance and health. It came ultimately from the religious conscience of ancient Israel, which sought to put it into effect within the confines of the nation itself. The true definition of 'neighbour' as 'he for whom the normal man feels instinctive sympathy at the most simple level, *i.e.*, every human being in need of what he can supply,' came not from our great Universities, but from an Asian scholar and leader, Jesus

[8] The series of reports published by the International Commission of Jurists (in their *Bulletin* and elsewhere) as the fruit of impartial enquiries into the failure of elementary principles of justice especially at political crises throughout the world stands as eloquent testimony to recurrent moral weakness irrespective of race, colour, or creed.

[9] *The Holy Bible*, *Leviticus*, xix. 18.

of Nazareth.[10] His positive teaching, 'All things therefore whatsoever ye would that men should do unto you, even so do ye also unto them: for this is (the teaching of) the Law and the Prophets,'[11] is the Golden Rule (often stated in the negative form, 'Do not do unto others . . .'), which he did not originate, for it existed, amongst other places, in the Code of Yājñavalkya (III, 65), which draws on very ancient material. It is not a timeless platitude,[12] but a challenge which is still largely unhonoured.

The great claims made upon the non-common-law world by the common law, with its assurance of freedom from exploitation or perversion of justice, are founded on the hypothesis that it puts the Golden Rule into practice. If the claim is well founded it is bound to influence other cultures and to hold up a mirror to other techniques. It is bound to penetrate, and has already penetrated, into juridical fastnesses where anything specifically English might have small claims as such. In so far as it has succeeded it has done so by its merit, and because the Rule of Law, often inconvenient to the 'Establishment' and to the 'Party,' is *true* in so far as it protects the individuals from among whom even Establishments are made up. *Dharma* (righteousness and law), as the Indian sages said long before Christ, *Dharma*, when protected, protects, for by it the weak overcome the strong.

But we have not done with the future if we merely hope that the Rule of Law will one day be universal. We must eliminate litigation between individuals in favour of reconciliation by an impartial agency charged with the wholesome duty of recalling citizens to their moral responsibilities.

As society became more complex and diversified we lost those comprehensive enquiries which we once had at the manor and hundred level and which were normal in oriental and African settings until very much later. At that stage it was practicable to review the personal records and merits of the parties to a dispute. It was practicable to determine whether those who asked for equity really *had* clean hands. Was their insistence upon rights not a mask for uncharitable motives? Calling for society's aid were they not defaulters in not first testing the limits of adjustment within their little world? In such a set-up insistence that wrong should be suffered without recourse to litigation[13] and that a firm friendly rebuke should be administered before methods of compulsion were employed[14] made very good sense.

[10] The parable of the good Samaritan, *New Testament, The Gospel according to St. Luke*, x. 29–37.

[11] *New Testament, The Gospel according to St. Matthew*, vii. 12. Compare xxii. 35–40: 'And one of them, a lawyer, tested him with this question: "Master, which is the greatest commandment in the Law?" He answered, "Love the Lord your God with all your heart, with all your soul, with all your mind." That is the greatest commandment. It comes first. The second is like it: "Love your neighbour as yourself." Everything in the Law and the Prophets hangs on these two commandments.' Naturally, for one cannot love God without loving his creatures—a truism which has proved to be remarkably elusive, though the comparatively trivial saying, 'Love me, love my dog,' would be comprehended at once!

[12] Compare the teaching of Hillel: *Babylonian Talmud*, tractate *Shabbat*, fol. 31*b*.

[13] St. Paul, *The First Epistle to the Corinthians*, vi. 5–9 (*New English Bible* translation).

[14] *The Gospel according to St. Matthew*, xviii, 15–17.

Cannot the same principles be applied across social barriers in a community which has become, in fact, a super-society, in which the mutual dependence of individuals has become much more real than it ever was in Galilee or Corinth? We can demand a great deal of each other as we cure each other's sick and educate each other's children. We can surely demand forbearance, some hesitation to gain at another's loss, and some suspicion of prestige-seeking as against each other. In the last we have the chance of excelling every ancient society, not excluding that of the early Christians.

Now a judgment in a civil action by no means attends to these requirements—on the contrary, it encourages private acquisitiveness and desire for revenge.[15]

Meanwhile, so long as determinations of 'our rights' continue to expose our individual weakness and moral poverty, judges there must be. But we respond to a primeval superstition, one which externalises an inborn intuition, when we believe that there is a judge above all judges. Law, for all its majesty, is a temporary expedient, and as such, is being judged.[16] The final decree passed in an actual lawsuit is law in its concrete form. Man, however, senses that above laws there is a standard, which is *just*.[17]

[15] Hence it is required that a candidate for the episcopate should not be litigious: St. Paul, *First Epistle to Timothy*, iii. 3, as understood by the canon lawyers (A. Barbosa, *De officio et potestate episcopi*, I, tit. ii, glos. xiv). This is a requirement which, unlike those relating to celibacy or matrimonial status, cannot be enforced by legal machinery in developed societies (which demand a strict system of pleading and proof), but many of St. Paul's recommendations were developed into law in the strict sense by the emperor Justinian in his sixth *Novella*.

[16] Hence the pre-Reformation practice of the English Church to proclaim from the pulpit once a quarter a general sentence of excommunication against not only those that withheld tithes and other rights of the Church but also those that purchased 'writs or letters of any lewd (*i.e.*, lay) court' whereby the Church court's process was restrained. On the assumption that that court could do right, coupling justice with mercy, resort to the common-law court merely to hinder this was sinful, and likewise any more direct means to frustrate the Church's internal system of discipline. Provincial 'constitutions' of the Archbishops attempted to deal with this problem (W. Lyndwood, *Provinciale*, *Const. Prov.*, pp. 21, 73–74). Canon law did not accept that any secular law could prevail over its own provisions: Gratian, *Decretum*, I *dist.* 10, *c.* 4. The solemn formulae, with book, candle, and bell (Sir Thomas Ridley, *View of the Civile and Ecclesiasticall Law*, 2nd. ed., Oxford, 1634, pp. 172 *et seq.*) ceased, partly because the ecclesiastical courts were adopted as limbs of the royal judicature, partly because sentences of excommunication lost their terrors in a dissolving society, and partly because of a reformed religious sense (*cf.* the *Commination* in the *Book of Common Prayer*, 1661, and its history at F. Procter and W. H. Frere, *A New History* . . ., London, 1914, p. 641, nn.). In India within living memory castes with sufficient social cohesion have passed resolutions excommunicating or fining any member who litigated in the state courts upon any family or social matter. Small wonder that the state sought to make excommunications unlawful, calling them 'caste tyranny,' and that when the Supreme Court upheld the practice of excommunication upon grounds of religious discipline only (in 1962) there was a general outcry that 'injustice' would result!

[17] Psalm lxxxii. Paulus, discussing the meanings of *ius* in Latin, frankly says that the *praetor* (below, pp. 7–8) is said to *reddere ius* (approximately, 'hand down law') even when his judgment is inequitable (or unjust): Justinian, *Digesta*, 1.1.11. The reason as explained by Hugo Grotius, *On the Law of War and Peace*, I, iv, 3, is that God requires that men should acquiesce in occasional failures of human justice, because of their obligation to obey the ruler, and that they should appeal solely to God for a remedy of their complaints. The general advance of democratic principles of government and the improved sensitivity of courts to the needs of the public since Grotius's day mitigate the chill of this teaching, but they do not diminish its essential relevance.

Thus, as we have seen, religion is not a true source of law, but, at most, part of the conceptual framework within which a legal system and legal propositions take their places; likewise beside the ultimate requirements of morality all such law is dwarfed, and in this conclusion it seems that Christians, Muslims, Hindus, and Jews are agreed. A superstition in which all the great civilisations are at one speaks for a constant factor of the human make-up which can only be ignored at one's peril.

Has one not heard people say, 'The judgment was carefully given, but was obviously unjust.'? Their confidence springs apparently from an inborn quality which any kind of education seems able to develop, provided the individual is in health.

One may hold on to this fact as to a reality whilst looking over the world's legal systems, admiring or deploring their attempts to effectuate the ideal. This fact religion itself relies upon and expresses eloquently. In this religion is objective, as it is in its constant demand for righteousness from the man who has it in his power to be unrighteous.

J. DUNCAN M. DERRETT

London, 1968

ROMAN LAW

J. A. C. Thomas

IF we leave aside the great systems of Hindu and Islamic law, the modern world may be divided into two broad groups of legal systems —the common-law countries which comprise the English-speaking world and territories which have formed part of the British Empire and Commonwealth; and the civilian countries which include continental Europe and many other—even Oriental—states which have, with westernisation, adopted occidental codes of law, like Japan and Turkey. To a greater or less degree, civilian systems stem from Roman law; or rather from revived Roman law.

For Roman law, in world history, had two leases of life and influence. In the first, of course, it was the living law of Rome and the Roman Empire, an existence which may be said finally to have come to an end with the compilation by the Emperor Justinian (A.D. 527–565) of the Code and Digest which contain the essential legacy of the imperial legislation and juristic writing respectively of Rome's past. Its second life began with the use and study of Justinian's works in the Italian universities of the eleventh century A.D., which spread thereafter throughout Europe (even, to an extent, into medieval England), influencing the development of juridicial terminology and thought and of the municipal legal systems of Europe down to the period of codification, which really starts with the French *Code Napoléon* of A.D. 1804.

While undoubtedly important in the history of modern western civilisation, the second life of Roman law is, jurisprudentially, less significant than its original existence. It was essentially an artificial creation of university professors, rationalising and generalising principles and rules to be found in Justinian's works (often with little regard to the original scope and purport of the material utilised), adapting them to the needs of modern life and so providing, in varying degrees of intensity, a common legal education and a kind of leaven in the development of the national legal systems of Europe. The original Roman law, on the other hand, from whose vast literature Justinian's compilation was culled, was a vital legal order which grew and developed as Rome herself grew and developed from a small agricultural community in central Italy to be the centre of a vast empire with a complex commercial economy and a multi-racial population. It is therefore with the original Roman law that this chapter is concerned.

The reign of Justinian, as said, marked the end of the first life of Roman law. In truth, it represented also an attempt to resuscitate, in the last brief glory of restored imperial power, a system which in fact had been in decline for more than two centuries. The creative and developing power of Roman law belongs to the Republic—making its first definite appearance with the enactment of the Twelve Tables (*c.* 450 B.C.)—and especially to the first phase of Empire, the so-called Principate, the period of 'classical Roman law' which ran from the beginning of our era until the middle of the third century A.D. Thereafter, there ensued a fifty years' period of instability throughout the empire which terminated with the accession of Diocletian (A.D. 284–304). In many respects, Diocletian was the last of the true Roman emperors, seeking to uphold the traditions of the past; but in truth, his reign is rightly regarded as inaugurating the so-called Dominate, the autocratic and bureaucratic administration which was the system of government of the increasingly enfeebled and Hellenised Empire of the fourth to sixth centuries, which, from the legal point of view, is universally known as the 'postclassical period of Roman law.'

The Romans were essentially a practical people; their genius lay not in theorising but in getting things done. The thoroughness and talent for organisation which took their armies throughout the western world and created an empire that endured for centuries, which made the construction of viaducts and roads, theatres and temples their principal artistic achievements, is manifest also in their supreme spiritual achievement, their law. If one accept Roscoe Pound's description of law as 'social engineering,' the harmony of this overall development is manifest. It is indeed ironical that the revived Roman law should be the creation of the universities, a 'book law'; because the true Roman law was essentially the creation of a legal profession, made by practitioners for practical application in a manner not dissimilar to that of the common law of England. Not until the postclassical period did law schools flourish, and their rise in fact coincided with the decline of Roman legal science. Moreover, it was a law made of the stuff of life and social *mores*: in the great days of Roman law legislation plays a minor role and, though the bulk of juristic literature was eventually considerable, it was a casuistic literature, leaving principles to be deduced from the mass of instances reported, rather than seeking to demonstrate accepted norms by scientific selection of illustrations of their operation. As the late jurist Paul says (Dig. 50.17.1),[1] 'The law is not to be taken

[1] The reference to 'Dig.' indicates the *Digesta* of Justinian in the *Corpus Iuris Civilis* (many editions).

from the rule but the rule is formulated from the law which exists.'

It is now time to leave general statements and to look more specifically at the manner of development of Roman law, at some of its principal underlying characteristics and some of its institutions and provisions.

While it is true that the enactment of the Twelve Tables marks the concrete existence of Roman law, it is also clear that, since the city reputedly existed from 753 B.C., there must have been law before this legislation. Initially, Rome was undoubtedly a monarchy in which the king exercised all the functions of government; but, though there are legendary reports of regal legislation, the law of the period was certainly customary. The king was indeed advised by a Senate and there was also an assembly of all the heads of families, *patres familiarum*, in the *Comitia Curiata*, but—to judge from its later historical function—this body was primarily concerned with ratifying the election of the king and with religious matters. The interpretation of the law was, at this time and for no inconsiderable period afterwards, the province of the pontiffs, the priests. In this, the Romans, no less than other peoples, exemplify the traditional early association of law with religion and morality.

In a way, it is this that gives particular importance to the Twelve Tables, which, at an early date, mark a clear distinction of law from religion. Of course, there were practical reasons for the legislation. From earliest times Roman society comprised two strata, the patricians and plebeians, the latter being conspicuously second-class citizens, with all offices—including the priesthoods—in the hands of the patricians. Frustrated by their ignorance of the law, especially the law of debt, the plebeians, by repeated secessions from the Roman community, won concessions from the patricians. The Twelve Tables represent a notable early advance for the plebeians and, understandably, were looked back to by later generations with the reverence (and exaggeration) which Englishmen give to Magna Carta. In truth, the Tables did not constitute a code of all the law then existing but rather a settlement of the legal points particularly in dispute between the two orders of Roman society. While, for example, detailed provisions on getting one's opponent before the court are included (*e.g.*, if he hides, one may lay hands on him; if he be ill, one must send a horse but need not provide a litter), nothing is said of *patria potestas*, the power of the head of a family. Still, the Tables marked a decisive point in the struggle of the orders: henceforth, the tide was set irrevocably in favour of plebeian freedom and, within a century and a half, they had all the offices of state, including the pontificate, open to them. The real development of Roman law was to occur in a free republic in which all offices were open to all free men.

At least in principle: for, throughout the republic in fact, it was the aristocratic upper class of society which still really held power and controlled the life of the city. The magistracies which replaced the monarchy (which fell traditionally in 510 B.C.) were generally held by members of families which had previously held office. Cicero, the great orator who attained the consulship, the highest office, in 65 B.C., could boast that he was the first 'new man' (*novus homo*) to do this in a generation (Cicero, *De Lege Agraria* II.1.3). Similarly, in the principal assembly of the Republic, the *Comitia Centuriata*, the voting system was such that the two wealthiest classes of society had an absolute majority. This doubtless led to the development of a special assembly of the plebeians, *Concilium Plebis*, which, from the beginning of the third century B.C. could enact measures of general validity and was thereafter the principal source of such legislation as appeared in the Republic. This dominance of, particularly, senatorial influence lasted into the Empire; it was not really until the second century of the Principate that inroads were made into this system of inherited social and political privilege.

In the light of this, it is not perhaps surprising that the principal characteristic of Roman legal development is authority: the system is based not on principle as such but on the authority of those who expound the law. The acceptance of authority is seen throughout Roman life and, indeed, makes it necessary immediately now to qualify the law with which we are concerned: it is Roman private law. In the constitutional sphere the magistrates had their various fields of activity and, within them, were the state: any transaction into which they entered as officials with anyone was inevitably a matter of public law, *ius publicum*, and outside the competence of the ordinary processes of litigation. Similarly, Roman criminal law was a very poorly developed system by comparison with the civil law. For the magistrate, armed with his authority, could deal summarily with anything which he regarded as infringing the interests of the state as represented by his particular function. Apart from some ancient crimes, this free administrative power of the magistrate represented criminal jurisdiction until the later republic, especially the last century B.C., when a series of statutes created certain offences and the courts to try them. Where these statutes did not apply, however, magisterial discretion still prevailed. In the Empire the pattern was substantially repeated, though with imperial officials exercising, in the emperor's name, the authority that had previously belonged to elected magistrates. Again, though, in the developed Republic, there were three assemblies capable of enacting legislation, their power was in truth considerably circumscribed. They had no legislative initiative: an assembly could meet only if and when convened by the appropriate magistrate and then only either to accept or to reject his proposal for legislation—there was no discussion, no power of amendment, etc. In effect, the measure gained its validity from the acquiescence of the assembly in the proposal which the magistrate himself had previously put before his associates in the Senate. The same authority we shall see also in private law with the singular position of the head of the family.

But our initial concern is with the manner of development of the law and its stamp of authority. Even after the Twelve Tables, much of the law was unwritten and its interpretation a matter for the pontiffs. While the early association with religion no doubt in part, at least, contributed to the traditional Roman respect for the law, it must also be noted that, like everything else about them, the state religion of the Romans was practical, and priesthoods usually went with political authority; Julius Caesar, for example, was chief priest, *Pontifex Maximus*. The two-fold aura of power which thus surrounded legal interpretation would naturally tend to cast such rulings in the form rather of fiats than of reasoned opinions. With the secularisation of legal learning which came in the third century B.C., the study and practice of jurisprudence was taken up, again naturally, by persons of the superior classes of society. Well into the first century of the Empire, the jurists were—with very few and notable exceptions —of senatorial rank, usually having held the highest offices of state: a conspicuous Republican family was that of the Mucii, the youngest and most distinguished of whom, Q. Mucius Scaevola, was consul in 95 B.C. and *Pontifex Maximus*, as had been his father before him. It could be expected that such persons would speak with the voice of authority, with that inborn sense of superiority which yet is devoid of arrogance. Men of affairs, they perceived the desirable solution of the problem before them and would simply advise that an action be or not be given, without staying to explain their ruling or, if they did seek to support their opinion, it was by reference to the fact that another had, on another occasion, given similar advice. Thus, *e.g.*, the late jurist Ulpian still says, 'If a partner inflict damage on the joint property, he is liable under the *lex Aquilia* and so say Celsus, Julian and Pomponius' (Dig. 17.2.47). It is interesting that this reliance on authority rather than principle is noted by perceptive non-jurists: Cicero, for example, writing to his jurist friend, Trebatius, then on military service in Gaul in winter, teasingly says (Cicero *ad Familiares* VII.10), 'I greatly fear that you are freezing in your winter quarters and so I think that you should build a blazing fire; Mucius and Manilius used to say the same.' The manner of juristic education again tended to favour the continuation of this manner of development. For there was no formal instruction. Young men of good family, themselves aspiring in due course to public office, would attend at the consultations of existing jurists—being accepted, by virtue of their social standing, both by the master and by his clients—and thus acquire their legal expertise from practice, rather like the pupil in a barrister's chambers.

This authority of the jurists was strengthened in two ways in the course of the Principate. In the first place, the first emperor, Augustus, instituted a system which conferred on certain jurists the honour of giving their opinions under the emperor's seal. Then, certainly from the latter part of the first century, jurists were regularly members of the emperor's cabinet, often holding the highest imperial positions. Of course, with the changing fortunes of the Roman body politic, new men, often of provincial and possibly humble origin, came to displace the old hereditary aristocracy of the city of Rome in the course of the Principate. But it can be fairly said that, throughout the period that Roman law flourished, the interpreters of the law were always of the ruling class (whatever it happened to be), men at the centre of political and social life; and their position stamped their technique and terminology with a general uniformity. It is indeed probably the continuity of their own public standing which, at least partly, explains their general indifference to public law and their ability to develop the private law in an atmosphere of secure permanence. Of course, if the jurists had continued simply, as in the republic, to make almost oracular rulings, Roman law—though it might have been practical—could hardly have become the great system that it did. In fact, while remaining casuistic, it became generally integrated through a factor important in the general cultural development of Rome, *viz.*, the influence of Greece.

There had naturally been contact between Greece and Rome for centuries, but, from 146 B.C., Greece was part of the Roman Empire and her culture was to permeate and dominate Roman civilised life. The Romans themselves recognised and accepted this—'Captive Greece took her fierce conqueror captive and introduced the arts into rustic Latium,' writes the poet Horace (*Epistles*, II.I.156). It was inevitable that educated Romans, schooled in Greek philosophy and scientific methods, should, sooner or later, utilise these aids in the study of the law, bringing order to collections of rulings. Already in the later republic, for instance, we find Servius Sulpicius defining tutorship of wards (Dig. 26.1.1pr), grouping together instances of Act of God (Dig. 19.2.15.2), and classifying four kinds of theft (Gaius III.183). In the course of the early Empire agreement is recognised to be the common feature of all the contracts known to the law (Dig. 2.14.1.3) and contract and delict as two species of the genus obligation. The Institutes of Gaius, an early elementary manual of Roman law dating from the later second century of the Empire which has come down to us independently of Justinian's compilation and so affords priceless direct testimony to the state of classical law, deals with the law on a threefold classification. All the law, we are told, pertains to persons or to things or to actions: the law of persons covers status and family relationships; the law of things is really the law of assets, of estate—ownership and possession, succession and obligations; the law of actions, of course, deals with the processes of litigation. And within each main head further classification is made—all men are free or slaves; obligations are created either by contract or by delict, etc. Again, classical jurisprudence worked out the essential characteristics of individual contracts and delicts and a comprehensive scheme of the standard of care required of parties to a contract. A person who did not benefit under a contract, *e.g.*, the lender of a book in loan, was liable only for fraud on his part; while a person who did benefit, *e.g.*, the borrower of the book or both parties in a contract of sale, had to show the standard of care of a good man, *bonus paterfamilias*, rather like the 'reasonable man' of the common law; and certain persons holding another's property by reason of a contract were absolutely liable if they did not restore the thing, unless some act of God or *force majeure* could be shown to relieve them of liability. Similarly, the common characteristic of the many instances of the delict *iniuria*, which ranged from trespass to land, defamation and imputations against chastity to assault and battery, was extracted as affront, deliberate insult to another. Principles were ascertained inductively from the mass of cases, so allowing for their further application to new situations in a manner also very similar to that of the English common law.

There was a further factor which made for the full splendour of Roman law in the last century and half of the Principate. As already indicated, the juristic method was essentially to think in terms of granting or withholding an action and of the redress to be obtained by action. The development of the law, in short, was through remedies. Until the later Republic, Roman law was confined to a restricted set of cumbrous modes of litigation, possibly suitable to a barely literate close community of farmers but far from adequate for an expanding sophisticated society. From the middle of the second century B.C., a new means of process was available which was virtually exclusive throughout the Principate. Under this new system the litigant would seek from the *praetor*, the magistrate charged with the administration of justice, a *formula*, *i.e.*, a written synopsis of the claim and any defence, addressed to the judge with instructions on how he should dispose of the issue. Let two examples suffice—'Let X be judge. If it appears that A ought to pay B 10 and there has been in the matter no fraud on the part of B, for the 10 condemn A to B; if it does not so appear, absolve (A)'; or on a sale, 'Whereas A sold to B a horse, whatever on that account B ought to give or do for A in good faith, for that, judge, condemn B to A. . . .' Henceforth, it would be the plaintiff's aim to persuade the praetor to grant a *formula*, even in respect of a claim for which no existing authority at law could be shown; conversely, the praetor himself, in the edict or programme which he issued at the commencement of his year of office, would intimate circumstances in which he was prepared to grant an action or defence: and the judge would decide the case as directed in the *formula*. Clearly, litigants would normally have no legal knowledge nor necessarily did the praetor or the judge: for Roman litigation was, in essence, a kind of arbitration before a lay judge. Herein really lay the unique power of the jurists. They would advise clients on their claims, the praetors—fellow citizens, usually, of equal standing—on the contents of their edicts and the judge on points of law, *e.g.*, what might be regarded as due 'in good faith' in the particular sale action before him. Since the praetor changed annually, it was theoretically possible for the edict to be completely changed from year to year; but of course, in the nature of things, praetorian modifications of the existing law were suggested because they were desirable and, once introduced, would be retained by successive praetors. The result of this process was that the jurists could function rather like an informal but very real standing commission for law reform, helping successive praetors to temper the possible severity and rigidity of the old civil law by the manipulation of the law of procedure. In this way, for example, there developed the dual system of ownership which is referred to later. But, in many ways, the law of succession presents the clearest illustration of the manner in which the praetor could modify the civil law in classical times. Strictly, a will had to be made by way of a collusive *mancipatio* (again discussed later; for the present, it is enough to say that it was a solemn form of transfer) by the testator of his estate to a friend: in practice, the praetor would confirm a document sealed by seven witnesses. Again, at civil law, rigorous provisions required that the testator expressly nominate as heirs those who became independent by his death or expressly disinherit them: in practice, even those who were expressly disinherited could get the will avoided by the praetor if they showed that they had been excluded without just cause from a share in the inheritance. Again, if there were a will which, for some reason, was invalid or if no will were made, the deceased died intestate and, under the civil law, those of his descendants who became independent at his death, having until then been members of his civil family, were entitled equally to the estate and, failing such person, his nearest relative through the male line. Here again, the praetor considerably altered the law in practice; for he would give possession of the estate to descendants of the deceased, whether they were still related to him by the civil link or not, in preference to other persons, even those entitled at civil law. In all these cases where the praetor adopted a course different from that of the civil law, the mechanics of the procedure were the same. He gave possession of the estate to those whom he was prepared to regard as entitled to the estate: if they should be sued by a civil action by those who were entitled under the civil law, he gave a defence in such action to the persons in possession under his authority. Since this would defeat the action of the civil titulary, his grant of possession was in effect a grant of the estate itself. It was, in effect, in this way that the old system of civil intestate succession based on relationship purely through the male line was superseded by a system based simply on blood relationship generally, a system made exclusive by Justinian. The unique interaction of the praetor and jurists is not the least explanation of the lack of legislation in classical Roman law: statutes were simply unnecessary because the law of procedure could be utilised to rectify substantive defects. It also led to the recognition of virtually two bodies of law, the *ius civile* or old civil law, and the *ius honorarium* or magisterial law, a circumstance which again prompts a comparison with the common law and the equity of England.

Clearly, while the praetor's edict remained in this way a potential source of creative law (possibly at the expense of full development of the civil law), jurisprudence could not undertake exhaustive definition and classifications of the law. Though, with the first stirrings of Greek influence, we find Q. Mucius Scaevola writing a book of 'Definitions,' we still find Javolenus in the late first century A.D. saying 'All definition in the civil law is dangerous for it is rare that there be one which cannot be upset' (Dig. 50.17.202). But the emperor Hadrian (A.D. 118–138) commissioned the great jurist Julian to consolidate the edict, and when his work was published (*c.* A.D. 130) no further alterations were allowed. The edict really thus became a permanent statute. Consequently, from this time Roman jurists were not only technically equipped by their education to regard their material as a whole but were also in a position so to treat it. Their function now was not, as previously, to amplify the body of the law, especially by the expansion of praetorian law, but to exploit to the full the existing corpus of law, both civil and praetorian, elucidating difficulties in existing literature, harmonising provisions of the civil and of praetorian law, extracting principles, etc., in the manner already described.

Before leaving the manner of development of Roman law, something must be said briefly of the sudden decline of jurisprudence from the third century A.D. Undoubtedly, the first factor was the nature of the Dominate which stifled independent legal initiative by the individual—emperors even regulated the use of existing literature—and, by the general levelling of all subjects before the almost divine majesty of the emperor, made impossible the continued prestige of the distinguished fellow-citizen on which the real strength of Roman legal development had so delicately yet firmly rested. In the later Empire individual enterprise could find an outlet only in the Christian church. Secondly, it must be conceded that later classical law probably carried in itself the seeds of its own destruction. So thoroughly did the great jurists do their work, especially Ulpian (*d.* A.D. 228) and his contemporary Paul, with their comprehensive commentaries on both civil and praetorian law, that there was little left for later lawyers—already necessarily inhibited by imperial power—other than making abridgments or further refining classical conceptions. This was, in truth, precisely the characteristic of the scholarship of the professors in the law schools of the East, which provided instruction for prospective advocates and officials in the later Empire. A system grounded on the authority of its exponents—and, moreover, an authority voluntarily recognised by fellow citizens in an essentially free society—could not outlive the circumstances in which it developed: when those conditions disappeared it too withered, becoming a subject for sterile study in academic institutions.

In the foregoing paragraphs an attempt has been made briefly to outline the manner of development of Roman legal science. It is now time to say something of its general characteristics at varying stages of Roman history.

Granted the essentially unwritten nature of the early civil law and the class of persons who were then and thereafter responsible for its interpretation, several features present themselves. In the first place, we find the traditional Roman virtues—meaning, of course, those of the noble Roman, idealised in, *e.g.*, the earlier books of Livy—transmuted into legal principles and institutions. Most notable, perhaps, is *fides*, almost untranslatable but signifying trustworthiness, fidelity. The Romans prided themselves on their reliability as compared with, *e.g.*, the Greeks and Carthaginians. Hence, with the earlier contracts, more specifically the verbal contract, *stipulatio*, a simple question and answer—'Do you promise to give me 10?' A. 'I promise'—the promisor would be bound to honour his undertaking, even though, perhaps, he was coerced or tricked into it. Having in fact given his word, he must do as he promised. In time, it is true, the praetor ensured that fraud or duress would be nullified by giving the promisor a defence if sued by action; but the civil position is instructive. *Fides*, indeed, became of itself the basis of the bilateral commercial contracts made necessary by and introduced for the commercial expansion which followed upon Rome's emergence as the dominant Mediterranean power after the first Punic War (265–242 B.C.). Again, the tutor who proved to have mismanaged his ward's affairs was not only cast in damages in the action on his tutelage but further stigmatised as *infamis*, infamous, which carried considerable legal and social disabilities; and the same was visited upon the depositee who betrayed his trust or the partner whose misconduct led to the dissolution of a partnership. At least in part, the same lofty concept of *fides* explains the remarkable liability of the judge. If a bad judgment were given—initially deliberately, but in developed law even through negligence—the party aggrieved had an action against the judge who had thus diverged from the standard required of his office. *Fides*, indeed, also explains the standard of the *bonus paterfamilias*, which, though really worked out in the contracts based openly on *bona fides*, goes back before their emergence and requires an exact degree of diligence and honesty from those subject to it. It further explains the bonds which exist between the patron and freedman after they have ceased to be master and slave and also the acceptance of *fideicommissa*, trusts. Because the Roman law of legacies was strict, regulating the manner in which such dispositions of property were made and also the size of legacies, the practice developed in the later Republic that a testator would devise his estate to an heir but then charge the heir to transfer the estate or a considerable part of it to some other person. In the Republic such charges, *fideicommissa*, as they were styled, constituted only a moral obligation for the heir—if he chose to ignore them there was no legal liability upon him for doing so. However, from the early Empire an heir who accepted the inheritance but who was also charged with such a trust was obliged legally to honour it, the example having been given by Augustus, who himself was made heir to a certain testator with a charge of this nature imposed upon him. In course of time, it is true, legal provisions ensured that such charges should not result in the heir's being deprived of all benefit from the estate; but the important thing is that, if the heir accepted the estate, he was now obliged to honour such claims upon his sense of duty.

Closely allied with *fides* is the strong Roman sense of the duties of *amicitia*, friendship. What other legal system would create a binding legal contract, mandate (*mandatum*), out of a voluntary undertaking to do something (anything that was legal and moral) gratuitously at the request of another, *i.e.*, in effect, an agreement to do a favour for another? Similarly, acting unasked on behalf of another—as, for instance, A's having B's roof repaired after a storm while B was away from home—created the no less legal relationship of *negotiorum gestio*, administering another's affairs. Mandate and *negotiorum gestio* are treated in considerable detail by the jurists; and sale became, in Roman hands, a legal relationship of the highest sophistication; by contrast, labour contracts and the contract of hiring generally are hardly worked out by the jurists. Not the least explanation of this phenomenon is that, in Roman society, everyone had—or could be supposed to have—friends regularly willing to give their services, whether on request or spontaneously, without expecting a reward. After all, disagreeable and menial tasks would be performed generally by slaves. Even when, in the Empire, changing economic conditions did lead to remuneration in fact for the performance of a mandate, the ideal conception of the contract was retained in that claims for such commission could not be made by the normal contractual action but had to be pursued by extraordinary process before the magistrate. And this very device of a mandate remunerated in fact, of itself, enabled the jurists to leave service contracts as such in their undeveloped form. There is perhaps another facet of the aristocratic formation of Roman law visible in this relative indifference to hiring in its multifarious applications—it is, in the main, the more modest strata of society that have to think of earning their livelihood by hiring out their labour, to find shelter in premises owned by another, etc.; and the law, though applicable to them, is not made by nor primarily for them. Again, in the field of security for obligations, it is a striking fact that personal security—guarantee in its various forms—was always more prominent and important in Roman law than was mortgage or any other form of real security. It was virtually a compliment to go surety for one's friend and, though it is clear that friendship in such cases must often in fact have been betrayed, the Roman answer was not to abandon the institution but, by a series of republican enactments, to introduce safeguards minimising the risks incurred by the surety. Suretyship is indeed the earliest contract of which we know and is found also in the oldest forms of litigation and execution of judgments. The judgment debtor, liable to personal seizure, *manus iniectio*, could make no defence himself: if there was anything to be said on his behalf it had to be said by another who, if unsuccessful, would take the debtor's place and, in earlier law, face death or foreign slavery in consequence. Yet we have no indication of unwillingness so to act for others: indeed, the Twelve Tables already contained provisions designed to prevent abuse of the system of defending judgment debtors.

Fides and *amicitia* give a moral basis to the law of relations usually between persons not of the same family and particularly in the law of obligations. Moreover, they are manifested essentially in the working out of individual institutions. Yet, above all, authority marks substantive law no less than the manner of its development. For the private law of Rome is really founded on a system of power relationships. In origin, the power of the head of the family over his children and descendants, of the husband over his wife, and of the owner over his property—whether human, *i.e.*, slaves, or not—was all of a kind. Naturally—and early—they became refined and distinguished as *patria potestas* over children, *manus* (power) over the wife, and *dominium* over property respectively. Still, marriage, the cardinal relationship of modern systems of personal law, to the Romans was important not as an institution in itself but as a means to the creation of *potestas* over issue of the union and, as a means of acquiring *potestas*, was no more significant than other means to the same end, *e.g.*, adoption.[2] Like the magistrate in the constitutional sphere, the *paterfamilias* was really the only person of legal constitutional standing in private law. He had complete domination over those in his power: children could be married, divorced, given in adoption, even put to death at his discretion, initially; equally, he owned all family property, and anything acquired by any member of the family automatically became his.[3] Again, with the passage of time, though extending into later classical law, his control became modified and its exercise restricted. Moreover, this dominance was in principle lifelong. Though means of terminating *potestas*, especially by emancipation, were devised, the *paterfamilias* originally retained his power until his death or that of those under him. Again, in the law of property the original absolute control of the owner enabled him to carve out lesser rights, *e.g.*, rights of way, estates for life, for others; but it was always such lesser rights which were identified and delimited, and so *dominium*, civil ownership—really the greatest of property rights—is never defined by the jurists and, moreover, is identified with the thing owned: one has one's thing and that 'having' is ownership. In the law of obligations Rome was, if anything, even stricter than English law in its refusal to allow benefits or duties to a third party by contract and also never achieved a really effective form of agency or assignment. While, in part, the use of members of the family and slaves as instruments in the making of contracts and the acquisition of property made a law of agency less necessary for the Romans, still the basic reason for the Roman

[2] The same view of the act of marrying a wife is to be detected in some Islamic territories and in Africa predominantly. *Ed.*

[3] The Aryans in ancient India subscribed to a similar concept of the father, but non-Aryan customs mitigated the severity of the doctrine in early pre-historic times. *Ed.*

position is the nature of the early obligation, which really placed the debtor in a position of subjection to his creditor. Though, in developed law, obligation is merely a legal bond, giving an action for damages in the event of non-performance, the early Roman law—which knew only unilateral obligations, *i.e.*, cases where only one party was under a duty to do something for the other—saw the debtor as a subjected person, a *persona obligata*. As in other fields of the law, he was put into the power of his creditor and, as he himself was a *paterfamilias*, this was an exceptional situation. It is also this exceptional character of the early obligation which explains the Roman failure ever to evolve a general law of contract, recognising only (and grudgingly) a series of separate contracts, stipulation, sale, hire, deposit, pledge, etc. One further consequence of this is that though, with the acceptance of agreement as the basis of all contracts, general principles could be—and were—worked out on factors vitiating consent, especially mistake, other contractual problems which, in modern law, are treated as general, such as frustration, the question of risk in contract, etc., cannot be treated generally in Roman law but have to be considered in relation to each individual contract. Yet even this seeming deficiency of the Roman law has its good side, for generalities often conceal traps.

Two other great qualities of Roman law seem almost self-contradictory—conservatism and capacity for change; yet, in fact, largely through the manipulation of procedure, they go harmoniously together.

Some illustrations may first be taken from family law. The full rigour of the ancient power of the *paterfamilias* might be at least bearable in an early peasant community where the family works as a unit on the holding and the army is merely a levy of the able-bodied males in times of emergency. But, by the end of the Republic, the typical Roman citizen was a city dweller in a commercial society who would wish to use his family dependants in business. In consequence, there developed the practice of giving a *filiusfamilias*—or slave—a fund, *peculium*, which he could administer himself: at civil law it was still the property of the *paterfamilias*, but, in practice, it was treated as the son's. Even so, contracts and other dispositions by the *filius* affecting the *peculium* would, at civil law, not bind the *pater*. However, the praetor would, in appropriate circumstances, give specially adapted actions to the third party against the *pater* in respect of the son's dealings with the *peculium*. Again, as the needs of Empire made necessary a standing professional army in which men might serve for twenty years or more, Augustus provided that the acquisitions of a *filiusfamilias* on service should be treated as a special *peculium* of which he was to be regarded as if he were a *paterfamilias* and in respect of which he could accordingly sue and be sued. In the later Empire this concession was extended to earnings in other imperial service. The result of these developments was that the civil-law position could in principle be left intact while, in the actual life of the law, *filii* could achieve economic independence despite being in *potestas*, and at the same time family dependants could be effectively utilised in commerce.

Turning to marriage, in earlier times it was normal for a wife to pass into the *manus* of her husband or, if he had one, his *pater*; but already the Twelve Tables provided that this would not happen if she spent three nights each year away from his house. As growing prosperity brought the possibility of wealth in the hands of independent women and also, it must be conceded, a decline in the moral standards of the upper strata of society, there understandably developed a predilection of women for the freer type of marriage: if not in *manus*, they retained their separate property and remained in their original family. By the end of the Republic it was accepted that marriage itself rested simply on the will of the parties to live together as husband and wife; and, once that willingness were withdrawn on either side, the marriage ended. Hence, from the late Republic, divorce—which, until then, was rare—was perhaps easier at Rome than in any other legal system. Though emperors, especially the later Christian emperors, sought to restrict divorce—mainly by penalties for capricious dissolution of marriage—divorce by mutual consent remained valid even under Justinian. The change in the conception of marriage brought with it further evidence of the adaptability of Roman law. In the early law it was usual for a dowry to be given to the husband which became his absolute property. With the growth of easy divorce, it became customary for the donor of the dowry (usually the bride's family superior or the bride herself) to exact an undertaking that, if the marriage should terminate, the dowry or a specified portion of it would be returned. Then the praetor came to give the ex-wife an action for the recovery of an equitable proportion of the dowry on divorce even though no express agreement had been made; and, by legislation, well-defined rules determined what was so recoverable in each case, with modifications according as there were children of the marriage and whether it was the conduct of the husband or rather that of the wife which precipitated the breakdown of the marriage. The consequent possible insecurity of tenure of the dowry by the husband led in turn to a reappraisal of his position during the marriage. Successive provisions restricted his ability to dispose of such property and, again by later classical law, he was more like a trustee with powers of administration than absolute owner of the dowry. But no direct interference with the civil law was made in effecting these substantive modifications of the law of marriage. In the field of adoption, again, Rome preserved right into the law of Justinian two separate institutions, *adrogatio* for the incorporation into the family of one who was already independent (*sui iuris*) and *adoptio* to transfer a *filius* or other dependant from one family into another. Originally certainly, they had different aims; *adrogatio* sought to provide a *paterfamilias* with an heir in the days before testation, while *adoptio* was a later institution initially to arrange a redistribution of the available labour force between families; but long before the end of the republic it was fully appreciated that, with the influx of slave labour, the real object of adoption was to establish a family relationship, and this could be effected by either institution. Only Roman conservatism satisfactorily explains the continued existence of two separate kinds of adoption.[4]

In the law of obligations the earliest contracts were all formal and unilateral—the question and answer in *stipulatio*, the written entry in the ledger in the literal contract, etc. With the change in Rome's economic position from the middle of the third century B.C., these formal transactions were insufficient for the increasing complexities of commercial life. At the same time, as already mentioned, obligations were, historically, regarded as exceptional. The Roman answer was—not a general law of enforceable promises such as has been developed in the common law; this would have been too great a departure—but to accept four new contracts of a wholly new kind, informal, bilateral, and based on good faith, the consensual contracts created simply by the consent of the parties, *viz.*, sale, hire, partnership, and mandate: *i.e.*, those which are barely sufficient for effective commercial life. If there were still any deficiencies they could be remedied by the use of *stipulatio*, by which any undertaking could be made binding. In this way, the legacy of the past allowed a restricted concession to the present. Two further developments follow. If *stipulatio* remained a verbal contract, its usefulness—considerable because of the simplicity of the contract—would be circumscribed. But the spread of literacy led to the practice of taking a note or record of the oral stipulation, and great weight was naturally given to such evidence of the transaction in the courts. Soon it became the practice simply to draft a document recording the terms intended by the parties and adding at the end that A had asked and B had promised: and the jurists fully recognised the utility of the practice. In theory, the document was only evidence of the verbal contract, but in effect a means had been achieved of avoiding the actual

[4] We may compare the varieties of adoptions in Hindu law and custom which in part correspond to the Roman forms. Religious, social, and economic motives played their respective parts. *Ed.*

question and answer and thus the necessary presence together of the parties. Meanwhile the broad regime of good faith gave the jurists scope in working out the range of the newer contracts, while the limited number of such contracts itself made it necessary that the lawyers should so exploit them to their full range. Taking sale as an illustration, the contract was in essence an agreement whereby the vendor promised to give possession of the thing sold to the buyer, who in turn undertook to pay the agreed sum of money. There was no inherent guarantee by the vendor that he had title to sell nor against defects in the thing sold. Accordingly, it became common to exact an undertaking by stipulation from the vendor that if the buyer were evicted by a third party he would be indemnified and also that the goods were free from specified defects. From the frequency with which such stipulations were taken in fact, the jurists came first to hold that the vendor must, by the good faith which regulated the contract, give such undertakings—*i.e.*, that he would be liable to an action on the sale if he refused—and, by the end of the classical period, that, since such stipulations could always be expressly required, they might be implied in good faith in the contract of sale itself. In this way, the contract of sale came to give, in itself, ample safeguards to the buyer. Certain other contracts were admitted by the civil law in the course of classical law, but it is the consensual contracts which constitute the greatest innovation of the law of obligations.

Again, in the field of property law the ancient law singled out certain things highly prized in the early community—slaves, horses, oxen, donkeys and mules, land in Italy, and rights of way over such land—as *res mancipi*, which meant that, for the transfer of ownership in such things, there was necessary a solemn transaction, *mancipatio*, a ceremony requiring the presence of five witnesses, a person holding a pair of scales, and the actual parties to the transaction. If *res mancipi* were merely delivered, *i.e.*, handed over, without *mancipatio*, ownership did not pass at once and the recipient would have to retain possession of the thing, for two years in the case of land or rights over land, for one year in the case of other things, before he became owner. While practicable in a small community where everyone was likely to know everyone else's business anyhow, the ceremonial of *mancipatio* would hardly commend itself to a more sophisticated society which values simplicity and prefers to avoid publicity in private transactions. In fact, in developed law the requirement was largely evaded because, though the thing delivered without *mancipatio* remained at law the property of the transferor during the relevant period of possession, the praetor would give the possessor a defence if he were sued for the thing by the transferor and also would give the possessor an action, fashioned on the claim for ownership, if the thing went out of his hands during the same period. In consequence, the possessor was fully protected until his holding ripened into full legal ownership. This was frankly recognised by the jurists and resulted in the existence, side by side, of two forms of ownership—civil and praetorian—while allowing the retention of the concept of *res mancipi* and the civil requirement of *mancipatio*, in principle, right down to the time of Justinian.

But not merely by the supplementation in this way of the civil law did the jurists ensure that the system was one capable of modern application. Where statute was concerned, they showed a nice sense of the art of interpretation, preserving the letter of the law while sometimes adapting the spirit; for they fully appreciated that 'it is impossible for laws and senatorial resolutions to be so framed as to cover all the possible cases which may at some time arise' (Julian, Dig.1.3.10). For instance, the praetorian ownership just referred to derived ultimately from a provision of the Twelve Tables: where property was mancipated, the legislation provided that, in the case of land for two years, in respect of other things for one year, the transferor would be liable for double the price if the transferee were evicted by another. This was interpreted as meaning that possession of the thing for the specified period gave the possessor a title which was unimpeachable: and this interpretation was applied also to cases where there was no *mancipatio* of a *res mancipi* and also to possession of things other than *res mancipi*. In consequence, possession for the appropriate period gave ownership by the process known as *usucapio* (literally, acquisition by use) not only where a *res mancipi* was transferred other than by *mancipatio* but also of other things, more particularly when they were transferred by one who was not their owner. True, in time, other requirements were necessary to ensure that the possession was one suitable to ripen into ownership—in particular, such acquisition of ownership of stolen goods was prohibited—but the evolution of *usucapio* allowed acquisition of title despite the lack of title in one's transferor: and it all derived from interpretation of the provision of the Twelve Tables. Another facet of this development which has practical economic consequences is that the ability to acquire ownership of a thing by possession for the appropriate period (*usucapio* is the technical term) regardless of the title of the transferor gave the Romans a means of safeguarding the security of commercial transactions despite the general tendency of Roman law to protect the position of the existing owner of property against all comers. For the person who has held, for one or two years as the case might be, a thing which his transferor in truth had no title to hand over to him becomes, by virtue of his possession, owner of the thing in question, and his capacity thereafter to pass on a good title to another person is not a problem.

Turning again to family law, the Twelve Tables provided also that if a *pater* mancipated his *filius* three times the *filius* should be freed from his *pater*. In the early Republic this was doubtless intended as a punishment for the *pater* who repeatedly enslaved his son to others. But with the possible need to distribute the labour force in an agricultural community, already in the days of pontifical interpretation, this provision was adapted to meet the needs of and to create the institution of adoption. The existing *pater* and the prospective adoptor would make three collusive *mancipationes* of the *filius*, so breaking the existing *potestas* over him, and the adoptor could then claim the *filius* as his own son before the praetor: for descendants other than actual sons, it was held that one such *mancipatio* was sufficient. Similarly, later, as family dependence grew irksome, the provision was adapted to allow emancipation of the children. Again there would be the necessary collusive mancipations, followed this time, however, by an assertion that the *filius* was *sui iuris*, independent. With the development of the *peculium* already referred to, it was usual for the *filius* to retain this fund on his emancipation. Hence, despite the theoretical life-long continuation of family subjection, in truth from the early Empire, a *filius* would usually be emancipated and set up in life on reaching relative maturity.

A further illustration may be taken again from the law of obligations, this time from delict. The *lex Aquilia* (*c.* 250 B.C.) provided redress if a person killed the slave or grazing animal of another and also if such property were not killed but mutilated or, generally, if other property were destroyed in certain ways. The original scope of the statute was limited; but, thanks to the interpretation by the jurists of the terms used for 'killing' and 'destroying' and to the activity of the praetor in giving special actions for situations where, though the exact provisions of the statute had not been complied with, nevertheless the same sort of damage had been done, the *lex Aquilia* became in fact, throughout classical law, the general basis of the law of damage to property, not merely intentional damage but also negligent.

Already several of the manifold uses of *mancipatio* have been indicated. Behind them lies a further quality of Roman law—its economy. *Mancipatio* was originally a cash sale, transferring ownership of the thing purchased, at a period when there was no coined money and the price was weighed out on the scales which were so important a feature of the ceremony. Very soon it became possible to make a gift, in effect, by weighing out only a token amount of copper and, with the development of true coinage, *mancipatio* became merely a ceremonial transfer of ownership, the real price in sale—where there was in truth a sale—being agreed and paid separately. But, as mentioned earlier, ownership was originally a form of undifferentiated power, and so *mancipatio* was utilised also for the transfer of other forms of civil dominance. Hence its use for adopting and emancipation previously mentioned and also to create *manus* over a wife. In this way, one institution was made to serve several related purposes. Again, in the field of obligations there were several recognised contracts: any agreement which did not fall into one of the categories legally accepted was, at civil law, ineffective. The praetor, certainly, gave actions in respect of some agreements not in these categories, but they were not thereby accepted as contracts. The reason is that they were all simply informal or, anyhow, new means of doing something for which provision was already made at civil law: for example, an informal agreement to pay another's debt could have been effected at civil law by suretyship. The civil law would not recognise a plurality of means to achieve the same end and so would not accept these so-called praetorian pacts.

One further and general evidence of adaptability remains to be mentioned. The earliest law was exclusively for Roman citizens, and traces of that exclusiveness always remain. For example, special consequences attach throughout classical law to 'legitimate' actions (*iudicia legitima*), *i.e.*, actions brought between two Roman citizens before a single judge within a mile of Rome, in short actions within the original ambit of Roman governance. But, from the third century B.C., Roman traffic with foreigners (which was a contributory to the evolution of the consensual contracts) was frequent and ever-increasing. One way to deal with this would have been the evolution of a system of conflict of laws such as is part of every modern system, whereby provision is made for the possible application of foreign law in a situation which, though it may involve a national or nationals of the state where the action is brought, none the less contains some foreign element. Again the Roman answer was different and characteristic. Roman law was nationalistic—and Roman relations with foreigners were usually the consequence of conquest. It would be unlikely that Roman jurists would take notice of foreign systems of law—nor did they. Even, for instance, after the general grant of citizenship to all free inhabitants of the Empire by the emperor Caracalla in A.D. 212, no hint is given in juristic writings of the possible difficulties arising from the consequent extension of Roman law as a whole to those who, at least hitherto, have been, in their own ordinary daily life, governed by their local rules and principles. The Roman method of coping with foreigners was to make applicable to them part of the general corpus of Roman law itself. Thus foreigners could use the less solemn transactions of the civil law—for example, the contract of stipulation except that the particularly Roman verb of promise, *spondere*, was reserved to citizens—and also the newer contracts based on good faith; informal modes of acquiring ownership, such as mere delivery, acquisition by finding, etc., but not *usucapio* or *mancipatio*. Similarly, in respect of foreign things, the furthest that Roman law would go was to allow the foreigner to have a Roman action for the assertion of title, with the additional direction to the judge that he was to decide as if the foreigner were a citizen. The institutions and procedures so open to foreigners were distinguished, within Roman law itself, as *ius gentium*, the law for all peoples, from *ius civile*, here meaning the law applicable only to citizens. In the later Republic and the Empire, of course, the *ius gentium* transactions were far more important in practice than those of the *ius civile* and, paradoxically, ceased to be relevant in their original connotation after Caracalla's provision really made the whole body of Roman law *ius civile*, since all free men were now citizens. Nevertheless, the distinction between *ius civile* and *ius gentium* is a basic feature of developed Roman law and a striking illustration of the system's capacity for adaptation and change.

The topics discussed in recent paragraphs exemplify the practicality of Roman law, so to speak in its substance. At this juncture we wish to consider this practicality from the standpoint of jurisprudence. In the system which developed as we have endeavoured to describe, the jurists, in the first place, showed little interest in legal history. Rules and institutions were accepted as in existence and simply made to work in current conditions. The uses of *mancipatio* and the adaptation of the Twelve Tables which have been mentioned were not deliberate reinterpretation of outmoded institutions but simply pragmatic employment of available means to achieve the desired end: Twelve Tables, republican enactment, juristic ruling, praetor's edict—all were merely existing law to the jurists. Secondly, classical jurisprudence did indeed develop well-defined conceptions and rules. Take, for example, the clear distinction between contract and conveyance: in modern English law the agreement for the sale of goods in itself generally transfers ownership of the goods to the buyer, while even the contract for the sale of land gives equitable ownership of the land to the purchaser; in Roman law, on the other, the contract of sale was merely the reason, the cause, for a subsequent transfer of ownership. But such rules and principles were never pressed to their logical conclusion when expediency or reason suggested a different result. The Digest contains numerous examples of jurists saying that, though principle requires a certain result, nevertheless for convenience (*utilitatis causa*) a different conclusion is accepted. To take an illustration; the Romans had a clear conception of possession which required a person to have factual control of the thing possessed with the intent to possess it: such factual control could be exercised through another, *e.g.*, a tenant. Now suppose that A is in possession of a piece of land because he has a tenant B occupying the land and B dies; really, though A may intend to continue as possessor, in truth he no longer has actual control, since the means by which it had been exercised no longer exists: nevertheless, it was accepted for convenience that he continued to possess unless, on hearing of B's death, he took no steps either to occupy the land himself or to put in another tenant (Africanus, Dig. 41.2.40.1). In a not dissimilar manner, Roman definitions of legal concepts and institutions generally lack scientific precision but none the less give a practical indication of what is in issue. To take one example, slavery is defined as 'an institution of the *ius gentium* whereby one man is subject to the ownership of another' (Institutes I.3.2): in fact, it was quite possible that a slave should have no owner—the real point is that the slave is the one class of human being who can be owned, and this is satisfactorily conveyed by the Roman definition.

Authority and practicality, conservatism and capacity for change, moral loftiness and controlled systematisation—these are perhaps the main features of the development of Roman law.

It would be impossible here to go into the institutions of substantive law further than has been attempted hitherto. Since, however, it has been frequently indicated that the law of procedure played a large part in the development of Roman law, something must here be said of actions.

The principal characteristic of the law of actions in the classical period is that, in theory, litigation still rested on the agreement of the parties to submit their dispute to an arbitrator by whose ruling they will abide. Though there are other views, it is fairly clear that the original mode of redressing grievances was self-help. Naturally, with the slightest degree of political development, such redress becomes undesirable; hence, the parties agree to submit their problem for decision to a third person, the state—initially through the king—merely seeing in the first place that there is such a dispute needing to be resolved. Of course, it early became established that parties must resort to litigation rather than indulge in self-help, but, nevertheless, the old initiative of the parties themselves remained manifest even in classical law. Hence the two-fold division of proceedings—the possible disputation before the praetor (*in iure*) seeking a *formula* (which is the developed representation of the state's establishing to its satisfaction that there is a claim to be dealt with), followed by the actual hearing of the action before a lay judge (*apud iudicem*)—and the need for the aggrieved person, who wishes to commence an action, *i.e.*, the potential plaintiff, himself to secure the appearance of his opponent before the praetor in the first place. Hence also the absence of any system of appeals in the formulary process. Obviously if parties can challenge the decision of the arbitrator whom they have accepted to settle their difference the whole basis of arbitration is destroyed. It was, indeed, doubtless the impossibility of appeal which led to the stringent liability, to which we have already referred, imposed upon the judge who gave a bad judgment.

Summons is the concern of the plaintiff. Naturally, in the developed law the praetor assisted the plaintiff in getting proceedings started, in that, if the defendant proved evasive or recalcitrant, the praetor would authorise the plaintiff to take control of his property or perhaps exact a penalty from the defendant for failure to appear. In the proceedings before the praetor, once started, the aim, as earlier indicated, was to persuade the magistrate to grant a formula addressed to the intended judge. In this, there is again a similarity with the early formation of the common law. The earliest *formulae* were simply remouldings of the ritual statements of the earlier procedures; but soon the praetor could grant new *formulae* as the earlier Chancery clerks granted new writs[5] and, equally, *formulae* already established provided the basis for the working out of their potentialities by the jurists in the same way as the accepted writs of the common law were worked out by the judges. Moreover, it meant that the plaintiff had to select the right action or, if none yet existed to cover his claim, to persuade the praetor that his complaint merited redress. There was no general overall process for approaching the courts, no uniform writ whereby a claim based on any branch of the law could be initiated.[6] For that, one had to wait until the Dominate, when the administration of justice was regarded as merely one aspect of the general business of government, when the whole dispute from the summons of the parties to the execution of the eventual judgment was managed by the imperial magistrate and when, with the disappearance of the old conception of arbitral litigation, the two-fold division of proceedings had vanished. The praetor, of course, granted his *formula*—whether it was based on a civil-law claim or was based simply on his own magisterial authority—on the assumption that each party could prove the facts on which he based his claim or defence. It was the function of the judge to hear the parties in fact establish their respective allegations and to decide the case: and in this, it is noticeable that the Romans had no clear rules of evidence

[5] See below, p. 183.

[6] So in ancient Hindu law the plaintiff was expected to state a case which the judge could recognise as falling within the eighteen titles of litigation. *Ed.*

such as exist in modern law; considerable laxity seems to have been shown in the matter of admissible evidence.[7]

Reference has been made to actions based on the civil law and those which derived simply from the praetor's authority. It was principally through the latter, which, sometimes, were adaptations of civil claims (like that given to the foreign owner of property mentioned earlier) and, more often, were introduced for the first time by the praetor in his edict, that the law was expanded and modernised; still, the jurists could also ensure the fullest scope to civil actions by, for example, working out the duties of the parties to sale, in respect of which, naturally, the civil actions of the buyer and vendor respectively were available, and acting similarly in respect of other civil remedies.

Consistently with the arbitral principle of litigation, the grant of a *formula* operated rather like the conclusion of a contract between the parties: it marked the joinder of issue between them and thereafter, whatever might befall in fact before judgment was given, the action was treated as though the situation of the parties and their dispute remained as at the time that the *formula* was issued. Again, as from that time, the cause of action on which the proceedings was instituted was extinguished; any attempt by either party to reopen the action after judgment could be met with the defence of *res judicata* as in modern law.

Once judgment was given and assuming that the plaintiff was successful, it was for the plaintiff himself to execute that judgment. Personal seizure of the judgment debtor, to make him work off the amount of damages awarded against him—for all Roman judgments were for money damages, there being no orders for specific delivery, etc.—remained possible, as it had been exclusive in the Republic. More often, however, the plaintiff would, with the praetor's aid, seek to realise the sum awarded to him by making the debtor bankrupt. Having been authorised by the magistrate to take over the debtor's property, he would arrange for its sale to someone prepared to pay the highest dividend to the creditors of the judgment debtor. If the latter co-operated in these proceedings he was immune from personal seizure thereafter, but not if he resisted.

In addition to procedure by way of action in this manner, however, there were other devices of developed law which also rested entirely on the authority of the praetor. Most notable are the interdicts. These were essentially summary orders by the praetor directed to one or both of the parties—*e.g.*, to restore land taken by force, forbidding either to use force to prevent continued peaceful possession of the

[7] Interest centred rather upon the standing of the witness, *i.e.*, his freedom from disqualification (as in canon law later an excommunicated person could not testify), a feature found also in the Islamic and Hindu systems. *Ed.*

land, to produce a slave who was being concealed, to allow the complainant to collect acorns which had fallen from his trees on to the other party's land, etc.; they were numerous and, as can be seen, diverse in their scope. If the order were complied with, then litigation by the usual processes of action could usually be avoided; in this way, interdicts served a function similar to that of the injunction found in the equitable jurisdiction of modern common-law countries.[8] The praetor could also, by restoring the parties to their original position, nullify transactions which had been induced by duress or fraud or into which a person under 25 had entered because of his complete lack of business sense.

In the later Empire many of the niceties of distinction of classical law disappeared. With the substitution of the unitary procedure of the Dominate for the two-fold system of the *formula*, the difference between actions based on the civil law and those granted by magisterial power had gone, so that, for example, agreements which had been enforced only by the praetor—no less than genuine contracts—came to be accepted as obligations. Similarly, *mancipatio* and *in iure cessio* having lost their significance with the complete protection of the person in process of *usucapio*, Justinian abolished the distinction of *res mancipi* and other things and *mancipatio* itself; the result was a unitary concept of ownership, in striking contrast with the dual system of classical law. The trend generally was in favour of a simplification of the law now that the procedural methods on which the careful distinctions of classical law were really based had ceased to function. There is no doubt that much that Justinian preserved in the Digest had no relevance, in its original context, for the conditions of the Emperor's own time. Yet it is Justinian's work which was the basis of the renaissance of legal studies. In the Code the territorial sovereigns of Christendom found an emphasis on the legislative power of the emperor and his own immunity from the provisions governing the conduct of his subject which provided them with ammunition both in their struggles to assert their temporal independence against the claims of the Papacy and in the maintenance of their authority within their own domains. By ransacking the compilation, the legal scholars of medieval and later Europe were able to formulate general definitions, *e.g.*, of property or obligation and rationalised principles, for example, of defects of consent in contract which have facilitated the eventual production of authoritative national codes of law since the early part of last century.

Contrasts have frequently been drawn between the authoritarian and rational temper of the legal systems of the European continent and the pragmatic nature of the common law, which has been

[8] See below, pp. 177–178.

developed by the essentially free activity of the legal profession. The historical utilisation of Justinian's compilation as a virtual compendium of law, all of equal date and equal validity, in no small measure explains the former. The development of the common law, however, bears a far closer resemblance to the emergence of the body of jurisprudence from which Justinian's work was composed. In the modern world the study of the *Corpus Iuris Civilis* is entirely historical, for European states have now long had their own national codes: it is not so much Justinian's work in itself but the insight that it gives into the thought and work of the great jurists of earlier centuries which is the centre of interest. To the English lawyer, this can give not only a lead in understanding the conceptions adopted by European systems but also a further guide to the appreciation of his own system of jurisprudence; for the continental, such study of Roman law can be an invaluable aid to understanding of the casuistic working of the common law. It has been said, paradoxically but aptly, of Justinian's compilation that 'the greatest codification of law that the world has known was never the law of any state at any time.' It could still be an indispensable source of mutual understanding and enlightenment for the lawyers of Britain and the continent as they proceed along the path towards the inevitable unification of Europe.

BIBLIOGRAPHY

Two good short introductions to Roman legal history are:

H. J. Wolff, *Roman Law, an Historical Introduction* (University of Oklahoma Press, 1951).

W. Kunkel, *Roman Legal & Constitutional History* (trans. J. M. Kelly) (Oxford University Press, 1960).

Kunkel's is the later and more authoritative work.

A larger work, giving a judicious discussion of disputed issues and full references to literature to the date of publication is:

H. F. Jolowicz, *Historical Introduction to Roman Law*, 2nd ed. (Cambridge University Press, 1952).

An excellent introductory survey of Roman private law is:

B. Nicholas, *Introduction to Roman Law* (Oxford, Clarendon Press, 1962).

The three most used elementary textbooks of substantive Roman law are:

W. W. Buckland, *Manual of Roman Private Law*, 2nd ed. (Cambridge University Press, 1939).

R. W. Leage, *Roman Private Law*, 3rd ed. (London, Macmillan, 1961).

R. W. Lee, *Elements of Roman Law*, 4th ed. (London, Sweet & Maxwell, 1956).

The principal merit of the last mentioned is that it contains a translation of Justinian's *Institutes.*

The standard comprehensive textbook of Roman law in English for those who wish to go further is:

W. W. Buckland, *Textbook of Roman Law from Augustus to Justinian* (Cambridge University Press, 1963).

A conspectus of the broad features of Roman law is to be found in:

F. Schulz, *Principles of Roman Law* (Oxford, Clarendon Press, 1936).

The same author makes a comprehensive and critical study of the forms of juristic literature and the various phases of Roman legal science in:

F. Schulz, *History of Roman Legal Science* (Oxford University Press, 1946).

A comparison of the leading principles and institutions of English and Roman law is given by a distinguished representative of each system in:

W. W. Buckland and A. D. McNair, *Roman Law and Common Law*, 2nd ed. (Cambridge University Press, 1952).

There is no complete English translation of the surviving Roman legal literature in Latin, but the first fifteen books of the Digest are translated in:

C. H. Morris, *The Digest of Justinian*, 2 vols. (Cambridge University Press, 1904, 1909).

The standard edition of Gaius's *Institutes* with translation and commentary is:

F. de Zulueta, *The Institutes of Gaius*, 2 vols. (Oxford, Clarendon Press, 1946–53).

JEWISH LAW

Ze'ev W. Falk

JEWISH LAW is an all-embracing body of religious duties, regulating all aspects of Jewish life. It comprises on an equal footing norms of worship and ritual, rules of private and social behaviour, and laws which are nowadays enforced by the courts. The system recognises distinctions between these classes of 'laws,' but they are all equally binding in conscience.

It is part of the law of modern Israel in so far as it forms the personal law[1] of Jewish citizens in matters of personal status. That means that it is used in questions of marriage and divorce, maintenance and alimony, legitimation of minors, 'inhibition' of (*i.e.*, protective restraint of the exercise of civil capacity by) incompetent persons,[2] and the administration of absent persons' property. Jewish law is also referred to in cases of Jewish religious charities and services, the interpretation of religious concepts, and in the matters of marriage and divorce of foreign Jews resident in Israel.

Its main application thus lies in the field of domestic relations, but some of its concepts have infiltrated other pieces of legislation, such as the *Joint Houses Law*, 1952, and the recent *Succession Law*, 1965. Modern Hebrew, again, drawing mainly upon the biblical and talmudic linguistic styles as its sources, has incidentally carried over some of the contents of the ancient law. For the judges, called upon to interpret a new term used by the legislature, often refer to its original meaning.

The jurisdiction in matters of marriage and divorce of Jewish citizens or residents is vested in the rabbinical courts. The members of these tribunals, always composed of three, are appointed by the President of the State on the advice of a committee from a panel approved by the Supreme Rabbinical Council. In all other questions concurrent jurisdiction has been granted to the ordinary civil and the rabbinical courts. The latter tribunals, moreover, are called to decide civil cases, if they are submitted to them under the provisions of the *Arbitration Ordinance*. Though no appeal lies from a rabbinical to a

[1] The definition of 'personal law' agrees substantially with that understood in South Asia, for example, in India and Pakistan, where the Hindu, Islamic, and Jewish systems are applied as personal laws. There, Jewish law is applied in few contexts, of which marriage and divorce are the principal. *Ed.*

[2] 'Inhibition' is an institution of civil law origin. *Ed.*

civil court, the Supreme Court sitting as a High Court of Judicature may issue directions to the rabbinical tribunals by orders of mandamus or prohibition.[3] Rabbinical judgments, moreover, can be executed only through the execution offices of the civil courts. The latter, for their part, sometimes refuse to act, if in their opinion the judgment was beyond the jurisdiction of the court.

Jewish law is applied by the rabbinical court in all cases and by civil courts in cases of personal status where the parties concerned are Israeli or stateless Jews. Its application, of course, is subject to statute, such as the *Succession Law*, 1965, the *Age of Marriage Law*, 1950, and the *Women's Equality Law*, 1951. Civil courts also pay respect to the rules of Private International Law and the law of evidence, so that their conclusions sometimes differ from Jewish classical sources, even where Jewish law is applied.

Outside Israel Jewish law is used on a voluntary basis by a considerable part of the dispersion. Orthodox, and to a certain extent conservative, Jews consider themselves bound to abide by the norms of Jewish law as part of their religious observance. Doubts and disputes are referred to a rabbi, acting as a jurisconsult as well as an arbitrator. In some countries, *e.g.*, the United Kingdom, the Bet Din (rabbinical court)[4] enjoys a certain status under civil law. In other systems the activity of these tribunals is based on the rules of arbitration and the social sanction of the Jewish community.

Jewish law does not claim universal or territorial validity. It is the personal law of all Jews without regard to their place of residence, citizenship, or even belief. This is the result of the biblical view identifying the religious with the political structure and defining allegiance to Israel as by descent or by proselytism. Even a non-believing or apostate Jew was considered to be bound by the law of his fathers, though some of its privileges were denied him. Ancient Israel was founded on a religious basis and on a sacred law. Contemporary Jewish law still disregards foreign law when dealing with the validity of legal acts. Thus when a marriage was celebrated by Jews before their immigration to Israel it will be recognised in Israel if the Jewish rites were observed though not the *lex loci celebrationis* (the requirements of local marriage law). On the other hand, such a marriage will not be recognised in the opposite case by the rabbinical court.

Most of the provisions of Jewish law do not apply to Gentiles living in the Jewish community. Ancient Jewish society, being of a uniform composition, did not think it necessary to provide special

[3] The orders are relics of the English-type legal administration of the Mandate period. *Ed.*

[4] The traditional spelling 'Beth Din' does not represent phonetically modern Hebrew pronunciation. *Ed.*

rules for them. The state of Israel, following the Ottoman Millet System,[5] is thus also in accord with Jewish tradition. Only a number of elementary norms, the so-called Noachide Commandments,[6] were to be imposed upon the non-Jewish residents. They included the prohibitions of murder, incest, idolatry, blasphemy, and theft, while other provisions of private law were inferred by the general commandment of justice, applying to them as well as to Jews.

From the point of view of Jewish law a person is Jewish if born to a Jewish *mother* or if converted to Judaism according to the traditional rites. This definition has been challenged by some of the immigrants, considering themselves to be Jewish though not complying with the rule. A decision taken in 1958 by the government caused a major crisis. It concerned an administrative ruling to register as Jewish any person claiming bona fide to be Jewish, provided that he had no other religion. The Prime Minister, consequently, consulted forty-five scholars in and outside Israel for their opinion in the matter, and the majority replied in favour of the traditional definition.

A similar question came up in the High Court of Judicature when a Carmelite monk of Jewish descent claimed the right of Israeli citizenship under the *Law of Return*, 1950, which reserves this right to Jews only. The government agreed to grant the applicant citizenship by naturalisation, and this view was upheld by the court. Under strict Jewish law, it is true, once a Jew always a Jew, even if one became an apostate, but the judges relied on popular feeling for the interpretation of this basic law of the state.

In order to study Jewish law we mainly rely on literary sources, for neither a state nor any other form of social structure has played a decisive role in the formation of its rules. It is learning rather than practice which has influenced legal creation, so that works of scholarship have often fulfilled the functions of both legislature and judiciary.

The earliest collection of Jewish laws is the Pentateuch, but to a lesser extent legal data can also be traced in the books of the Prophets and the Writings. Modern scholars study these sources against the background of other ancient eastern law collections, for example, the Codes of Hammurabi and other monarchs of the Babylonian and Assyrian empires and the Hittite laws. Post-exilic Jewish tradition, on the other hand, interpreted Scripture in the light of the so-called Oral Law, which was ascribed together with the Pentateuchic laws themselves to the divine revelation at Mount Sinai, and thus became part of God's 'covenant' with his people.

[5] That system, based on the Islamic concepts then accepted by the Turkish empire, allowed to each religious community its own (personal) law and its own community court. *Ed.*

[6] In theory applied to the descendants of Noah and to Gentiles only after the Law was given to the Jews at Mount Sinai. *Ed.*

The Oral Law was indeed transmitted in the academies at least as from the Babylonian Exile (586–537 B.C.), though in its present form the greater part dates from Hasmonean and later times. The material originally remained an oral tradition so as to distinguish it from Scripture. The idea may also have existed that oral traditions could be tested in the academy as in court, whereas any written source did not lend itself to cross-examination. The Oral Law was gradually committed into writing, this process taking from A.D. 200 till the Middle Ages.

Ancient pieces of this pattern can be traced in the *Midrash*, *i.e.*, the commentaries to the legal parts of the Pentateuch, in passages of the Septuagint (the ancient and most celebrated Greek version of the Hebrew Bible), the Apocrypha, the Dead Sea Scrolls, in Philo and Josephus (first-century Jews of Egypt and Judaea respectively). Where this pattern is used, the biblical phrase is followed by a short explanation mentioning parallel texts and alternative interpretations.

While the earliest traditions have been preserved anonymously, those dating from the second century before the Christian era onward were transmitted in the names of their authors. At that time the Oral Law had increased to such an extent that it could no more be contained in a commentary upon Scripture. There was need for a new literary genre, the *Mishnah* (agreeing partly with what are called 'traditions' in the New Testament literature),[7] which, though literally secondary to Scripture, became the primary textbook in the academy.

In his *Mishnah* the author aimed to collect all those traditions which he considered of legal relevance. The book now known by this name was compiled by the patriarch Judah about A.D. 200 from earlier books of the same genre. Unlike the *Midrash*, running parallel to the biblical text, the *Mishnah* aims at a systematic arrangement. Thus the six Orders of the book deal with the following topics and are named accordingly: Seeds (Agricultural Commandments), Festivals, Women (Family Law), Torts (and other provisions of law), Sacred Things, and Ritual Cleanness. Each Order is divided into tractates, being sub-divided into chapters and passages.

Since the *Mishnah* was an anthology of earlier sources, the author left out other material, which was then called *Baraita* (external tradition). Many of these teachings have been preserved in later literature such as the *Talmud* compilations. A special collection of this material has come down to us under the title *Tosefta* (Supplement), and should be dated in the third or fourth century A.D. Its arrangement follows that of the *Mishnah*, but it is both a commentary upon and a collection of additional versions concerning the

[7] See particularly *The Gospel according to St. Matthew*, ch. xv. 2–6, and *The Gospel according to St. Mark*, ch. vii. 3–13. *Ed.*

questions discussed in the *Mishnah*. Often one view is presented in the *Mishnah*, while the alternative one appears in the *Tosefta*.

The minutes, as it were, of the Palestinian and Babylonian academies during the study of the *Mishnah* form the contents of the Palestinian and Babylonian *Talmud* respectively. Beside the discussion of the meaning of the *Mishnah* text and its parallel passages, opinions, decisions, and controversies are cited in the *Talmud*, many of them being rather loosely connected with the text under consideration. After having been discussed by successive generations and various schools the text of the Palestinian *Talmud* was compiled at the beginning of the fifth century and that of the Babylonian counterpart at its end. It took another century to add numerous scholia and to establish the final form of the Babylonian *Talmud*.

The study of both compilations, especially of the latter, which is held in greater esteem, has been going on till our times. An observant layman should spend part of his day in the study of these sources. Hundreds of commentaries were written for this purpose, to explain the meaning of *Mishnah*, *Tosefta*, *Talmud*, or *Midrash*, or any part of them.

Another branch of Jewish legal literature, having started after the *Talmud* and developed to this very day, are the Responsa ('replies,' or juridical 'opinions'). They are rabbinical opinions collected by the writers or their disciples for guidance in similar cases. Several thousand books of this type have so far been published, and a great many are still in manuscript. This literature is also of great historical value, as it shows practical problems at certain times and places.

The increase of legal material called for systematic treatises codifying the rules which were of practical application. Each codification on its part was followed by a number of commentaries taking care of interpretations, recent developments, and a general discussion of the subject matter. The most systematic code is the *Mishneh Torah* (Second to the Law) by Moses Maimonides (1135–1205) and the most authoritative one is the *Shulchan 'Arukh* (The Set Table) of Joseph Qaro (1488–1575). This work is used by present-day judges and rabbis, of course always subject to the later commentaries and responsa.

Mention should be made of three projects which are in the course of realisation at Jerusalem. There is first the collection of Judgments of the Rabbinical Courts of Israel, comprising seven volumes. A digest of the responsa literature arranged as a commentary to Qaro's code is in progress and already covers the foundations of family law. A Talmudic Encyclopaedia, also in progress, aims at a systematic presentation of all legal rules and institutes in their classical and post-talmudic development.

This may help us in showing *where* the law can be found. However, in order to understand the creation of individual rules or institutes and the ways in which the law is found, we must say something about the legal sources of Jewish law.

The average man thinking of 'law' usually recalls statute law, which is the creation of a human legislator. Jewish law, on the other hand, is partly understood as the literal word of God and partly its divinely inspired interpretation. Being a sacred law, it originally included certain irrational forms of law- and fact-finding. The chastity of a suspected wife, for instance, was to be established by an ordeal, and legal questions were sometimes decided by reference to a 'heavenly voice.' About A.D. 100, however, these techniques were replaced by rational modes of legal thinking. In a discussion taking place in the academy one of the sages had produced various miracles in favour of his view and a divine voice had declared its truth. Thereupon rose another sage to dismiss this kind of proof, for 'the law is not in heaven.' Divine law, then, is but the existential result of human reason and 'the sage is greater than the prophet.'

While a distinction was made by the rabbis between the commandments defining the duties towards God and those concerning one's fellow man, both were considered equally to be of divine origin. However, there existed another distinction, namely between biblical and rabbinical norms, the former normally being of absolute validity. Thus in cases where the judge's course is not clear on the facts a lenient decision would be taken in cases of the latter group, but not of the former. In the course of time rabbinical norms, being covered by authority under biblical law, became partly incorporated into the biblical category itself. Thus rules which were created by the rabbis came to be described as part of the law given to Moses at Mount Sinai.[8]

Nevertheless, the sages remained aware of the legislative role played by man. Although biblical law was thought to embrace all problems and to be complete, the need was admitted for human legislation to interfere from time to time. According to rabbinical theory, the divine law already foresaw the possibility of a delegated legislation by the religious leadership with the sanction of communal consent. In order to safeguard the strict fulfilment of the law, the 'men of the Great Synogogue' had added numerous provisions 'to make a fence about the Law,' *i.e.*, protectively to elaborate or extend it, so that breach of the biblical law was more easily avoided. Informal gatherings of pietists in the third century B.C., as well as the Gerousia

[8] The Church had acute difficulties with some of these extra-biblical rules, a fact which partly explains the extent of the Gospels taken up with apparently purely juridical controversy. *Ed.*

(assembly of elders) and Synedrion (Council) of the following centuries, were thus, the authors of many law reforms. Some of these innovations must have caused the great rift between Pharisees and Sadducees during the second century B.C. and the disputes between the schools of the great teachers Hillel and Shammai in the century following.

After the destruction of the temple in A.D. 70 legislative power was vested in the central academies of Palestine and Babylonia. It was exercised under the leadership of the learned heads till the eleventh century, *i.e.*, as long as the spiritual centre of Judaism remained in the east. Thereafter each local community or group of communities claimed the right of legislation for its own members to control their behaviour for the common good and loyalty towards tradition. In most cases this power was vested in the rabbinical leadership, which, however, acted in close collaboration with the lay representatives of the communities.

A piece of legal theory concerning legislative power evolved around the so-called Prosbol formula introduced by Hillel towards the end of the first century B.C. Under the biblical law of the Sabbatical year a creditor lost his right of action, though he had granted the loan shortly before the seventh year. Obviously, this law, instead of assisting the poor debtor, precluded him from obtaining any credit. It was therefore practically abolished by Hillel by a formula we shall examine below.

Without going into the details of form, talmudic scholars of the fourth century then asked themselves how Hillel had been able to do this. One of them replied that a rabbi could abolish a *positive* (not a negative) duty of biblical law, but he could not legalise the breaking of a biblical injunction. Hillel's act had been of the first category, for he had abolished the duty of remission of debts. According to an alternative attempted explanation, which avoids this casuistry, rabbinical reforms were legitimate if concerning matters of property but not matters of religious commandments or personal status. Rabbinical authority in the former field stems from the power of requisitioning private property which is vested in the rabbinical court. Under this power the rabbis were entitled to take away property from its legal owner and transfer it to a person whom they thought fit. Thus biblical provisions of property and contract law could be changed by the rabbis.

Another occasion for the study of the formal basis of rabbinical legislation arose out of a reform in the law of divorce. According to classical law, a wife had little chance to obtain a divorce against the husband's will unless she could show that her grievance was expressly mentioned in the sources. During the seventh century, then, the

Babylonian academy allowed the claim for an immediate divorce even against the husband's wish. This reform was introduced lest such a wife turn to the Muslim judge to get the right denied to her by rabbinical justice.[9]

The decision was later criticised by the French scholar Jacob Tam (1100–1171), before whom this precedent was cited. The editors of the Babylonian *Talmud*, he replied, were the last ones entitled to introduce innovations in the law. He admitted that post-talmudic sages could reform property law. Thus they had allowed the creditor to levy distress upon the personal property of a deceased debtor, not only upon his real (or immovable) property as prescribed by the *Talmud.* This change had become necessary because the majority of Jews were no longer land-owners as foreseen by the earlier rule. But post-talmudic lawyers, said Jacob Tam, were not competent to give effect to an invalid bill of divorce. After the final edition of the *Talmud* until the coming of the Messiah (in the indefinite future) no such authority had been conferred upon the rabbis. Therefore the divorce performed under the authority of this reform was in his view totally void.

Even in the field of pure property law rabbinical legislation did not go unchallenged. We have just mentioned, for instance, the post-talmudic extension of the liability of assets for a deceased person's debts. Moses Maimonides nevertheless advised the readers of his code to provide for this event by an express clause in the contract creating the debt. This was preferable, in his opinion, to relying upon the juristic provision, for post-talmudic authorities did not enjoy the legislative powers of the ancient Synedrion, even in property cases.

Indeed, quite a number of legal rules and institutes owe their existence to contractual practice. Sometimes a clause which was current among a certain community was later interpreted by the scholars. Thus at the end of the first century B.C. a marriage clause of Alexandrian Jewry was used by Hillel to prevent the law's producing undesired results. According to talmudic law, a betrothal could not be dissolved without a formal divorce: this hit any subsequent union, and its offspring would be illegitimate. The rule being violated by the Alexandrian community endangered the possibility of intermarriage between this important part of Jewry and their Palestinian brethren who kept to strict law. Hillel, then, found in the marriage contract a provision delaying the full effect of the betrothal until the nuptials had taken place. Thus where the betrothal was broken off informally, it was not a violation of a proper betrothal but rather of a contract to

[9] On the wife's rights to divorce at Islamic law—limited indeed but less so than at Jewish law—see below, p. 73. *Ed.*

make a contract. The law was thought to have been changed by convention.

But there existed limitations to this form of quasi-legislation also. During the second century A.D. discussion went on in the academy, whether a wife could forgo her matrimonial rights by a clause in her marriage contract. While Meir invalidated any contracting out of biblical law, his colleague Judah allowed contractual arrangements of property relations. Sometimes the rabbis assumed the existence of a tacit condition implied by the court rather than by the parties themselves. The name given to this type, *viz.*, 'condition of the court,' pointed to its real function, which was a reform of the law.

The conventional character and origin of the ordinances which were made by medieval communities can be inferred from the fact that they were simply called *haskamah* (convention). Being promulgated by the assembly of the householders or at least of their representatives, these ordinances were based on consent rather than authority.

For until the twelfth century communal laws were thought to be binding by either of two forms. The rule could be made by the rabbinical head of the community in his capacity as successor to the Synedrion, the idea being that the local leader had all the powers of the ancient central authority. But the rule could also be derived from the wishes of the public, which until the twelfth century had to be ascertained by a unanimous vote. Some of the rabbis, then, recognised the right of the majority of the 'good people' to impose their decision upon the whole. Nobody, moreover, was allowed to claim exemption from a communal decision for having failed to take part in the vote.

Some communal ordinances were called *cherem* (excommunication) or *qenas* (fine), both referring to the sanctions imposed upon any eventual transgressor. The former was by no means of mere social effect, but it implied a strong sacral punishment. It was therefore thought to affect even undetected offenders. It was the people who were entitled to add new provisions to the sacred law, and their innovations were covered by the original sanction.

However, the main way of legal creation was interpretation. As already mentioned, the Oral Law had developed between the fifth and the first centuries B.C. through the study of Scripture. Teachers of the law, scribes, and men of the Great Synagogue explained the difficult passages of the text, creating in fact many new rules and institutes. Take, for instance, the provision of Deuteronomy (xxiv. 17) that you shall not take a widow's garment in pledge, which lends itself to different interpretations. By a reasonable argument the injunction could be limited to the poor widow, while a stricter form of interpretation would extend its application to all widows, rich as well as poor.

Seven 'measures' were used by the rabbis during the first century B.C. for the interpretation of the text, some of them perhaps being derived from Hellenistic rhetoric. The rules of interpretation are mainly based on reason, for instance, the deduction *a minori ad maius*, but some are just ascribed to tradition.[10] A rule of the former category, therefore, may be applied to any text to find the law, while those of the latter one may apply only to a fixed number of passages.

Apart from the interpretation of Scripture, logic may also be used for the solution of legal problems. Thus legal rules may be derived from reason as well as from tradition. Sometimes the same rule is explained in both ways, as for instance, the transfer of rights under a deed by delivery of the deed to the transferee. The editor of the Babylonian *Talmud* based this form of transfer both on tradition and on logic.

An important source of law are the practical decisions in the academy or in court, which are then cited by way of precedent. The *Mishnah* includes a tractate called *'Eduyot* (evidences), forming a collection of decisions which were taken in the academy about A.D. 100. Each of these decisions was preceded by the evidence produced by a scholar for a certain law, which was then discussed and examined by his colleagues. Having satisfied themselves of the validity of the tradition, the members of the academy proclaimed its admission into the body of the *Mishnah* collection.

A good example is the case of the wife returning from abroad without her husband and claiming that her husband has died. The school of Shammai were ready to accept her words and permitted her remarriage. The school of Hillel, on the other hand, rejected this decision. They relied on the original case, where the wife had come to court after having been away for a short while only, *viz.*, after having been together with her husband at the harvest. Under these circumstances one had relied on the wife's pleading, for the truth would easily turn out. The Shammaites, then, had extended the original decision so as to include any similar case, while the Hillelites insisted

[10] *Middot*, or rules of interpretation, are discussed succinctly by H. L. Strack, *Introduction*, pp. 93 *et seq.* and 285 *et seq.* They include *analogy* (based on similarity of terms in two texts), 'constructing a family' (*i.e.*, extension of a rule to a number of connected provisions though it is found in relation to one only of them), inference from the general to the particular and vice versa, and deduction from the context or proximity of other material. As time went on, the systematic elaboration of rules of interpretation continued. Thirty-two *middot* are listed at length, including that which attributes amplifying or restricting force to various particles (like 'also') and that which allows a point to be transferred from a less appropriate to a more appropriate context. In *haggadic* hermeneutics even more methods are available, including variant readings of the Hebrew text.

on the original facts to draw the mitigating conclusion. We would say that the argument of the two schools concerned the *ratio decidendi* of the precedent, that is to say the reasoning which had led to it.

This case shows also the tendency of taking a lenient view in order to facilitate remarriage. Both in the academies and in the courts, indeed, a tendency towards mitigation often prevailed over strict law. This tendency, which may be compared with equity, is the cause of various deviations from the rule of law. At the beginning of the second century A.D., for instance, Aqiba and Tarfon took opposite points of view when discussing the priority among creditors where the estate turned out to be insolvent: 'He who died leaving a widow, a creditor and heirs surviving him and leaving a deposit or a loan with a third party—Tarfon said: It should be given to the weakest. Aqiba said: There is no pity in the administration of justice, therefore the heir shall have it, for the others need to take an oath before collecting, but not the heir.'

Many of the more progressive rules of Jewish law, especially in the field of torts, derived from what was called 'celestial' as distinct from 'human' justice. The former was a body of rules created and observed by the pietists beyond the general law. The Pharisees adopted some of these provisions of law into ordinary jurisprudence. Examples are the right of pre-emption[11] over a neighbour's property and the relief granted to the debtor against foreclosure proceedings, which are both modifications of the positive Scriptural law in favour of equity.

For a man was asked 'to do what is right and good in the sight of the Lord' or, according to another definition, to keep 'within the border of the law,' *i.e.*, to refrain from insisting on the use of his rights to their full extent.

In fact, present-day rabbis often base their decision on fairness rather than on formal legality. While the law is, thus, corrected in individual cases, an orthodox rabbi will not agree to the change of the norm itself. The courts go out of their way to permit remarriage of a woman whose husband may be presumed to be dead without positive proof being forthcoming. But they will not seek a general solution to the problem by way of legislation.

Reference is made in legal sources to lay tribunals administering informal law. Most cases of private law were settled by way of compromise. Originally, this practice was severely criticised by the rabbis who claimed the jurisdiction for those learned in the law. Gradually, however, the rabbis themselves tended to prefer compromises to decisions, for they were afraid of the responsibility for judicial errors.

[11] *i.e.*, to insist on purchasing from the seller in preference to any would-be purchaser who has no better right to acquire the land, *i.e.*, as owner of adjacent property. *Ed.*

Thus there was little reason to abolish the lay jurisdiction, and it has indeed existed beside the Rabbinical courts for most of the time.

In the fourteenth century, for example, the Rabbi of Toledo mentioned in a responsum the argument of a layman and tried to refute it. This man had relied on the law of reason as a source equal in authority to that of religion, and he had used its arguments to find the law. This was obviously the result of the standard of education prevailing among the upper classes of Spanish Jewry, which gave them the opportunity of comparison and entering into a discussion with the rabbi. Italian Jews, too, referred commercial disputes to lay arbitrators, and even the national board of Polish Jewry (between 1580 and 1764) maintained concurrent systems of lay and rabbinical jurisdiction.

Another way whereby public opinion impressed the administration of justice was through the recognition of custom as a legal source. The *Talmud* even knows a saying that 'custom abolishes law,' which may originally have been an anti-rabbinic slogan. However, the maxim was admitted into the law, though its application was mainly limited to matters of property. Only in one case is reference made to custom with regard to a religious commandment, *viz.*, the form of the 'unshoeing' ceremony liberating the childless widow from the duty of marriage with her deceased husband's brother (*Deut.* xxv). On that occasion it was said that even the prophet Eliyahu (Elijah) would not be listened to, if he made a decision contrary to custom.

In most cases, on the other hand, custom is disregarded if it contradicts the law. The rabbis, thus, reserved to themselves the right of opposing what they call an 'erroneous custom.' The ideal application of custom as a source of law would be in private law, where there exists a lacuna or gap among the legal norms.

A variety of local customs was mentioned during the first century A.D. in matters of domestic property law. The editor of the *Mishnah* explains the conflict of his sources as the result of differences between the customs of Judaea and Galilee. Similar varieties were later noted between the customs of the Palestinian and Babylonian communities.

The courts, then, had to take account of specific norms applying to one or both litigants. The problem arose, how to deal with a person moving from one community to another; should he obey the former custom or abide by the rule of his new residence? Palestinian custom, in most periods, claimed superiority over the Babylonian one, though much depended on the court where the conflict arose.

Difficulties were felt when western Jewry emerged as an independent group, *i.e.*, from the tenth century onward. Both the Palestinian and the Babylonian academies sent envoys to the far brethren, to win the spiritual supremacy over, and the financial support of, the new dispersion. North African and Spanish Jewry eventually accepted the Babylonian influence, while the Balkan, Italian, French, and German communities tended to follow Palestinian customs.

Nowadays Jewish practice differs among the offspring of these communities, which have been dispersed over the greater part of the world. Thus we have different customs of eastern European, German, Spanish, Middle Eastern, North African, and Yemenite origins, each being preserved by the members of the synagogues. Among the Yemenite Jews, for instance, bigamy is still legal under certain circumstances, while the Spanish synagogues accord succession rights to women as well as to men. This, of course, presents great difficulties to the rabbinical authorities of Israel when justice has to be done to the various exiles ingathered in their new homeland. Little by little the new Israeli community has tended to create a custom of its own, which, as in the cases of bigamy and succession rights, have sometimes (as we shall see) been sanctioned by state legislation. The new custom of Israel, moreover, has already influenced part of the dispersion and will eventually, it is thought, restore the unity of Jewish law.

Being a sacred law system, talmudic jurisprudence has little understanding of law reform. A person is asked to observe the letter, not only the spirit, of the law, though conflicts may arise between them. Owing to the multiple changes of historical circumstances, during three millennia, there was often felt a need for change in the law. Such change often took the form of a legal device or fiction, rather than of legislation. Thus a person was thought to be able to obey the letter of the law without having to violate a vital interest.

An oath, for instance, could not be broken under any circumstances. When the tribes had sworn to withhold their daughters from marrying the Benjaminites they could only circumvent it by kidnapping the maids at Shiloh (*Judges* xxi). In post-exilic times, likewise, vows and oaths could be dissolved by an ordained rabbi if it could be shown that the person who had made them had overlooked a certain material fact. By this device almost each vow or oath could be annulled on the basis of error. Yet the *Mishnah* still declares this practice to be 'flying in the air' without proper support from Scripture.

Another example is the Prosbol-clause, already mentioned. The utopian norm of the Sabbatical year providing for the remission of debts had a detrimental effect. For during the months prior to the seventh year nobody would grant a loan which would be legally irrecoverable, so that the poor were worse off than without this law. The reform of Hillel, already mentioned, consisted of creating a fictitious application to the court for execution proceedings starting before the Sabbatical year. Once this application was made, the debt was deemed to be actionable at any time, even after the seventh year.

When dealing with certain biblical narratives and other traditions the rabbis came to notice their being at variance with established norms. Instead of assuming a violation of the law, they developed the idea of emergency powers existing beside the ordinary norms, so as to meet the needs of a grave situation. Thus Maimonides in his code describes the talmudic law of evidence, declaring confessions to be inadmissible. He then cites two biblical cases where the accused was found guilty on his admission and was consequently executed. These cases, he explains, reflect a royal privilege of disregarding normal rules, a privilege granted in order to prevent High Treason.

Similar privileges were conferred on the courts of later generations for the purpose of securing the maintenance of the law. At the beginning of the second century B.C. a Hasmonean tribunal inflicted severe punishments against Hellenistic transgressors of the law. The rabbis did not justify these hard sentences under the ordinary rules, but referred to 'the needs of the hour.' According to this idea, a court may punish, at its discretion, any act harmful to the community, though such an act was not expressly dealt with by the law. The judges, thus, serve as a kind of legislators in retrospect.

Reception of foreign rules, finally, has played an important role in the development of rabbinical jurisprudence. During the greater part of its history Jewish law evolved under unfavourable circumstances. Living in a Gentile state, even observant Jews would prefer such forms of contract as were actionable under civil law. Similar tendencies made themselves felt in criminal and administrative matters. Thus rules and institutes of Gentile law gradually became part of Jewish practice and even theory.

Pecuniary fine as a mode of punishment, for instance, is due to borrowing from Persian law. Local Jewish judges after the Babylonian exile were expressly authorised by the government to impose this penalty, and the rabbis, thereafter, derived this innovation by interpretation from a biblical passage. We have already mentioned the fear of the Babylonian academies lest a wife turn to the Muslim judge to obtain a divorce against her husband's wish. In these cases the applicant's conversion to Islam would be the means to change her position in law. Jewish law, then, had to give in to prevent this danger. The enforcement of monogamy by medieval German communities is another example for this process. While defending their judicial and religious autonomy, the rabbis had virtually to accept certain parts of substantive law from outside.

In spite of these border-line influences, Jewish law has preserved its special character. Having undergone three millennia of development in the four corners of the world, the law has kept its peculiarities, distinguishing it from other legal systems.

The divine origin of the law, to begin with, has played a decisive role in the formation of the various rules. Rights of property, for example, are restrained in favour of persons in need of special care. Money is therefore to be lent without interest, merchandise is to be sold at a reasonable price, real property rights, as well as credits, are to be released in the seventh year, part of the income belongs to the poor, the sale of land is subject to the right of pre-emption, and many similar rules.

The ideology behind all this is religious rather than social. Society adopts the religious view that there does not exist any full ownership. All a man's property is but a kind of holding from the Lord who is conceived for this purpose as a sovereign in a feudal system.

The sacred law made the idea of justice more important than strict legal concepts. Hence the law became adaptable to new circumstances without being tied too much to dogmatics. While the concept of property originally covered only objects of physical enjoyment, it could easily be extended to include credits, commercial interests, and monopolies. During the Middle Ages unfair trade practices were treated under the law of theft, the goodwill of the plaintiff being considered the victim of the offence.

The main concern of criminal law are the offences against God, including murder, sexual offences, and disrespect towards the parents. It is these acts which are the concern of the community to prevent and punish, because they endanger the covenant between God and Israel. Offences against the person or property, on the other hand, are treated by private law, the object of which is restitution, not punishment. Sometimes, though, the wrongdoer must pay more than the actual damage to the person wronged, to atone for the misconduct. The under-elaboration of offences against society and a certain failing to understand crime and its social implications may be due to living under laws administered by Gentile governments. But the religious basis of the Jewish law can have been a factor even here: the categories were fixed.

A similar reason may be presumed for the fact that the law of contracts deals with dispositions and liabilities respecting property rather than with personal obligations. Legal rules apply to changes of ownership and agreements affecting the status of goods. Human relations and promises, on the other hand, are still based on religion rather than on law. Only at a late date was a legal action created to effectuate such objects.

The sacred character of the law makes the process of law-finding quite difficult and dangerous. The judge is to consider himself 'as if a sharp sword is lying upon his neck,' which is a form of describing his responsibility. An error of law is dreadful not only as regards the wronged party but, even more, regarding the divine law itself. Small wonder that, though the opinions of highly regarded rabbis are frequently cited as instances, not all such decisions are in themselves sources of law.

Moreover, often a point of law has not been covered by a clear statement in written or oral law. A controversy may have developed on such a point between individual scholars or factions. There is indeed hardly a rule of Jewish law without any difference of opinion. The major task of the scholar and judge, therefore, is to arrive at a decision between conflicting views.

During the second century A.D. this state of affairs was contrasted with an ideal past in which each dissension might be brought to an end. It was then the task of the Synedrion to make a decision which would be obeyed by all quarters. For whenever opinions differed a vote was taken and the majority prevailed. Commenting upon this ideal solution, the source laments the situation in his own generation: 'But when there arose many disciples of Shammai and Hillel who had not served their teachers enough, they increased dissension in Israel and created two legal systems instead of the original one.' Thus after the already existing cleavage between the Pharisees and Sadducees this new dispute threatened the unity of the former faction itself. The disciples of the two teachers had established two independent schools and had not convened the Synedrion to bring their controversies to an end. The followers of each of these schools were thus asked to keep to the rules laid down by the school.

In the course of time this variety of opinions was held to be advantageous also, making Jewish law flexible. The *Talmud* itself records a heavenly voice as saying to the two schools, 'Both these and those are the words of the living God.' As a scholar of the third century says, the law had been able to subsist just because of its opinions, not because of its decisions. Each question should be dealt with in various, even conflicting, directions, though practice had to be guided by the majority decision.

After the Synedrion and the central academy had ceased to exist the *Talmud* had to adopt various rules for practical guidance in controversy. The views of some rabbis should always be preferred to those of their colleagues, and conflicts of opinion should be construed in favour of the defendant. For the latter would then be arguing the view in his favour, while the onus of proof lay upon the plaintiff. If the matter was one of a biblical duty, positive or negative, the stricter and more comprehensive view (as we saw above) should be followed. Therefore whenever a doubt arises as to the validity of a divorce the woman cannot remarry until the act of divorce has been repeated according to law. In the case of a rabbinical commandment, on the other hand, the more lenient view was to prevail, and technical distinctions could more readily be relied upon.

The power of delivering binding decisions and of imposing fines or other penalties was reserved to ordained rabbis. In theory, a chain of succession had existed without break since the moment when Moses had authorised Joshua (*Deut.* xxxi. 23). In spite of the various persecutions, the same process of ordination from teacher to disciple existed in various forms until the destruction of the Palestinian community by the crusaders. A hundred years later Maimonides incorporated in his code the opinion that ordination could be reinstituted by the unanimous decision of the Palestinian scholars. An attempt was indeed made in 1538 in Safed by a Spanish rabbi Jacob Berab. One of the four scholars ordained by a conference under his chair was Joseph Qaro, the author of the code. However, the rabbis of Jerusalem did not recognise the act, which in their view should be postponed till the rebuilding of the Temple.

The French and German communities, meanwhile, had a system of authorisation of their own. Nobody was to act as a rabbi or to perform marriages and divorces unless he had been licensed by his teacher. This system has been in force up to the present, and it forms the basis to the marriage and divorce legislation for Jews in modern Israel.

But already at the beginning of the thirteenth century a French scholar denied the legitimacy of rabbinical authority. Even a disciple could dissent from the teaching of his master, he claimed, 'for the tractates, commentaries, "novels" and treatises are the teachers and all depends upon reason . . . even a disciple may contradict his teacher, if he is able by dialectics.'

The study of the law, in fact, has never been the monopoly of a hierarchy, but on the contrary it has been the duty of every individual. The *Talmud* and the other legal works are studied in the synagogues and in private circles all over the world. Though priests, scribes, and rabbis have fulfilled certain functions, they have never excluded the layman from the interpretation of the law. In the dispersion, moreover, the decision delivered by the rabbi is essentially private, his authority is based only on his learning and piety, and a layman may resort to any scholar in whom he has confidence.

Post-talmudic law, on the other hand, should be understood as a reaction to anti-traditional tendencies. Already during the first century B.C. the Sadducees had expressed their opposition to the Oral Law and had insisted on the validity of biblical norms only. During the eighth century A.D. Anan ben David reopened this criticism of tradition, thus founding the Qara'ite movement. According to his view, everybody was asked to 'search the Scripture diligently and not to lean upon my opinion.' The reaction of the Pharisees, the scholars of the *Talmud*, and the post-talmudic rabbis was in the opposite direction. While basically agreeing with the rational character of the law, they tried to strengthen the unity of practice in the dispersion. Therefore a kind of hierarchy, headed by the Babylonian academies, came to lead Eastern Jewry.

As far back as during the Babylonian exile the internal religious and legal autonomy of the Jewish community had been recognised by the government. The national leader was the Exilarch, and parallel offices existed in the communities of Egypt and the rest of the dispersion. The holders of these offices, existing in similar forms under the Persian, Greek, Roman, and Muslim rulers, enjoyed jurisdiction over their flock in matters of their ancestral law. In the Christian world, likewise, the local rabbis assumed such power by virtue of government privileges.

In addition to the political necessity for a centralised representation, the Qara'ite danger fostered the hierarchical organisation of rabbinical Judaism. But there were also other factors curtailing the basic freedom of learning and opinion within the realm of Jewish law, making it as static and inflexible as it is today.

Printing, to begin with, helped to spread the code of Joseph Qaro in all quarters of the Jewish world. Hence questions were decided according to one comprehensive standard work, the views of which became, as it were, canonised. This was all the more so as a result of the belief in a continued decadence of the generations since the early teachers. The limitations of contemporary rabbis were, thus, taken for granted, and little could be expected from them. Only in exceptional cases was there readiness to assume the existence of improved conditions, as compared with the time when a certain rule was first laid down, so that it would be reasonable to change it.

Moreover, the rigidity of present-day jurisprudence is a reaction to the Jewish Reform movement of the last hundred and fifty years. Orthodox rabbis, feeling the danger of Reform to the existence of Jewry in the dispersion, reject even just criticism and positive suggestions. The founder of modern orthodoxy, Moses Schreiber of Pressburg (1763–1839), declared 'any innovation to be against biblical law.' In his view, the only thing to do to combat violations of the law was to add restrictive measures, but never to amend the law itself. We will come back to this view, when speaking of the problems of future development. Meanwhile, however, some general remarks on the development of Jewish law in the past may be appropriate.

Studying the classical sources, such as the *Mishnah*, one has great difficulty in distinguishing between theoretical and practical jurisprudence. A rule, for instance, providing for an individual warning of the accused before he commits the offence as a prerequisite of his conviction seems to have had little basis in reality. It must rather have been an academic theory, a criticism of the harshness of applied criminal law, or a pious wish. This may be an indication for the late dating of the norm, namely after the abolition of the criminal jurisdiction of the Synedrion. At that time the rabbis could afford to hold such an extremely mitigating view, thereby criticising the judicial practice of the Roman procurator. A similar situation had perhaps existed before 76 B.C., when the Synedrion was controlled by the Sadducees. Thus the rule is to be understood as a demand for leniency rather than as a legal norm. On the other hand, there are indications for the practical application of certain rules. A casuistic formulation of the fact that a passage is found in a responsum raises a presumption in favour of the realistic background, while the contents of commentaries and codes may be the result of academic reasoning.

But the modern development of Jewish law does not always result from systematic thinking. Owing to the multiplicity of opinions, most authors have adopted an eclectic method. Some of them count the opinions of the earlier authorities in order to decide according to the majority rule. Hence the same author sometimes contradicts himself by following this more or less arbitrary way of decision. The study of legal theory is thereby hampered. When making decisions on practical problems, moreover, the rabbi tends not to rely on a single view only but to justify his decision also according to the opposite view. This, again, gives Jewish law an empirical rather than systematic character, and often blurs the classical concepts.

Often the formulation of a rule is the result of sociological not legal considerations. During the fourth century the rabbis discussed the negligence of a person who had acted in order to protect another person from an illegal assault. One of the scholars held the former person not to be responsible for damage caused by his action, even if damage was caused to the victim or to an innocent bystander: 'This is not strictly the Law, but otherwise nobody would intervene to preserve anybody from danger.' Rather than insist on some dogmatic theory, this jurist took a practical course.

In general, however, the rabbinical attitude is dogmatic and does not rely on historical considerations. The law is given 'for ever to be observed throughout their generations by the people of Israel.' Dealing, for instance, with marriages out of the faith, Ezra applied the law of Deuteronomy, although the socio-political situation had changed. The Gentiles and Samaritans of the fifth century B.C. were not the inhabitants of the land of Canaan at the time of the conquest. Nevertheless, the right to intermarry with the former was prohibited under the Deuteronomic law. The opposite view was taken by Joshua ben Chananyah about A.D. 100, when asked whether an Ammonite convert should be allowed to marry into a Jewish family. 'Are Ammonites and Moabites still in their countries?' he replied, 'Sennacherib, King of Assyria, has meanwhile come up and mixed all the nations.' Thus the biblical injunction was practically abolished on historical considerations.

Such an attitude as the last was by no means the rule; most rabbis rather emphasised the divine origin of the law and its immutability. We have already said that the whole of Jewish law is permeated by religious considerations. Each transaction or obligation is measured by the standard of the sacred code, the result being such norms as the prohibition of interest, the demand of adequate consideration or the duty falling upon children to pay their father's debt. Especially matrimonial relations have always been understood against the background of religion.

Instead of the modern classification of acts into legal and illegal ones, Jewish law distinguishes between obligatory, meritorious, allowed, forbidden, and invalid acts. Sometimes religious penalties fulfil the function of civil sanctions, in other cases the latter are inflicted for religious transgressions. There are also basic duties and injunctions which are inculcated by celestial punishment as their only sanction.

In theory, the ancient Jewish state was but a means in the realisation of theocracy. Royal power was based upon the election of the king by God and upon the covenant of vassalage declaring the mutual rights and duties of God and king. However, while Scripture aims at the religious interpretation of history, it preserves at the same time various references to secular law and government. The king was elected by the people as well as by God, and beside the covenant making the king a vassal of God there was a covenant between king and people. This covenant, in fact, preceded the theory of the social contract and of the modern constitution. Rabbinical law, as already mentioned, has always had regard for public opinion and has recognised custom as a source of law. Though little distinction was made between religious and civil laws, the division into holy and secular matters was important in administration. Thus Jehoshaphat, when establishing a supreme court, appointed the chief priest as its president 'in all matters of the Lord,' while the ruler of the house of Judah was to preside 'in all the king's matters' (2 *Chron.* xix. 11).

Such a separation of powers was certainly fostered under the

Hasmonean regime. While the pietists and the Pharisees advocated the supremacy of the Synedrion, a king like Alexander Jannai (103–176) did not surrender his prerogatives. The constitutional struggle following this dispute has left various imprints in the law. The Pharisees, consequently, called for the abdication from either the royal or priestly office, though the two had been combined for several generations. 'You have enough with the crown,' they said, 'leave the diadem of priesthood to Aaron's offspring.'

According to their opinion, moreover, 'one does not go forth to war without the consent of the Synedrion,' and even the king can be summoned before the court to be charged with the commission of an offence. In this last matter, at least, the Pharisees had to give in, so that a later maxim has exempted the king from the jurisdiction of the court.

We have found Jewish law sometimes to be influenced by Gentile law. The theoretical basis of this process of reception was the recognition accorded by the rabbis to royal power. Jeremiah (xxix. 7) had advised the exiles to 'seek the welfare of the city where I have sent you into exile.' This was interpreted by the Babylonian scholar Mar Samuel in the third century B.C. that 'the law of the realm is law.' The Jews were, thus, to abide by the royal laws as well as by their own, for political power was thought to have been granted by God. The maxim mainly related to the duty of taxpaying, but it was also invoked in civil cases where one of the parties could show the state law to be in his favour. A French rabbi of the twelfth century offered the following explanation for the validity of the king's laws: 'All the people of the realm willingly accept the royal laws and make them valid.' A German colleague, on the other hand, relied on the feudal concept for justification of the power of legislation: 'All the land belongs to the king and the king may therefore expel the transgressor.'

This theory, then, was also mentioned when the power of Jewish kings was examined. A minority of scholars were ready to recognise the legislative acts of future Jewish kings on similar grounds. The majority, however, denied the legitimacy of lay legislation. Unlike the Gentile king of their age, went their argument, the kings of Israel would not be entitled to expel any citizen from the land. For every Jew was legally owner of a minimum share in the holy land and could not be deprived of this right by his ruler. The only form of legislation, therefore, was that promulgated by the rabbis or by the community itself.

These discussions had little practical application until the modern age. There was no question of any Jewish authority, rabbi, or layman, trying to abrogate Jewish law itself. The law was believed to be of divine origin and the rabbinical interpretation was accepted. The situation changed, however, as a result of the civil emancipation of the Jews starting in the late eighteenth century. Having become equal citizens, many of the French, German, and Italian Jews changed their traditional style of life in order to assimilate and to join Christian society. For these intellectuals and well-to-do upper-class people the Jewish law and tradition was but an obstacle to progress. The modernists did not limit themselves to changes in private life, but put pressure also upon the rabbis to make them agree to various legal reforms. Both ritual and law were to be modernised and adjusted to westernised society.

Similar demands were made by Napoleon. A Synedrion was convoked on his orders in 1807, representing the rabbis and laymen of French Jewry, to deal with various practical problems arising from Jewish emancipation. The members of the convention were expected to take a lenient stand on civil marriage and divorce and on marriage out of the faith, as established by the constitution. The majority, indeed, declared intermarriage to be compatible with Jewish law, though they held that a rabbi could not officiate at the ceremony. They also agreed to the abolition of Jewish judicial autonomy, referring all disputes, of Jews as well as of Christians, to the ordinary courts of the land.

The majority of the rabbis outside this Synedrion and the Jewish masses strongly opposed such suggestions. Their leader was the above-mentioned Moses Schreiber of Pressburg, who organised the orthodox reaction. The liberals, on the other hand, did not only establish synagogues of their own, but advocated various reforms in the law. Few of them, it is true, were as extreme as Samuel Holdheim (1806–1860), calling for the abolition of Jewish marriage and divorce altogether, legalising intermarriage, and advocating the repeal of Jewish legal autonomy. The law of the realm was sanctioned by Jewish law. Therefore, said Holdheim, if conflict arose between the two systems the law of the realm was to prevail. Thus, by making use of a talmudical rule, the whole of Jewish law might be put out of action.

World Jewry is nowadays divided into orthodox, conservative, and liberal communities, beside the considerable number of people without any synagogue affiliation. In Israel, on the other hand, only the pattern of oriental and eastern European orthodoxy is recognised, though there exists a small number of non-orthodox synagogues. Almost all the rabbis and all the rabbinical judges belong to the orthodox group, which is also supported by the religious parties accounting for about 15 per cent. of Parliament. Preserving a fundamentalist attitude towards law, these circles work for the state to become a theocracy, perhaps qualified by certain liberal and democratic tendencies.

The majority of Israel's population, on the other hand, has voted for the general parties, which have not endorsed the orthodox point of view. This is all the more remarkable, since the problems of state and religion have always raised the deepest emotions and have provoked the only major ideological conflict. Many of the observant laymen refuse to render assistance to the religious establishment, and thereby wish to dissent from the status quo. Intellectuals from various quarters, secular judges, and politicians have often asked for changes in the religious organisation of the Jewish community and in the institutes of Jewish law.

Two important reforms of Jewish law are, indeed, due to the British government of Palestine. According to the request of Jewish secularists, the government demanded that the rabbinical assembly accept two changes in their judicial practice before being given legal status. A rabbinical court of appeal was to be established, and a right of appeal was given to litigants in the rabbinical court. The other reform dealt with the law of inheritance, which did not, originally, provide for the wife and daughters. This disqualification was to be abolished, unless all the parties had agreed to the distribution according to the former rule.

The majority of the rabbis, wishing to receive the official status, acceded to these conditions, which were then made law. A minority, however, dissented from what they called a breach of tradition. They established an independent orthodox community, headed by a court which acted only under the Arbitration Ordinance without compulsory jurisdiction. The government recognised the marriages performed by their rabbis but not their divorces.

In the State of Israel the exclusive jurisdiction of the official rabbinical courts was extended to all Jews, whether citizens or residents, but this jurisdiction was limited, on the other hand, to cover matters of marriage and divorce only. Questions of constitutional, criminal, or private law have been determined in accordance with the law which was in force up to the establishment of the state, and statutes have mainly been modelled after western patterns.

On a number of occasions even the rules of family law have been reformed by the legislature. Needless to say, the Rabbinate and the religious parties opposed each of these bills, which, consequently, took the form of compromises. Thus it was provided that women should enjoy equality of status regarding polygamy, guardianship, maintenance of children, succession rights, and matrimonial property. The age of marriage was raised to seventeen and the age of majority to eighteen. Provision was made for the adoption of minors (a novelty), and common-law marriages[12] were recognised for the acquisition of pension rights, names, and inheritance. Following an international convention, finally, a law enabled the civil courts to issue declarations of death, to be used in succession cases, though not for remarriage. The usual formula of compromise in statutes of this kind is a proviso that nothing in the law should affect the rules of marriage and divorce.

There exist, however, various problems making the application of Jewish law difficult and shaking the equilibrium of state and religion. In matters of marriage and divorce, as already mentioned, no respect has been paid, so far, to the status acquired abroad. This is rather unsatisfactory in a country of immigrants. Non-believing Jews, moreover, will not for long renounce the possibility of marrying out of the faith or of choosing a spouse in contravention of religious injunctions. Difficulties have also been experienced where a marriage should be dissolved without the agreement of one of the parties or where divorce is not feasible under talmudical law. These problems will probably be the cause of the introduction of civil marriage and divorce, at least as an alternative to the present system.[13]

Even more complicated is the question who is a Jew, which is asked for purposes of immigration, registration, capacity of marriage, and jurisdiction. Instead of the objective criterion of Jewish tradition, the national feeling and the bona fide declaration have been advocated by secular circles. Again, some account will have to be taken of the cases of proselytism originating with the views of non-orthodox rabbis abroad, who had admitted converts somewhat too generously for the liking of the scrupulous.

Finally, the monopolistic status of the orthodox community and rabbinate will not be maintained for very long. The democratic and liberal state will ultimately grant a certain measure of recognition to Jewish dissident groups. The orthodox community itself, moreover, will have to adjust its constitution to democratic practice, thus gradually taking into account the non-observant membership. The equality of women, likewise, will then be extended so far as to make them eligible for legal and religious office.

What are the chances for an evolutional adjustment of Jewish law to the modern state? Much seems to depend on rabbinical education and the future type resulting therefrom. The new religious leader will have to speak a common language with the public at large, to carry his listeners away by his personal example, and to apply a certain dose of criticism to holy tradition. Let us hope that the modern

[12] That is to say marriages founded on the consent of the spouses *de facto* without ceremony of any kind.

[13] An innovation which the experience of India would seem to encourage. *Ed.*

state will be patient enough to wait for this leader to rise. It would be a tragic break with the whole past and with the dispersion, still considerable at present, if Israel were to declare itself to be purely secular and abolish Jewish law. The future of the Jewish state depends on the preservation of its cultural identity and on the religious continuity of the chosen people.

BIBLIOGRAPHY

The principal texts are to be found in:

The Babylonian Talmud, trans. I. Epstein (London, Soncino Press, 1939–48; index volume 1952).

H. Danby, *The Mishnah* (Oxford, 1933).

Moses Maimonides, *Mishneh Torah*, in the course of translation by various authors (New Haven, Yale Judaica Series).

Joseph Qaro, *Shulḥan 'Arukh*, trans. J. L. Kadushin, 4 vols. (New York, Jewish Jurisprudence Co., 1915–28).

L. Finkelstein, *Jewish Self-Government in the Middle Ages* (New York, Feldheim, 1964).

Works of reference include:

The Jewish Encyclopaedia (New York–London, 1901–6).

The Universal Jewish Encyclopaedia (New York, 1939–43).

Ze'ev W. Falk, *Hebrew Law in Biblical Times* (Jerusalem, Wahrmann Book, 1964).

G. Horowitz, *The Spirit of Jewish Law* (New York, Central Book Co., 1953) (a succinct and comparative survey of the rules of law as well as their leading principles).

Family and succession laws are dealt with in:

L. M. Epstein, *The Jewish Marriage Contract* (New York, Jewish Theological Seminary, 1927).

L. M. Epstein, *Marriage Laws in Bible and Talmud* (Cambridge, Mass., Harvard University Press, 1942).

Ze'ev W. Falk, *Jewish Matrimonial Law in the Middle Ages* (London, Oxford University Press, 1966).

R. Yaron, *Gifts in Contemplation of Death* (Oxford, Clarendon Press, 1960).

The law of obligations and property is covered by:

I. Herzog. *The Main Institutions of Jewish Law*, 2nd ed., 2 vols. (London, Soncino Press, 1967).

For the predicament of Israel we may consult:

G. Tedeschi and U. Yadin, *Scripta Hierosolymitana XVI: Studies in Israel Legislative Problems* (Jerusalem, Magnes Press; London, Oxford University Press, 1967).

The beginner's best guides to the literature and its techniques are Z. H. Chajes, *The Student's Guide through the Talmud*,[1] trans. J. Shachter (New York, Feldheim, 1960) and H. L. Strack, *Introduction to the Talmud and Midrash* (Philadelphia, Jewish Publication Society, 1945, and Meridian Books, New York, 1959). M. Waxman, *History of Jewish Literature*, 5 vols. (New York, T. Yoseloff, 1950) is important for post-talmudic literature.

Various studies deserving special note include D. Daube, *Studies in Biblical Law* (Cambridge University Press, 1947), J. J. Rabinowitz, *Jewish Law* (New York, Bloch, 1956), which shows how Jewish business usage influenced the development of commercial law throughout Europe, and even affected the growth of the English law of securities for loans; B. Cohen, *Jewish and Roman Law*, 2 vols. (New York, Jewish Theological Seminary, 1966), which is a collection of profound comparative studies; and S. Belkin, *Philo and the Oral Law* (Cambridge, Mass., Harvard University Press, 1940), which illuminates Alexandrian Judaism.

The religious outlook of the rabbis and their handling of the sacred text in *haggadah* is expounded in M. Kadushin, *The Rabbinic Mind*, 2nd ed. (New York, Blaisdell Publishing Co., 1965). The predicament of modern Israel is handled in A. Rubinstein, 'Law and religion in Israel,' *Israel Law Review*, ii (1967), pp. 380–414

ISLAMIC LAW

N. J. Coulson

ISLAMIC LAW (known in some parts of the world as 'Muhammadan law') is a body of rules which gives practical expression to the religious faith and aspiration of the Muslim. Total and unqualified submission to the will of Allāh is the fundamental tenet of Islam, and the law which is associated with the religion defines the will of Allāh in terms of a comprehensive code of behaviour covering all aspects of life. *All* aspects of life: for ritual practices, such as prayer, fasting, alms, and pilgrimage, the subjects of permissible foods and styles of dress, and social etiquette generally are as vital and integral a part of the system as those topics which are strictly legal in the western sense of the term. Known as the 'Sharīʿa,' a derivative of an Arabic root word meaning 'track' or 'road,' this law constitutes a divinely ordained path of conduct which guides the Muslim towards fulfilment of his religious conviction in this life and reward from his Creator in the world to come.

From the advent of Islam in early seventh-century Arabia the task assumed by Muslim jurisprudence was the discovery of the terms of Allāh's law for Muslim society. Legal scholarship gradually built up a corpus of doctrine, and by the end of the tenth century Sharīʿa had achieved a definitive formulation in legal manuals composed by individual jurists. Throughout the medieval period this basic doctrine was elaborated and systematised in a large number of commentaries, and the voluminous literature thus produced constitutes, in sum, the traditional textual authorities of Sharīʿa law.

As the expression of the ideal Islamic way of life, traditional Sharīʿa doctrine must form the focal point of any enquiry into law in Islam. But for two principal reasons the medieval legal manuals are far from presenting a factual picture of the laws that govern the lives of Muslims today.

In the first place law in contemporary Islam is by no means exclusively Islamic. Inevitably perhaps, in Islam as in other philosophies of life, there has always existed some degree of conflict between theory and reality and of tension between the religious idealism of the doctrine and the demands of political, social, and economic expediency. On grounds of practical necessity Muslim states and societies have recognised and applied laws whose terms are contrary to the religious doctrine expounded in the medieval legal manuals.[1] Within the vast geographical spread of Islam and the many different peoples who make up its four hundred million adherents, customary law has always controlled many aspects of life. And in recent times an ever-increasing field of legal relationships has become governed by laws imported from foreign, and particularly European, sources. Behind this complex diversity of current legal practice the Sharīʿa may stand as a symbol of the ideological unity of all Muslim communities and, in so far as it is applied in practice, may be regarded as the common law of Islam. Nevertheless, Sharīʿa doctrine forms only part of the law applied by Muslim courts.

The second reason why the medieval Sharīʿa texts can no longer be regarded as complete authorities for current law in Islam is the fact that the doctrine they expound does not today have a paramount or exclusive validity as the expression of Sharīʿa law. In several Muslim countries laws now apply which are at variance with the dictates of the traditional authorities but which purport none the less to represent a legitimate version of Allāh's law. These recent developments have given to Islamic law a new historical perspective. Sharīʿa doctrine, which grew to maturity in the first three centuries of Islam and which then remained essentially static for a period of ten centuries, appears now in the course of further evolution.

It will be evident from these introductory remarks that Sharīʿa law today has been conditioned by a legal history in Islam extending over almost fourteen centuries. Accordingly, this review will adopt a basically historical approach to the subject. By what process of growth did Sharīʿa doctrine attain its traditionally authoritative expression in the medieval legal manuals? To what extent and for what reasons has legal practice in Islam diverged from the dictates of this Sharīʿa doctrine? On what basis and with what effect has the traditional doctrine today been superseded in those fields of law which are still formally governed by the Sharīʿa? It is in the answers to these three broad questions that lies the key to an appreciation of the nature and role of Islamic law in contemporary Muslim society.

For the first community of Muslims, founded in Medina under the leadership of the Prophet Muhammad in A.D. 622, Islam meant obedience to the will of Allāh transmitted to His community through His messenger in a series of revelations which occurred piecemeal throughout Muhammad's lifetime and which, duly collected and written down, form the *Qurʾān*. As the very word of Allāh himself, the *Qurʾān* is, historically and ideologically, the primary expression of the Islamic law.

[1] We find the same in Jewish law, above, pp. 48–49. *Ed.*

But the *Qur'ān* is not essentially a legislative document. It contains a great number of moral precepts of a general nature, relating to such matters as just retribution, fairness in commercial dealings, and compassion for the weaker members of society, but these norms are not generally translated into any legal structure of rights and duties. Thus, wine-drinking and usury are simply declared to be 'forbidden.' Polygamy is permitted, a husband being allowed to have up to a maximum of four wives concurrently, provided he treats his wives with impartiality; but nothing is said as to the precise legal significance of this proviso or as to any remedies a wife may have in the event of its infringement. In short, the *Qur'ān* is not a code of law (in the sense that it does not attempt to be comprehensive) but the basic formulation of the Islamic religious ethic.

Certainly the *Qur'ān* does contain many regulations of a more strictly legal tone. These range over a wide variety of subjects and constituted far-reaching reforms of the customary tribal law of Arabia. New criminal offences, with attendant penalties, were introduced—such as the penalty of flogging for fornication and for an unproved accusation of illicit sexual relations. The legal status of women was greatly improved in a variety of respects, *inter alia* by the rule that the dower, or payment made by the husband in consideration of marriage, belonged to the wife herself and not, as was common previously, to her father or other guardian who had given her in marriage. And yet most of these rules have the appearance of *ad hoc* solutions for particular problems. There is no real attempt in the *Qur'ān* to deal with any one legal topic or relationship comprehensively. Its regulations set out to modify the existing customary law in certain particulars rather than to supplant that law with an entirely new system.

The general nature of Qur'anic law is aptly illustrated by the provisions relating to the institution of divorce by unilateral repudiation, or *talāq*. Under the patriarchal customary law of Arabia the right of a husband to terminate his marriage at will by simply repudiating his wife was undisputed. The *Qur'ān* makes no attempt to deprive husbands of this power, but simply urges them not to abuse it, speaking of 'releasing wives with consideration' and 'making a fair provision' for wives who are so repudiated. An existing legal institution is subjected to new moral standards directed solely, so far as the *Qur'ān* itself is concerned, at the individual conscience.

Up to the year A.D. 661 Medina continued to be the centre of Muslim activity. During his lifetime Muhammad was accepted as the supreme arbitrator of the community and solved legal problems, as and when they arose, by interpreting the relevant Qur'anic revelations. After the Prophet's death in 632 the mantle of his judicial authority was assumed by the Caliphs, who succeeded to political leadership, and their decisions, together with those of the Prophet, marked the beginning of the growth of a body of law which supplemented and expanded the general precepts of the *Qur'ān*.

The fundamental problem facing the Prophet and his successors in their judicial capacity was the precise determination of the relationship between the new Qur'anic provisions and the traditional standards of the customary law. One of the spheres in which the conflict and tension between the old and the new orders of society was particularly apparent was the system of inheritance. Since the pre-Islamic Arabian tribe was patrilineal and patriarchal—its solidarity stemming from the tie of blood relationship that existed between a group of males who traced their descent, through male links, from a common ancestor—succession to property at death was traditionally confined to male *agnate* relatives, or *'asaba*. The *Qur'ān*, however, laid repeated emphasis upon the closer family tie that existed between parents and their children and envisaged this narrower group, within which the female was given a higher and more responsible status, as the proper unit of Muslim society. In accordance with this policy, the *Qur'ān* gave rights of inheritance to certain close female relatives—the wife, daughter, mother, and sister—by prescribing fixed fractional portions (*farā'id*) of the estate as their entitlement. But the absence in the *Qur'ān* itself of any specific regulations dealing with the rights of inheritance of male agnate relatives as such created the problem of the relationship between the old tribal heirs and the new heirs nominated by the *Qur'ān*. Because rights of inheritance were intimately bound up with the structure of family ties and responsibilities, and because the influx of new wealth from the military conquests had produced a popular concern with the manner of its distribution, the problem was one of considerable practical importance; and the decisions on the subject attributed to the Prophet and the Medinan Caliphs provide significant examples of the process of early legal development.

In the case of the estate of Sa'd, the widow of the deceased complained that all Sa'd's property had been claimed by his brother, as his nearest male agnate relative, to the exclusion of herself and her two daughters. The Prophet ordered that, in accordance with the Qur'anic provisions, the widow should receive one eighth of Sa'd's estate, the two daughters their prescribed collective portion of two thirds, and the brother the residue—a share of five twenty-fourths of the estate. This decision laid down what may be termed the golden rule of the Islamic law of inheritance: that those relatives nominated by the *Qur'ān* first take their prescribed portions and the male agnates then take the residue. In this way the two distinct classes of heirs—the new Islamic heirs and the traditional heirs of the customary law—were merged into a composite system of succession.

Sa'd's case clearly shows that the rights of the traditional heirs—in the present instance the agnatic brother who alone would have inherited under the customary law—were now seriously diminished by the Qur'anic regulations. And yet the significant fact is that the brother was allowed to inherit at all when the deceased was survived by daughters. For the *Qur'ān* expressly declares that a brother does not inherit 'when the deceased is survived by a child.' The word 'child' was apparently taken to mean 'male child,' so that a brother would be excluded from succession by a son of the deceased but not by a daughter. Such considerations make it plain that the early authorities regarded it as proper to interpret the Qur'anic precepts in the light of the accepted standards of the customary law. In fact, the Islamic law of inheritance was so developed on this basis that the '*asaba* generally retained a predominant position as legal heirs. The Qur'anic heirs were simply superimposed upon the customary system and confined strictly to the portions prescribed for them by the *Qur'ān*. Although their portions are a first charge upon the deceased's estate, no Qur'anic heir can totally exclude any male agnate from succession. Where, for example, a deceased is survived by his daughter and a distant male agnate cousin, the daughter will take only her prescribed portion of half and the cousin the remaining half as residuary heir. This restrictive interpretation of the Qur'anic provisions and the perpetuation of the traditional standards of the customary law was by no means confined to inheritance, but was a central feature of general legal development in the Medinan period.

Under the hegemony of the Umayyad dynasty (A.D. 661–750) Islam was transformed from the small and closely knit religious community of Medina into a vast military empire with its central government at Damascus. Local governors were appointed to control the affairs of the conquered provinces, and it became standard practice for the local governor to delegate his judicial powers to an official known as the *qāḍī*. It was the activities of the *qāḍīs*, or judges, that produced a growing diversity in Islamic legal practice.

The first reason for this was the fact that the extent to which decisions were based upon the text of the *Qur'ān* or the precedents of the early Medinan authorities depended upon the degree of knowledge and piety possessed by the individual *qāḍī*. Moreover, the precise interpretation of those rules often produced difference of opinion, even among the judiciary of one particular locality. Verses of the *Qur'ān*, for example, urge husbands to make 'a fair provision' for wives they have repudiated. Ibn Hujayra, who was *qāḍī* of Cairo from

688 to 702, considered such provision to be obligatory and fixed its amount at three dinars. But in 733 a later *qāḍī* of Cairo, Tawba ibn Namir, decided that the Qurʿanic injunction was directed only to the individual's conscience and that a husband who refused to pay such compensation could not be compelled to do so. Under Tawba's successor, payment once again became a strict legal obligation.

The second reason for diversity in legal practice lay in the fact that the *qāḍīs* saw themselves essentially as the spokesmen of the local customary law, which varied considerably. In Medina, for example, where society had preserved the traditional standards of Arabian tribal law, no woman could contract a marriage on her own account but had to be given in marriage by her guardian. In the Iraqian locality of Kufa, on the other hand, the admixture of diverse ethnic groups in a predominantly Persian milieu produced a cosmopolitan atmosphere in which women occupied a less-inferior position than they did in Medina, and the *qāḍīs* of Kufa upheld the right of an adult woman to conclude her own marriage contract without the intervention of her guardian. Moreover, it was through this recognition of local norms and standards that elements of Byzantine, Roman, and Persian law were absorbed into Islamic legal practice in the conquered territories. The recognition by *qāḍīs* in Iraq of the age of twenty-five as the age of emancipation from guardianship of property revealed the influence of the Roman law of *curatio*, while in Medina the *qāḍīs* continued to observe the customary Arabian rule that guardianship terminated upon the physical puberty of the ward. As a result of these diverse influences and local standards, Islamic legal practice under the Umayyads lost the unity and cohesion it had enjoyed during the Medinan period.

From the year 720 the mounting wave of political hostility against the Umayyads, condemned as rulers whose Arab kingdom had lost sight of the fundamental principles of the religion, found a particular expression in the field of law. Pious scholars, concluding that the practices of the Umayyad courts had failed properly to implement the spirit of the Qurʿanic precepts, began to give voice to their ideas of standards of conduct which would represent the systematic fulfilment of the true Islamic religious ethic. Grouped together for this purpose in loose studious fraternities, they formed what may be called the early schools of law. These schools mark the true beginning of Islamic jurisprudence, and their development derived a major impetus from the accession to power of the Abbasids in 750; for the legal scholars were publicly recognised as the architects of an Islamic scheme of state and society which the Abbasids had pledged themselves to build. From Abbasid times onwards it is upon the jurist, or *faqīh* (pl. *fuqahāʾ*), that attention must focus; for it was the *fuqahāʾ*

who formulated the doctrine, which it was simply the task of the *qāḍī* to apply.

Of the many different schools of law which existed in the various territories of Islam at this time the two established at Medina and Kufa were particularly important. The objective of both these schools was identical: it was to formulate the ideal scheme of Islamic law. Institutions and activities were systematically reviewed in the light of the principles enshrined in the *Qur'ān* and the precedents of the early human authorities and approved or rejected on that basis. But because, within those limits, the individual jurist was free to exercise his personal reasoning (*ra'y*), and because the thought of the jurists was naturally conditioned by their particular social environment, the corpus of legal doctrine which gradually evolved in the school of Medina differed to no small degree from that of Kufa. Outside the common ground of the explicit provisions of the *Qur'ān* and the accepted precedents of the early authorities, local custom was ratified by the doctrine just as it had been recognised in the judgments of the Umayyad *qāḍīs*.

Thus, following the established practice of the courts in the two localities, Kufan doctrine allowed an adult woman to conclude her own marriage contract, while Medinan doctrine required the contract to be concluded by the marriage guardian. With the advent of the literary period in law, the notion of local allegiance, upon which the different schools of law had originally been founded, was replaced by the personal authority of the authors of the first legal treatises. Malik ben Anas (*d.* 796) had produced the first compendium of Medinan doctrine and the Medinan school became known as the Maliki school. In Kufa the prolific author Shaybani had attributed the authority for his writings to his master Abu Hanifa, and that school accordingly became known as the Hanafi school.

Increasing attention was now given by the jurists to the question of the authority of the doctrine and the sources from which it was derived; and this jurisprudential debate produced further conflict and disagreement both between and within the different schools. At root the debate turned upon the scope that was to be allowed to the personal reasoning of the jurists in their attempt to ascertain the terms of Allāh's will. The originally accepted freedom of speculation (*ra'y*) in the absence of any explicit text of divine revelation began to be questioned, and many argued that reasoning should be more disciplined and by way of deduction (*qiyās*) by means of analogy from established rules. In the Hanafi school, for example, the rule that the minimum dower payable by the husband on marriage was ten dirhams was the acknowledged result of *ra'y* on the part of a jurist who did not 'think it proper that a marriage should be contracted for less than this sum.' In the Maliki school, on the other hand, an attempt was made to base the rule of the minimum dower on *qiyās*. A rough parallel was drawn between amputation of the hand, as the penalty prescribed by the *Qur'ān* for theft, and the loss of a woman's virginity as the physical result of marriage. Since the Prophet had ruled that the penalty of amputation was not applicable unless the stolen goods reached a minimum value of three dirhams, the same sum should represent the minimum consideration payable by the husband in respect of marriage!

However, a much more radical attitude towards juristic reasoning was adopted by the so-called *ahl al-ḥadīth*, or 'supporters of Traditions.' This group of scholars, representing opposition to the current legal method of both the Hanafi and the Maliki schools, maintained that the use of juristic reasoning in any form was both illegitimate and unnecessary. Outside the *Qur'ān*, they argued, the only true source of law lay in the practice of the Prophet Muhammad, the one person who was qualified to interpret and explain the divine will. His practice, or *sunna*, was to be found in Traditions, or *ḥadīth*, which described what the Prophet had said or done on particular occasions. And since the *Qur'ān* had declared that 'man was not left without guidance,' the *sunna* of the Prophet was without doubt comprehensive. It was simply the task of the jurists to discover this *sunna*, through the *ḥadīth*, rather than to indulge in speculative reasoning as to what Allāh's law might be.

The conflict of principle between the generality of jurists and the *ahl al-ḥadīth* had now shown that the basic dilemma of legal theory lay in determining the precise relationship between divine revelation and human reason in law. And it was at this point that the scholar Shafi'i emerged as the most influential figure in the history of Islamic jurisprudence.

Shafi'i was the first jurist to expound, systematically and unequivocally, the principle that certain knowledge of Allāh's law could be attained only through divine revelation. Outside the *Qur'ān*, he maintained, the only other legitimate material source of law lay in the decisions and precedents of the Prophet Muhammad. Muhammad was Allāh's chosen instrument, not only the mouthpiece to transmit Allāh's word of the *Qur'ān* but also the infallible exponent of the sacred law in matters not specifically regulated by the *Qur'ān*. The Prophet's legal activities were divinely inspired. His practice, as ascertained through reliable *ḥadīth*, was the divinely ordained *sunna*, explaining and supplementing the *Qur'ān* and ranking alongside it as an equally authoritative source of Allāh's law.

Where problems arose which were not specifically solved by any text of the *Qur'ān* or *sunna*, Shafi'i accepted the necessity for reasoning, but only in the strictly disciplined and subsidiary form of reasoning by analogy (*qiyās*). He roundly condemned the methods of juristic reasoning which were current in the early law schools as attempts to rationalise the ends or purposes which the law should serve and formulate the appropriate legal rule thereby. For, Shafiʿi argued, the purposes that law should serve were a matter for Allāh alone. The function of jurisprudence was not to make law but simply to discover it from the substance of divine revelation and, where necessary, apply the principles enshrined therein to new problems by analogical reasoning.

Shafiʿi's avowed aim in thus formulating a firm theory of the sources from which law should be derived was to instil into Muslim jurisprudence a uniformity which was conspicuously lacking at this time. Diversity in the law had arisen from the recognition in the legal method of the early schools of local and personal criteria—the tradition of a particular locality and the individual opinions or collective consensus of its scholars. In his doctrines, *viz.*, of one valid tradition—the *sunna* of the Prophet—a systematic method of reasoning and a consensus of the whole Muslim community, Shafiʿi was replacing the local and limited elements in current jurisprudence with concepts of an application and validity universal for Islam. A statement in his *Risāla*—the work he composed in Cairo, where he spent the last five years before his death in 820—serves as a summary of his doctrine and the purpose which inspired it. 'On points on which there exists an explicit ruling of Allāh or a *sunna* of the Prophet or a consensus of all the Muslims, no disagreement is allowed; on the other points scholars must exert their own judgment in search of an indication in one of these three sources. . . . If a problem is capable of two solutions either opinion may be held as a result of systematic reasoning; but this occurs only rarely.'

Shafiʿi's legal theory, in setting the authority of law on to an altogether higher plane, expressed the fundamental aspirations of Muslim legal philosophy and was assured of eventual acceptance.

Many scholars now devoted themselves to the task of documenting the *sunna* through the collection and classification of *ḥadīths*, and during the latter part of the ninth century several compilations of *ḥadīths* were produced which claimed to have sifted the genuine from the false. Two such manuals in particular, those of al-Bukhari (*d.* 870) and Muslim (*d.* 875) have always enjoyed a high reputation as authentic accounts of the *sunna* of the Prophet.

But despite this activity in support of Shafiʿi's doctrine, his dream of a basically uniform and common law for Islam was not to be realised. In fact, as a result of his work two more schools of law were formed in addition to those which already existed.

Those who were prepared to accept absolutely the precise terms of Shafi'i's doctrine were a minority and formed the Shafi'i school, while from a group who carried the doctrine of the authority of *ḥadīths* to even more rigid extremes the Hanbali school originated. Its founder, Ahmad ben Hanbal (*d.* 855), rejected human reason in any form, including *qiyās*, as a source of law and insisted that each and every legal rule could find its requisite authority only in the *Qur'ān* or the *sunna.*

The established schools of the Malikis and Hanafis, on the other hand, while unwilling to deny the authority of Prophetic precedents, were equally unwilling to revise their existing body of law in the light of those precedents. But they managed to reconcile their existing law with the fundamental dictates of Shafi'i's theory. From the great mass of *ḥadīths* which had now been 'discovered' and put into circulation, support for their particular doctrines could usually be found, and the effect of *ḥadīths* which contradicted their established doctrine could be minimised through juristic interpretation.

Once this process of adjustment was complete, the Hanafis and Malikis formally acknowledged the principle of the supreme authority of *ḥadīths*. The Hanbalis, on the other hand, also modified their original position by recognising that *qiyās* was a necessary instrument in the elaboration of the law. And thus, by the end of the ninth century, Muslim jurisprudence as a whole had succeeded in absorbing the master's teaching in a form acceptable variously in the four schools.

The classical legal theory, which grew from the developments described, consists of the formulation and analysis of the principles by which comprehension of the terms of the divine law is to be achieved. The general process of endeavour to comprehend the divine law is termed *ijtihād*, and in defining the course that this must follow classical jurisprudence followed Shafi'i's doctrine; for the *mujtahid* (the scholar exercising *ijtihād*) must first seek the solution of legal problems in the *Qur'ān* and the *sunna*, and failing any specific regulation therein must then use the method of analogical deduction or *qiyās*. But in regulating the effect of such *ijtihād* and evaluating its results in terms of the authority which they should command as expressions of the divine will, classical jurisprudence wrote an extremely important supplement to Shafi'i's legal theory in its doctrine of *ijmā'*.

Ijmā', as defined by the classical jurists, is the agreement of the qualified legal scholars in a given generation, and such consensus of opinion is deemed infallible.

In the attempt to define the will of God, the *ijtihād* of individual scholars could result only in a tentative or probable conclusion termed *ẓann* (conjecture). Where, however, such conclusions were the subject of general agreement by the scholars they then became incontrovertible and infallible expressions of God's law. *Ijmāʿ* thus guarantees the totality of the results of *ijtihād* legitimately exercised. Consensus of opinion produces certain knowledge of God's will; but at the same time, where no consensus is in fact achieved, variant opinions are recognised as equally valid attempts to define that will.[2]

The effects which flowed from this doctrine of *ijmāʿ* have dominated Islamic legal history since medieval times. In the first place *ijmāʿ* operated as a permissive principle to tolerate variations in substantive legal doctrine between the different schools and individual jurists. The acceptance by Muslim jurisprudence of the phenomenon of variant versions of Sharīʿa law is reflected in the alleged words of the Prophet Muhammad: 'Difference of opinion within my community is a sign of the bounty of Allāh.' With a philosophy of candid pluralism, the four schools of law—Hanafis, Malikis, Shafiʿis, and Hanbalis—are blended together as inseparable manifestations of the same single essence under the blanket authority of the principle of *ijmāʿ*.

Geographically, from medieval times onwards, the division between the schools was well defined, inasmuch as the courts in different regions of Islam had gradually come to apply the doctrine of one particular school—whether as a result of the voluntary adoption of a school by the population of a given area or because the political authority appointed judges who were wedded to the doctrine of a particular school. Thus, broadly speaking, Hanafi law came to predominate in the Middle East and the Indian sub-continent, Maliki law in North, West, and Central Africa, and Shafiʿi law in East Africa and parts of the Arabian peninsula, Malaysia and Indonesia. The Hanbali school did not succeed in gaining any real territorial dominion until it was officially adopted by the political Wahhabi movement in the eighteenth century, since when it has been the law applied by the courts in Saudi Arabia.

It is true that the several schools have the same fundamental structure of doctrine and the same basic legal institutions. At the same time, from the examples of the differences between the Malikis and the Hanafis which have already been given and from others which will appear in due course, it is clear that the schools represent essentially distinct systems whose individual characteristics were fashioned largely by their circumstances of origin and growth. The philosophy of the mutual orthodoxy of the schools should not

[2] This accords with the Jewish belief that discordant opinions are equally 'words of the living God.' See above, p. 43. In Hindu law jurisprudence is in theory a unity, though variant practices may be valid as *customs*. *Ed.*

obscure the fact that geography and history created a four-fold division in the legal practice of Sunni Islam.

Sunni, or 'orthodox' Islam, is the term used to distinguish the vast majority of Muslims from certain minority groups or sects of Muslims who diverge from the Sunnis on basic theological issues and tenets.

Among these important sects the numerically strongest group is that of the Shi'a, who oppose the Sunni belief that Muhammad was the last person to have contact with the divinity and maintain that after his death divine inspiration was transmitted to the line of his descendants through his surviving daughter Fatima. These descendants of the Prophet are recognised by the Shi'a as rulers, or Imams, by divine right. The Shi'a possess their own particular version of Sharī'a law, and at this point a brief comparison between their law and that of the Sunnis on the subject of inheritance may serve to illustrate the extent of the divergence between them.

Although there are many aspects of the laws of inheritance upon which the Sunni schools are divided among themselves, the fundamental scheme of succession is common to them all. In particular, they all subscribe to the basic principle that it is the male agnates who have pride of place as legal heirs. In total contrast, Shi'i law wholly repudiates the criterion of the agnatic tie. 'As for the male agnates,' the Shi'i Imam Ja'far is alleged to have said, 'dust in their jaws.' According to Shi'i law, all relatives, male and female, agnate and non-agnates, are integrated into a single system of priorities, under which parents and lineal descendants exclude brothers and sisters and grandparents, who in turn exclude uncles and aunts and their issue.

It is perhaps in the position of the female and non-agnatic descendants of the deceased *vis à vis* the collaterals that the divergence between the two systems is at its most apparent. In Sunni law the daughter does not exclude male agnate collaterals, however remote,[3] while daughter's children, male or female, are totally excluded by any male agnate collateral. In Shi'i law, on the other hand, any lineal descendant will totally exclude all collaterals from inheritance.

This distinction has both a social and a juristic significance. From the standpoint of social relationships Sunni law, recognising the claims of the agnate collaterals, embodies the concept of the extended family or tribal group. Shi'i law, on the other hand, rests firmly upon the predominance of the narrower tie of relationship existing between parents and their issue. From a juristic standpoint the fundamental question involved is the interpretation of the *Qur'ān*. The Sunnis clearly regarded the Qur'anic regulations as piecemeal reforms to be superimposed upon the existing customary law, impliedly

[3] For example, a father's father's brother's son's son's son.

endorsed by the *Qur'ān* unless it expressly rejected it. Hence the fusion in their scheme of inheritance between the male agnates, the old heirs of the customary law, and the new heirs specified by the *Qur'ān*. The Shi'a, on the other hand, regarded the Qur'anic provision as constituting an outright break with past practice and laying down the first principles for the elaboration of an entirely novel system of law. From these first principles in the matter of succession, which stress the rights of female relatives and nowhere indicate the pre-eminence of the agnate relationship as such, they constructed a law of succession which ignored the criteria of the tribal customary law, and which they claimed was more in conformity with the spirit and intendment of the *Qur'ān*. The individual approach of the Shi'i jurists here certainly serves to underline the fact that it had consistently been the accepted *modus operandi* of Sunni jurists to interpret the *Qur'ān* in the light of the conditions and mood of their social environment.

To return now to the effect of the classical legal theory upon Sunni law, the consensus of opinion, as has been explained, endorsed the variant doctrines of the four schools as equally legitimate. But *ijmā'* also operated as a prohibitive and exclusive principle. For once *ijmā'* had cast the umbrella of its infallible authority not only over those points which were the subject of a consensus but also over the existing variant opinions, the contemporary situation was irrevocably ratified inasmuch as to propound any further variant opinion was to contradict the *ijmā'*, the infallible expression of God's will, and so to be guilty of heresy! Hence the right of independent effort, or *ijtihād*, to ascertain Allāh's law disappeared. *Ijmā'* had set the final seal upon the doctrine which, as it existed in the early tenth century, was represented as the culmination of the quest to express the law in terms of the will of God; and Muslim jurisprudence recognised that its creative force was now spent by declaring that 'the door of *ijtihād* was closed.'

This phenomenon ushered in the era of *taqlīd*, or 'imitation.' Henceforth jurists no longer had the right of *ijtihād* but were simply 'imitators,' bound to accept and follow the doctrine established by their predecessors. Legal literature, from the tenth century onwards, was confined to a succession of increasingly exhaustive commentaries upon the works of the originators of the doctrine, and adhered not only to the substance but also to the form and arrangement of the works of the past masters. By the fourteenth century various legal texts had appeared which came to acquire a particular reputation in the different schools and areas of Islam and which represented for each school the authoritative statement of the law ratified by the *ijmā'*.

Classical jurisprudence had therefore obliterated the real origins of a large part of Sharīʿa doctrine, which, as has been seen, lay in local customary practice and the personal reasoning of individual scholars. Through the doctrine of *ijmāʿ* each and every particular legal rule had become identified with the command of God. Law, in theory, had not grown out of society; it had been imposed upon society from above. Knowledge of the true values and standards of conduct could not be attained by human thought or experience but only through divine revelation, and acts were good or evil exclusively because God had attributed this quality to them. In the Arabic legal manuals lay the perfect expression of God's law. And it was, as so elaborated, an immutable system; for after the death of the Prophet Muhammad there could be no further communication of the divine will to man. In short, law, in the classical concept, is the comprehensive and divinely ordained code of duties expounded in the legal manuals; and to its eternally valid dictates the conduct of a Muslim state and society is bound to conform.

Sharīʿa law as so embodied was doctrinaire and idealistic in the sense that its authority did not lie in the fact that it had been or was observed by the courts, but in the arguments of the scholars as to why it ought to be observed. The question that now arises, therefore, is how far the doctrine of the Sharīʿa texts was applied in practice. Since the *qāḍī* was the single organ for the application of the Sharīʿa, the question may be answered in terms of the extent and nature of the jurisdiction of the *qāḍīs*' tribunals or the Sharīʿa courts.[4]

As delegates of the political ruler, in whom was vested supreme executive and judicial power, the *qāḍīs* never formed an independent judiciary. The jurisdiction of the Sharīʿa courts was always subject to such limits as the political sovereign saw fit to define, and when a clash occurred between the terms of the Sharīʿa and the interests of government it was perhaps inevitable that the political sovereign should curtail the powers of his Sharīʿa courts and recognise alternative organs of jurisdiction.

One of the most serious limitations upon the practical efficiency of the Sharīʿa courts lay in the rigid system of procedure and evidence, applicable both in civil and criminal cases, by which they were bound. The burden of proof was strict, and the party who bore it, usually the plaintiff, was obliged to produce two male, adult, Muslim witnesses, whose moral integrity and religious probity were unimpeachable, to testify orally to their direct knowledge of the truth

[4] It will be observed that there was a fundamental difference between the lay *iudex* of the Roman system and the learned *qāḍī*: in Islam the responsibility for law existed at the decision-making level; hence the process of putting the divine will into effect was feared. This tended to increase the difficulty of accepting legislation as a method of law reform. *Ed.*

of his claim. If the plaintiff or prosecution failed to discharge this burden of proof the defendant or accused was offered the oath of denial. Properly sworn on the *Qur'ān*, such an oath secured judgment in his favour; if he failed to take it, judgment would be given for the plaintiff or prosecution, provided, in some circumstances, this side in turn took the oath. Such a system or procedure and evidence may have reflected the religious idealism of the scholars; but it was largely because of the often impractical burden of proof that was imposed upon a plaintiff, and the corresponding ease with which unscrupulous defendants might avoid a civil or criminal liability which reason declared to exist, that the Sharī'a courts proved an unsatisfactory organ for the administration of certain spheres of the law.

Criminal law and land law were the obvious spheres in which political interests could not tolerate the cumbersome nature of Sharī'a procedure; and as a general rule the authority to try such cases was delegated by the ruler to officials other than the *qāḍī*. The powers of those officials are best termed, collectively, as *Maẓālim* (lit.: 'complaints') jurisdiction. Exercised by an official known as the *Ṣāḥib al-Maẓālim*, this jurisdiction so developed in scope as to constitute serious competition with the Sharī'a tribunals and to create a clear dichotomy in Islamic legal practice. All functions in the Islamic state were theoretically religious in nature. But the distinction between the *Maẓālim* and Sharī'a jurisdictions came very close to the notion of a division between secular and religious courts, the *qāḍī* being regarded as the representative of God's law, and the *Ṣāḥib al-Maẓālim* as the mouthpiece of the ruler's law.

Government interests had thus, generally speaking, confined the jurisdiction of the Sharī'a courts to the province of private law. But it remains to observe that even in the sphere of family law, which is regarded as an essential and integral part of the religious faith, Sharī'a doctrine has been by no means universally applied throughout the Muslim world. For many peoples who came to accept the religion of Islam, Sharī'a law, based as it was upon the customs of those localities in the Arab world where the law had originated, was often wholly alien to the traditional structure of their societies. And this resulted in their continued observance of customary law to the total or partial exclusion of the Sharī'a. Thus the Berber peoples of North Africa, who include almost half of the Muslim population of Morocco, have been governed down to the present day by a customary law applied through official tribunals which is often at great variance with Sharī'a doctrine—one of its consistent features being the denial of rights of inheritance to women. In the Indian subcontinent the communities of the Isma'ili Khojas, the Bohoras, and the Cutchi Memons continued for some considerable time after their conversion to Islam from Hinduism to be governed by the Hindu law of testate and intestate succession, and thus retained the power, in outright contravention of Sharīʿa principles, to will away the whole of their estate. In northern Nigeria and in Kashmir immovable property passes in accordance with custom. Muslim society as well as Muslim government could not always support the principle of the exclusive jurisdiction of Sharīʿa tribunals.

Within the accepted bounds of their jurisdiction, the courts of the *qāḍīs* also deviated in certain limited respects from the strict doctrine of the Sharīʿa texts on the ground of social or economic necessity. This was particularly the case in the realm of civil transactions, where the doctrine expounded by the classical jurists was of a highly idealistic character. Here, the twin basic prohibitions of *ribā* (illicit profit) and *gharar* (uncertainty) had been developed to a degree of systematic rigour which eliminated any form of speculative risk in contracts and which postulated standards totally unrealistic in the light of the practical demands of commercial and economic life. Sharīʿa courts therefore in certain instances recognised and applied elements of the local customary law. One example of this is provided by the agricultural contract of *khamessa* in the practice of the Maliki courts in north-west Africa. Under this contract the tenant retains a quota part of four-fifths of the produce of the land which he occupies and works, the remaining fifth representing the rental required by the land-owner. Such a type of land tenure contravenes two cardinal principles of strict Sharīʿa doctrine—namely, that rental should not consist of foodstuffs and that its precise value should be known and determined. But the existence of *khamessa* in this area was widespread, and indeed something of an economic necessity in a society which possessed little floating capital, and from medieval times onwards it was universally recognised by the Sharīʿa courts.

In other cases the courts recognised certain devices or stratagems (*ḥiyal*), which were designed to circumvent rules of the strict Sharīʿa doctrine which had proved insupportable in practice. Thus, despite the prohibition of *ribā*, a loan with interest could be effected in a way in which the mutual obligations arising thereunder would be enforced by a Sharīʿa court. This was by the simple device of a double sale. L, the lender, would purchase from B, the borrower, an object for an agreed price of £X, payable immediately in cash. B would then contract to repurchase this same object from L for a price of £$X + Y$ (Y representing the agreed rate of interest) payable by a future specified date (the term of the loan). Hanafi and Shafiʿi courts generally accepted the validity of such *ḥiyal*. But the Malikis and Hanbalis, displaying a greater concern for the real intention behind overt acts, roundly condemned this manipulation of the letter of the law to achieve a purpose fundamentally contrary to its spirit.[5]

Developments of this kind in legal practice were often supported, if not initiated, by those scholars who were regarded as the guardians of Sharī'a doctrine—particularly the *muftis*, or jurisconsults, whose formal opinions (*fatwās*) upon the legal issues involved in a factual situation were largely responsible for so accommodating the classical doctrine to the needs of Muslim society. But such concessions to practical necessity were always made reluctantly and by way of exception to the general rule that the courts were rigidly bound to the doctrine of the classical manuals. Any departure from the strict terms of the authoritative texts constituted a deviation from the ideal standard.

During the nineteenth century the impact of Western civilisation upon Muslim society brought about radical changes in the fields of civil and commercial transactions and criminal law. In these matters the Sharī'a courts were now wholly out of touch with the needs of the time, both in their procedure and in the doctrine which they were bound to apply.

The Sharī'a law of civil obligations, based upon the comparatively simple commercial activities of medieval Arabian society and involving a total prohibition of any form of interest on capital investment, was quite incapable of catering for modern systems of trade and economic development. Equally insupportable in the modern state was the criminal law of the Sharī'a. In the first place the fixed, or *ḥadd*, penalties for certain offences, such as amputation of the hand for theft and stoning to death for adultery, were no longer generally acceptable from a humanitarian point of view. Secondly, homicide under Sharī'a law is essentially a civil injury rather than a crime, the prosecution of the offence depending upon the wishes of the relatives of the victim, who might either demand the death of the offender in retaliation, require him to pay blood-money as compensation, or pardon him altogether. Reasonable though such a notion of homicide might be in the context of a tribal society, it was no longer suited to the modern state. Finally, outside the six specific *ḥadd* offences (wine-drinking, fornication, theft, slander, highway robbery, and apostasy), Sharī'a law allows the judge an almost unfettered discretion in the determination of offences and the punishment therefor. Such arbitrary judicial power held little appeal for those Muslim peoples which began to be influenced by western ideas of criminal law.

[5] Plainly in their regions the social and economic implications of usury were more disagreeable, and the loss to be suffered by totally prohibiting usury was less, than would have been the case in other regions where lending money at interest was not viewed as exploitation of one who needed capital. *Ed.*

As a result of these considerations the nineteenth century witnessed the abolition of the Sharīʿa criminal law and the law of civil transactions in most Muslim countries and a large-scale reception of codes of European law to replace it. Thus, with the notable exception of the Arabian peninsula, where the Sharīʿa still remains formally supreme in all fields of law, the application of Sharīʿa law in Islam has been broadly confined, from the beginning of the present century, to the realm of family law.

But here also the impetus for reform was soon felt. Sharīʿa family law, as has been seen, reflected to a large extent the patriarchal scheme of Arabian tribal society in the early centuries of Islam. Not unnaturally certain institutions and standards of that law were felt to be out of line with the circumstances of modern Muslim society, particularly in urban areas where tribal ties had disintegrated and movements had arisen for the emancipation of women. At first Muslim society in this respect seemed to be faced with the same apparent impasse between the changing circumstances of modern life and an allegedly immutable law as had caused the adoption of western codes in civil and criminal matters. Hence the only solution which seemed possible to Turkey in 1927 was the total abandonment of the Sharīʿa and the adoption of Swiss family law in its place. No other Muslim country, however, has as yet followed this example. Instead, traditional Sharīʿa law has been adapted in a variety of ways to the circumstances of contemporary society. It is therefore the striking phenomenon of the recent evolution of Islamic family law that is our final, and at the same time our most important concern, since it is towards a proper appreciation of the significance of these modern developments that this review of Islamic legal history has been mainly directed.

In the Middle East the dominating issue from the outset has been the question of the juristic basis of reforms—that is to say, granted their social desirability, their justification in terms of Islamic jurisprudential theory. Reforms in the Middle East have, of course, come into effect as laws promulgated by the authority of the state, and in this sense it is not improper to refer to them as modernist legislation. But they do not represent independent law-making in the fullest sense of the term. They represent (or purport to represent) Allāh's law, or that version of the Sharīʿa which the political sovereign commands shall be observed, and the preamble to the 'legislation' invariably explains the juristic principles which underly its authority as such an expression of the Sharīʿa.

During the early stages of modern reform the doctrine of *taqlīd*[6] was still formally observed, and the traditional view that the authority

[6] Above, p. 66.

of the medieval legal manuals was paramount and exclusive was not openly contradicted. The fundamental basis of reform lay in the doctrine of *siyāsa*, or 'government,' as expounded in the traditional texts of jurisprudence and in the particular principle that the political authority, although having no legislative power in the real sense of the term, nevertheless has the right, and indeed the duty, to make administrative regulations to secure the effective application of Sharī'a law by the courts. Such administrative regulations, or *qānūn*, as used by the reformers, take one of two forms.

In the first place they may relate to the system of procedure and evidence by which the Sharī'a courts are bound. The courts are instructed not to entertain cases which do not meet certain procedural requirements. In its simplest form this type of regulation was used to make documentary evidence necessary in certain classes of case. For example, under traditional Sharī'a law a marriage or divorce can be, indeed ideally ought to be, proved by oral testimony. But the Egyptian *Code of Organisation and Procedure for Sharī'a Courts* of 1897 provided that 'no claim of marriage, divorce or acknowledgement thereof shall be heard after the death of either party unless it is supported by documents free from suspicion of forgery.' However, the same type of regulation has been used to more interesting effect in Egypt to deal with the problem of child marriage.

The Egyptian *Code of Procedure for Sharī'a Courts*, 1931, consolidating a number of previous provisions on the subject, enacted that no disputed claim of marriage was to be entertained where the bride was less than sixteen or the bridegroom less than eighteen years of age at the time of the contract. Although this had developed out of regulations which had initially been procedural—forbidding the courts to entertain claims arising out of marriages which had not been registered and at the same time ordering the competent officials not to register marriages between parties who were below the stated ages—it now clearly affected the traditional substantive right of a marriage guardian to contract his minor ward in marriage. A marriage concluded between minors was still perfectly valid, but would not, if disputed, be the subject of judicial relief from the courts. In theory, the doctrine of the classical authorities was not contradicted, but in practice an attempt had been made to abolish the institution of child marriage.

In India, by way of contrast with this indirect method of reform, the traditional Hanafi law was directly superseded by the legislation of the *Child Marriage Restraint Act*, 1929, which (as amended) prohibited the marriage of girls below the age of fourteen and boys below the age of sixteen, under pain of penalties.

The second aspect of the use of governmental administrative power to achieve reform in the Middle East lay in directives to the courts as to which particular rule among existing variants they were to apply. Traditional Sharīʿa law is, in effect, a comparative legal system in itself. Not only are there four separate schools of Sunni law, but variations between individual jurists of the same school led to the expression of the law in terms of the majority and minority view, the intrinsically sound opinion, and the opinion of less strong authority. This comparative aspect of Sharīʿa law was greatly stimulated from the late classical period onwards by works of scholarship devoted to the general topic of variations in Sharīʿa doctrine. For example, a famous legal treatise of the twelfth century called *al-Mughnī*, the work of the Hanbali scholar Ibn Qudama—is a critical assessment and comparison of the variant doctrines of the different schools and jurists. With the development of this kind of study came a further breakdown of the barriers between the schools, which classical legal philosophy already held to be equally legitimate versions of the Sharīʿa. Jurisprudence recognised that the 'correctness' of a ruling or opinion was a relative term, that each variant could find its own particular justification, and that no single view could claim, as against all others, to be sacrosanct.

This background enabled jurists of the Middle East to support the principle that government might freely choose, not only from the opinions of Hanafi jurists but also from the four streams of Sharīʿa doctrine as a whole, that rule which was deemed to be most suited to the circumstances of contemporary society, and then order the courts to apply that rule to the exclusion of other variants.

One of many examples of this process of 'selection' is provided by Egyptian legislation of 1920 concerning divorce. The traditional Hanafi law in force up to this time did not allow a wife to petition for divorce on the ground of any matrimonial offence committed by the husband, a situation which it was recognised was causing great hardship to abandoned or ill-treated wives. Maliki law, however, does give a wife the right to dissolution of her marriage on the grounds, *inter alia*, of the husband's cruelty, failure to provide maintenance and support, and desertion. Accordingly, the Egyptian legislation codified the Maliki law as the law henceforth to be applied by the Sharīʿa courts.

It is once again instructive to compare the position of Islamic law in this regard in the Indian sub-continent. Here, substantially similar reforms in the law of divorce were effected by the *Dissolution of Muslim Marriages Act*, 1939. But while the Indian reformers claimed to be adopting Maliki rules, many provisions of the Act were in fact contrary to basic Maliki principles. The Act is therefore best regarded as yet another example of the Indian Legislature directly overriding the traditional Sharīʿa law.[7]

As long as the process of 'selection' was confined to a choice between variant opinions which Sunni jurisprudence recognised as equally authoritative, the reformers could perhaps properly claim that they were still observing the doctrine of *taqlīd*. But such a claim became more dubious when the reformers proceeded to embody in their codes rules for which the only authority was a sectarian school or the individual opinion of an isolated jurist and which were in conflict with the accepted doctrines of the four Sunni schools as a whole. In their search for authority the legislators were foraging beyond the bounds traditionally established by the *ijmāʿ*. Finally, they resorted to the activity termed *talfiq* (literally 'to make up a patchwork, to piece together'), under which legal rules were ostensibly constructed by the combination and fusion of juristic opinions, and of elements therefrom, of diverse nature and provenance. The result was the formulation of a rule for which no precise authority existed either in the view of any one school or individual jurist. When this stage was reached it was clear that such mobility and capacity for change as the corpus of Sharīʿa doctrine contained within itself had been fully exploited. The claim of *taqlīd* (imitation) had become little more than a formality.

During the past two decades the doctrine of *taqlīd* has been openly challenged to an ever-increasing degree. On many points the law recorded in the medieval manuals, in so far as it represents the interpretations placed by the early jurists upon the divine texts of the *Qurʿān* and the *sunna*, has been held no longer to have a paramount and exclusive authority. Modern jurisprudence has claimed the right to renounce these interpretations and to interpret for itself, independently and afresh, the original texts of divine revelation: in short, to re-open the door of *ijtihād*[8] which had been in theory closed since the tenth century. History records the names of certain scholars, such as the Hanbali Ibn Taymiyya of the fourteenth century, who had never accepted the doctrine of the closure of the door of *ijtihād*, and in the last years of the nineteenth century the great Egyptian jurist Muhammad Abduh had advocated the reinterpretation of the *Qurʿān* and the *sunna* in the light of modern conditions as a basis for legal reform. Similarly, scholars like Iqbal in India had argued that the exercise of *ijtihād* was not only the right but also the duty of present generations if Islam was to adapt itself successfully to the modern world. But this thesis, representing an outright break with a

[7] The examples illustrate India's debt to common-law post-Reformation principles of statute-making. Parliament can legislate validly on matters of conscience also. *Ed.*

[8] Above, p. 63.

legal tradition of ten centuries' standing, naturally engendered violent controversy, and only in most recent times has it been given practical implementation.

The developing use of *ijtihād* as a means of legal reform may be seen through a comparison of the terms of the Syrian *Law of Personal Status*, 1953 with those of the Tunisian *Law of Personal Status*, 1957 in relation to the two subjects of polygamy and divorce by repudiation (*ṭalāq*). The unrestricted right of a husband to marry up to four wives concurrently and his absolute power to discard a wife at will by unilateral repudiation of the marriage were uncontested by any Sunni school. As the twin pillars of the patriarchal system of Sharīʿa family law they have naturally attracted great attention from modern reformers.

As regards polygamy the Syrian reformers argued that the *Qurʾān* itself urges husbands not to take additional wives unless they are able to make proper provision for their maintenance and support. Classical jurists had construed this verse as a moral exhortation binding only on the husband's conscience. But the Syrian reformers maintained that it should be regarded as a positive legal prerequisite of marrying polygamously and enforced as such by the courts. This novel interpretation was then coupled with a normal administrative regulation which required the due registration of marriages after the permission of the court to marry had been obtained. Article 17 of the Syrian law accordingly enacts: 'The *qāḍī* may withhold permission for a man who is already married to marry a second wife, where it is established that he is not in a position to support them both.' Far more extreme, however, is the approach of the Tunisian reformers. They argued that, in addition to a husband's financial ability to support a plurality of wives, the *Qurʾān* also required that co-wives should be treated with complete impartiality. This Qurʾanic injunction should also be construed, not simply as a moral exhortation, but as a legal condition precedent to polygamy, in the sense that no second marriage should be permissible unless and until adequate evidence was forthcoming that the wives would in fact be treated impartially. But under modern social and economic conditions, declared the reformers, such impartial treatment was a practical impossibility. And since the essential condition for polygamy could not be fulfilled, the *Law of Personal Status* of 1957 briefly declares: 'Polygamy is prohibited.'

With regard to unilateral repudiation by the husband, the Syrian law introduced a bold innovation when it provided that a wife who had been repudiated without just cause might be awarded compensation by the court from her former husband to the maximum extent of one year's maintenance. The reform was once again represented as giving practical effect to certain Qurʿanic verses which had been generally regarded by traditional jurisprudence as moral rather than legally enforceable injunctions—those verses, namely, which enjoin husbands to 'make a fair provision' for repudiated wives and to 'retain wives with kindness or release them with consideration.' The effect of the Syrian law, then, is to subject the husband's motive for repudiation to the scrutiny of the court and to penalise him, albeit to a limited extent, for abuse of his power. Once again, however, the Tunisian *ijtihād* concerning repudiation is far more radical. Here the reformers argued that the *Qurʿān* orders the appointment of arbitrators in the event of 'discord' between husband and wife. Clearly a pronouncement of repudiation by a husband indicated a state of discord between the spouses. Equally clearly the official courts were best suited to undertake the function of arbitration that then becomes necessary according to the *Qurʿān*. It is on this broad ground that the Tunisian *Law of Personal Status* abolishes the right of a husband to repudiate his wife extra-judicially, section 30 of the Law enacting that: 'Divorce outside a court of law is without legal effect.' Although the court must dissolve the marriage if the husband persists in his repudiation, it has an unlimited power to grant the wife compensation for any damage she has sustained from the divorce—although in practice this power has so far been used most sparingly. In regard to polygamy and *ṭalāq* therefore, Tunisia had achieved, by re-interpretation of the *Qurʿān*, reforms hardly less radical than those effected in Turkey some thirty years previously by the adoption of the Swiss civil code. In Pakistan a new interpretation of the original texts of divine revelation was the declared basis of the reforms introduced by the *Muslim Family Laws Ordinance* of 1961, although the provisions of the Ordinance in relation to polygamy and divorce by repudiation are much less radical than the corresponding Middle Eastern reforms, since a second marriage is simply made dependent upon the consent of an Arbitration Council, and the effect of a husband's repudiation is merely suspended for a period of three months to afford opportunity for reconciliation.

However, recent judicial decisions in Pakistan have unequivocally endorsed the right of independent interpretation of the *Qurʿān*. For example, in *Khurshid Bibi* v. *Muhammad Amin* (1966)[9] the Supreme Court held that a Muslim wife could as of right obtain a divorce by payment of suitable compensation to her husband. This decision was based on the Court's interpretation of a relevant Qurʿanic verse. But under traditional Sharīʿa law this form of divorce, known as *khulʿ*, whereby a wife pays for her release, is a contract between the spouses and as such entirely dependent upon the husband's free

[9] [1967] *Pakistan Legal Decisions*, 97 (S.C.).

consent. The present attitude of the courts towards this fundamental question of the authority of the traditional Sharīʿa manuals contrasts sharply with previous practice. In *Aga Mahomed* v. *Koolsom Bee Bee* (1897)[10] the Privy Council had declared that 'it would be wrong for the court . . . to put their own construction on the Koran in opposition to the express ruling of commentators of such great antiquity and high authority.'

Such has been the broad progress to date of the reform movement which has enabled modernist jurisprudence to solve the immediate problems of Islamic personal law. It should not, however, be supposed that modernist legal method has as yet approached the stage of formulating a firm and systematic scheme of the principles upon which it rests. While there has been a clear progression in jurisprudential thought over the past decades from the doctrine of *taqlīd* to the principle of fresh *ijtihād*, independent interpretation is by no means generally or consistently invoked as the one fundamental basis for reform. Traditionalist and modernist elements at present lie in uneasy juxtaposition, often within the ambit of a single piece of legislation. It is for this reason that the reforms often consist of *ad hoc* and partial remedies for particular mischiefs rather than a comprehensive reformulation of basic principles. The whole traditional scheme of Sunni inheritance, for example, rests on the concept of the extended or tribal family. But in many Muslim societies today the unit is the narrower family group of parents and their children. Accordingly, a number of important reforms in the laws of inheritance have been directed towards increasing the rights of succession of this more restricted family group. However, the basic rule which entrenches the rights of the tribal heirs in Sunni law is that a daughter of the deceased does not exclude from succession any male agnate collateral relative. And yet it is only in Tunisia and Iraq that this rule has as yet been superseded and daughters have been given absolute priority in succession over the brothers or more distant agnate relatives of the deceased. In Iraq the reform was achieved by adopting as the national law the Shiʿi system of succession. In the context of Iraq this was not so radical a step as it might be elsewhere, since approximately half the population of Iraq are in fact Shiʿis. In Tunisia the reform was grounded upon the Qurʿanic text, which declares that a brother or sister has no rights of inheritance in the presence of 'a child' of the deceased. But elsewhere in the Muslim world the traditional law in this regard has proved too deep-rooted to challenge, however much it may be felt to conflict with the present notion of family ties.

[10] L.R. 24 Ind. App. 196; A. A. A. Fyzee, *Cases in the Muhammadan Law of India and Pakistan* (Oxford, Clarendon Press, 1965), pp. 1–4.

Because the relative strength of modernist and traditionalist attitudes differs from country to country, the substance of current Islamic law varies considerably in the different parts of the Muslim world. Moreover, external influences have produced diversity in the manner and form of its application. In the Middle East, primarily because of French influence, Sharī'a law has been largely codified. In the Indian sub-continent, on the other hand, the application of Islamic law follows the English legal tradition. Subject to the various statutory enactments, the courts administer Islamic law as a case-law system on the basis of the doctrine of binding precedent. But it is only in India and Pakistan, Egypt and Tunisia that Sharī'a family law is now applied as an integral part of the national law through a unified court system. Elsewhere, the Sharī'a courts remain as a separate system of jurisdiction, distinct from those courts which apply the secularised civil and criminal law.

Despite this complex variety of form and substance, however, the fundamental purpose of current Muslim jurisprudence is the same in all countries and communities. It is to cater for the needs and aspirations of present-day society through laws which can claim to express the command of Allāh. Reform of the traditional law as it has so far developed still involves great problems of principle and practice. A hard core of traditionalist opinion still adamantly rejects the validity of the process of *ijtihād*, on the ground that the texts are merely being manipulated to yield the meaning which suits the preconceived purposes of the reformers, and that therefore, contrary to fundamental Islamic ideology, it is social desirability and not the will of Allāh which is the ultimate determinant of the law.

As regards the practical effect of legal reform, there exists in many Muslim countries today a deep social gulf between the Westernised and modernist minority and the conservative mass of the population. And reforms which aim at satisfying, and are largely inspired by, the standards of progressive urban society have little significance for the traditionalist communities of rural areas. It is also often the case that the *qāḍīs*, through their background and training, are not wholly sympathetic with the purposes of the modernist legislators.

Such problems are, of course, inevitable in the transitional stage of social evolution in which Islam now finds itself. But the one supreme achievement of jurisprudence over the past few decades has been the emergence of a functional approach to the question of the role of law in society. Jurisprudence has discarded the introspective and idealistic attitude which the doctrine of *taqlīd* had imposed upon it since early medieval times and now sees its task to be the solution of the problems of contemporary society. It has emerged from a protracted period of stagnation to adopt again the attitude of the earliest

Muslim jurists, whose aim was to relate the dictates of the divine will to their own social environment. It is this attitude alone which has ensured the survival of the Sharīʿa in modern times as a practical system of law and which alone provides its inspiration for the future.

BIBLIOGRAPHY

A general survey of the Islamic legal system, covering its historical development, jurisprudential theory and the most important spheres of the substantive law, is contained in the three following works:

J. Schacht, *An Introduction to Islamic Law* (Oxford University Press, 1964).

J. N. D. Anderson, *Islamic Law in the Modern World* (New York and London, 1959).

N. J. Coulson, *A History of Islamic Law* (Edinburgh University Press, 1964).

The student is referred to the bibliographies of these books, particularly for the numerous articles written by J. N. D. Anderson on the subject of modern developments in the law.

J. Schacht, *The Origins of Muhammadan Jurisprudence* (Clarendon Press, Oxford, 1950) is the fundamental work of modern research on the early development of legal theory written by the pioneer scholar of this subject.

Abdur Rahim, *Muhammadan Jurisprudence* (Madras, 1911) is a sound analysis of traditional legal theory.

Farhat J. Ziadeh, *The Philosophy of Jurisprudence in Islam* (Leiden, 1961) is an English translation of the Arabic text of an outstanding Muslim jurist of the present time, Sobhi Mahmassani.

Law in the Middle East, ed. M. Khadduri and H. J. Liebesny (Washington, 1955), is a work of composite authorship which includes chapters by Muslim scholars and western orientalists on the various spheres of substantive Islamic law, traditional, and modern.

A. A. A. Fyzee, *Outlines of Muhammadan Law* (Oxford University Press, 1955), is the standard text book dealing with Islamic law as it is applied today in India and Pakistan.

The Encyclopaedia of Islam (1st ed., Leiden, 1913–42; 2nd ed., Leiden and London, 1960), contains numerous articles on individual legal topics.

HINDU LAW

J. Duncan M. Derrett

HINDU LAW is applied as part of the law of the land to over 400,000,000 Hindus in India, Pakistan, Burma, Malaysia, Singapore, Aden, Kenya, Uganda, and Tanzania, but not (curiously) in Ceylon. Its name derives from its being applied to Hindus rather than from its historical connection with a religion. In those territories it is a *personal law* (as is Muhammadan law) in the sense that the individual carries with him the law of his religious community, which the law itself defines as that of the 'Hindus.' The statute law, except that which amends personal laws, will be common to all inhabitants of the territories concerned, as also will be the rules of common law and equity in so far as these were formerly introduced by the foreign rulers and continue in vigour.

Hindu law is not a territorial law, and, subject to variations which are of little intellectual significance, a Hindu, so long as he remains a Hindu and does not voluntarily subject himself to a general statute with contrary effect,[1] will be governed by this system whether he lives in, *e.g.*, Delhi, Rangoon, or Dar-es-Salaam. As there are two major 'schools' of Hindu law, differing in minor aspects of marriage and inheritance, and certain even less important differences of sub-school within the major school as to, *e.g.*, females' rights in family property, it would be more correct to say that a Hindu carries with him not merely 'Hindu law' but rather the Hindu law of his school or sub-school, but the distinction hardly signifies in the context of this book. In territories other than those listed above, Hindu law is referred to as the law of the domicile in the appropriate context where a conflict of laws arises. It may be referred to in order to determine the rights and capacities of non-Ceylonese Hindus when these, or their successors in title, litigate in an appropriate matter before a Ceylon court; and nowadays the large number of Indians in Britain gives rise to frequent proof of Hindu law before our courts. The matters in which Hindu law governs Hindus will be mentioned below: they constitute the scope of their personal law.

Those who are governed by Hindu law range in race and intellect from the geographically most remote and historically most backward

[1] *Special Marriage Act*, 1954. Marriage under this statute takes the individual out of the Hindu law for all purposes except membership of the joint family and adoption.

to the world's most adaptable and sophisticated people. 'Hindu' does not, of course, mean an Indian, but a person belonging to a community like an originally Indian caste (even if not in India) or tribe, family, or other social unit (including Sikhs and Buddhists), which does not profess any of the Muslim, Christian, Zoroastrian (Parsi), or Jewish religions. 'Hindu' means in practice an Indian by racial extraction who is not a member of any such non-Hindu community. A child of a non-Hindu father by a Hindu mother may well be brought up as a Hindu, and will normally be governed, unlike his father, by the Hindu personal law.

To be a Hindu for legal purposes it is not necessary that the individual should hold any belief, though the vast majority of 'Hindus' adhere to the basic religious postulates of the indigenous Indian civilisation. A few of the more generally significant of these will appear below, for we should not ignore them. Attempts have been made to avoid responsibilities by pleading that the individual did not believe in the Hindu trinity of gods or by pleading a conversion to another religion: happily these attempts have uniformly failed. Conversion *to* Hinduism is recognised for legal purposes, provided that the conversion is a reality, so far as concerns the social group to which the individual purports to belong.

The law is as old as the Indian civilisation, and traces of the rules are found in the Vedic literature of about 1500 B.C. Respect for elders, mercy, charity, and good government are eloquently insisted upon in the famous inscriptions of the emperor Aśoka,[2] whose military and subsequently missionary career in the third century B.C. is somehow of a piece with India's exhortations to herself and others in modern times. The fundamental rules of law and their spiritual supports are available in texts which are usually dated between 500 B.C. and A.D. 200. Exact chronology is defied by these traditional materials which had so long a working life. Some of the postulates—as, for example, the division of function between the judge who reached, and the assessor who recommended, the judgment—may have had a centralised origin: the basic structure can hardly have emerged in separate areas and periods independently. The 'eighteen titles of law,' or 'footings of litigation' as the chapters of court-law are called, must have been the child of one brain, or of a small number of brains in one place. But the materials themselves developed independently, called forth by the urge felt in many social groups and small kingdoms to be better informed about *duty*, which is the system's key word. The intellectual élite, the Brahmin caste, developed this science. It was called *dharma-śāstra*, 'science of righteousness.' It contained

[2] See N. A. Nikam and R. McKeon, *The Edicts of Asoka* (Chicago/London, Phoenix, 1966).

many rules of government and law, besides many intricate provisions which would not be tolerated by, nor be useful to, others than the Brahmins themselves, to whom ritual purity was important as a qualification for employment or pension. Naturally no one asked then, any more than anyone asks now, to be governed by a law which was not righteous, and righteousness (being an ideal) was hard to divine in a complicated issue. There was ample work for juridically interested scholars, and their products are available in numbers and weight from the fifth century of our era to as late as the 1830s.

When the Portuguese, the French, and the British acquired territories in India, and especially when the British East India Company became *de facto* sovereign of Bengal, Bihar, and Orissa in 1765, the need to administer justice devolved (however unpalatably) upon the unqualified and at first reluctant European adventurers who found themselves vested with political power. It will be obvious that it is highly undesirable that judges should lay down law which will not apply to themselves or their friends; still more that they should judicially legislate for folk they feel inferior to themselves; but in the circumstances no alternative was possible, and much of the history of Hindu law, especially its alleged rigidity during the British period, is to be attributed to this. Parliament soon supported the East India Company, and eventually courts of an English type were set up throughout British India, which itself rapidly grew in extent. These courts had from the first the advantage of a fused system of law and equity.[3] Later the states under British paramountcy set up courts of their own, following the procedure and the law of the British Indian courts. Appeals from British Indian High Courts were heard by the Privy Council in London, and from French Indian territories matters went to the Cour de Cassation in Paris. The *dharmaśāstra* could thus hardly be expected to stop still, though the foreign judges used to obtain opinions on the personal law from native professors appointed to the courts for the purpose (the Pandits) up till 1864, when judicial knowledge of the system was (with some temerity) assumed. Indians were exposed not only to a partially competent judiciary but also to a new economy and to the social effects of such changes. The French purported to keep in touch with the customs of the people. The British developed 'Anglo-Hindu' law, which, while based on the texts and commentaries by native authors, gradually became a new entity. The Privy Council made it in a myriad of cases, while no one was responsible for overall clarity or consistency. Principles of common law, and more especially equity, were injected, sometimes unconsciously, and the *dharmaśāstra* was reanimated so

[3] See below, p. 177.

far as the natural conservatism of lawyers and the especial caution of Privy Councillors would allow.

The Anglo-Indian legal system as a whole was not a little seasoned with the contribution of Scottish members of the Privy Council. It was accepted at its face value by the Indian public, whose confidence rested upon a widespread belief that their judges turned first for their law to the ancient books containing the distilled learning of the pre-British periods. Not a few of these had, by 1864, been translated competently from the original Sanskrit.

However, elements in Indian society envied English freedoms as against Indian self-restraint and conservatism, and gradually piecemeal amendments were made to enable people to live less hampered by the ideals of altruism (living for the people to whom you 'belong' rather than for yourself) which, at bottom, had in practice kept Indian castes apart. Tentative steps taken before Indian Independence in 1947 led to a desire for thorough reform, and this was carried out in 1955 and 1956. But modern Hindu law in India is only partly founded on the so-called 'Hindu Code' of those years. Aspects of the personal law were drastically altered, but what of the remainder, especially that governing the joint family which it was not thought prudent to touch? This remained as before, subject to judicial construction of the 'Code.' To the dilemma this creates we must return. Meanwhile the contemporary Hindu law has its roots in the *dharmaśāstra*; in the Anglo-Hindu law which is still to be consulted outside India and rules even in India in the chapters untouched by the 'Code'; and in the statutes forming the 'Code' itself. The practitioner must ask whether the 'Code,' or any of the enactments of East African legislatures, is applicable to the problem before him; if not he will consult the Anglo-Hindu law. In the rare cases where the point is not covered by unimpeachable judicial authority he may have recourse to the original treatises of the *dharmaśāstra*, taking care to observe the interpretations placed upon them by jurists whom the courts have consulted, especially that remarkable polymath, P. V. Kane.

The sources of Hindu law are sometimes complicated and not seldom recondite. But could it have been otherwise? Native lawyers controlled the system for not less than two millennia, and Europeans and western-trained Indians have administered it to a rapidly changing society for a further two centuries.

Thus Hindu law has always been a book law. The written texts of the leading fundamental jurists, namely those passing under the names of Manu, Yājñavalkya, Nārada, Brihaspati, and Kātyāyana (all of whom wrote before the end of the third century A.D.) were themselves the fruit of attempts to collate, combine, and systematise maxims, propositions, and reflections (not to speak of the inevitable and sometimes beautiful exhortations) which had already been handed down as an oral 'literature' for centuries. For example, the maxim 'things enjoyed through favour are never lost to their owners' needed to be moulded and formed into a sufficiently weighty part of a developed law regarding acquisition by a non-owner possessing adversely to the true owner. The jurist's task was to take an institution, to fix it in words, to categorise it, stamping it with approval, or expounding it in such a manner as to limit its practice so as to conform to overriding moral requirements. Marriage by capture, and the remarriage of the deceased's brother's widow, are instances where ancient customs, enshrined in complacent maxims, were subjected to tendentious revision by zealous reformers.

Jurists had a wide grasp; their insinuations could turn an insecure custom into a regulated—but then secure—institution of law. The mental power required was of exceptional dimensions. Succeeding generations refined and explored but did not question the essentials. One can sense a lack of originality; but their inheritance, which had to be grasped as a whole, dwarfed attempts at improvement. Some of the ancient rules which survive in the books seem footling; but a primitive society was not offended by the incongruous if it expressed what they took for granted and thought important.

The *Manu-smriti*, the 'Laws of Manu' to which Sir William Jones gave celebrity in 1794 and which should be consulted now with Georg Bühler's translation, is a work of elaborate editorship, requiring in its exponents as much interpretative skill as the author himself possessed. The maxims and poetical moral precepts which he rightly expected his readers to memorise were seldom of his own composition: what he took from antiquity, the folk-memory of a self-conscious prestige-bearing element in the population, he fitted so as to accord with the needs of his own age. The verses were singly and collectively known as *smriti* ('memory'). They were the bed-rock of juridical argument, the scholars' armoury, the committee of discipline's bible, the judge's reasons. Though they were evidently composed by men, they could be trotted out like holy scripture, a status understandable in materials of such great age.

Smritis tended to proliferate, and bogus examples could ingenuously be cited as if from an ancient source. If they met the needs of the relevant social group they could not be contradicted. Centres of scholarship, such as Benares, to which students from every quarter resorted, specialised in collecting and digesting such *smritis*. The digest-maker certified the genuineness of his collection. Such a one was Lakshmīdhara (tenth–eleventh centuries A.D.), characteristically a minister of a Hindu kingdom. While he arranged his material under their topics and subheadings, he coloured them by their very juxtaposition, silently adjusting their scopes, interpolating in his own voice only the occasional explanation of an obsolete or ambiguous Sanskrit term.

Commentaries were written for the guidance of penance-committees and for judicial assessors. The basic text was chosen for its local currency and for the scope it gave the commentator. While nominally expounding it he would enrich it with explanations and supplement it with quotations from other *smritis*, which, as often as not, threw more than mere illumination upon the text—they sometimes added a new dimension. He often discussed variant readings and different juristic interpretations. Some of these hide, under discreet and technical evaluation of sources, an attempt conclusively to deal with a practical issue. Rightly, established authors refuse to reconcile divergent texts, or to elaborate on well-known propositions, when the subject-matter has definitely ceased to be of practical significance: some rules relating to impurity or penance, to ordeals, or to discriminatory punishments have fallen totally out of use—and the scholar declines to include them in his bulky work. Men wanted to know their law shortly and comprehensively. Vijñāneśvara's *Mitāksharā* combined terseness with dialectical minuteness, professional skill, and educational endeavour, and it became popular throughout India (early twelfth century). Not all its successors valued terseness where juridicial skill could find a public, and Devanna-bhatta's *Smritichandrikā* (thirteenth century) is a vast affair, while even more vast is Mitra-misra's *Vīramitrodaya* (seventeenth century)—the one from the South and the other from the North of the peninsula. Some five thousand authors worked prior to the British period and shortly after it commenced, but not all their texts have survived.

Much more effort would have been put by the foreign powers into learning the *dharmaśāstra* if all the Hindu law had been enforced after they acquired their jurisdictions. It turned out that it would be applied as a matter of course only in the following matters: adoption, inheritance, and succession, the joint family, guardianship, maintenance of dependants, marriage and matrimonial causes, questions of caste discipline (which were soon placed primarily within the castes' own care), and religious and charitable endowments and trusts. Part of the law of debts was allowed to remain Hindu in character; and the common law of India relating to *benami* transactions, that is to say, nominal transfers to persons who were bare trustees for the actual purchaser, and also relating to pre-emption of landed property[4] survived as topics of indigenous law. A comprehensive search

[4] See p. 38, n. 11. In India co-owners but not (now) neighbours have this right.

through the Indian law books was never made, and government took hardly any part in acquiring, publishing, or translating manuscripts of the *dharmaśāstra*. Works on specialised topics such as inheritance and adoption were translated, but sometimes only in part, and without reflecting the balance of Hindu scholarly opinion. A work commissioned from the very learned Jagannātha (fl. *c.* 1790) did contain a substantial treatment of contracts,[5] but, largely because of its intellectual modesty, it was not appreciated. It does not surprise us to find that as Indian businessmen dealing with Europeans acquired a tolerance of English law, the Hindu law of contracts withered away before its English counterpart, from which it did not differ radically, and was eventually replaced by Indian statutes.

The case-law based on the Sanskrit sources never contemplated diverging from them. But the system was strengthened and made more easy to imbibe by importations from the English legal atmosphere into which it had been, as it were, transported. It was asked, for example, whether a killer could succeed to the estate of his victim. The Sanskrit texts appeared to be silent on the point. The rule excluding unrighteous persons from inheritance was not cited in any book on the judge's table, and the common-law rule was applied as a stop-gap. Naturally Indian jurists would not have allowed a killer to succeed: in fact, their outlook, tempered with the normal deference to local wisdom, would preclude even disobedient children from inheriting. But this went too far. The Anglo-Indian judges could not measure the appropriate degree of disobedience, and that would-be rule was silently abolished. A further example would be that of the unchaste widow. The *śāstra* intended her to be divested of her husband's estate, and custom would have agreed. But the courts in British times were hostile to the divesting of a vested title, and averse to a rule which would encourage perjury by those of the woman's 'in-laws' who would take the property in default of her. Accordingly, it was decided that though a widow would lose her husband's estate if she *remarried* (should any caste permit her to do so), and she might not inherit at all if she were unchaste at the time of her husband's death, her unchastity the day following his death could not deprive her of the inheritance. This illustration of the weakness and complexities of the Anglo-Hindu system—an instance now happily obsolete in India—will serve to give an adequate impression of the result of applying an Asian book-law at the hands of foreign judges.

Meanwhile there was a positive aspect. The sources required to be

[5] H. T. Colebrooke, *A Digest of Hindu Law on Contracts and Successions with a Commentary* . . ., vol. 1 (Madras, 1964).

developed. There was no effective provision for attachment and sale of a debtor's property: indeed, attachment before judgment though present in some ancient treatises had not been developed. It was an expedient the usefulness of which soon struck English lawyers, and it had repercussions on the substantive law, as so many movements in the realm of procedural law tend to have. To substantive changes due to the British we shall return presently.

The resulting amalgam deserved, and acquired, a long series of authors in English, not to speak of the occasional French treatise. Nowadays the authors who command the attention of practitioners include the formerly academic treatise of J. D. Mayne, who started as a professor of philosophy in Madras but found law more profitable; the summary of the case-law with notes of the effect of statutes compiled by the indefatigable Parsi, Sir Dinshah F. Mulla; and the more recent but highly readable and comprehensive textbook of N. R. Raghavachariar. The differences of opinion between the High Courts, particularly those of Calcutta, Madras, and Bombay, give rise to intriguing problems as to the requirements of the hypothetical 'true' Hindu law, which the Supreme Court is now steadily clearing up.

An academic interest in India's ancient jurists has never failed since Europe first became aware of their existence. Their ideas and institutions cement the accepted linguistic and religious bonds between the Aryans of India and their cousins who founded western civilisation. But an academic interest in modern Hindu law was slower in growing, as foreigners tended to stumble at the amateurish incongruities illustrated above, and the Indian public was uncomfortably digesting statutory amendments of the ancient system. Teachers are not agreed as to what the spirit of the new system is, or whether it has intellectual continuity with the past. Advocates, who are much nearer to the effects of the legislation, prefer, as usual, to give their minds to winning their clients' cases.

The pace and impact of the controversial legislation may be compared with that in a comparable field in English law. It is well to look into this before we go back, as shortly we must, to the constant ingredient in Indian legal thought, the *dharmaśāstra* itself. For the standing as well as the pervasive quality of the latter is illuminated by the attempts to rescue the public from its detailed rules. We may take as example the rights of women, always a sensitive issue. In 1929 sisters were made heirs on an intestacy, for the first time in some schools and much higher in the order of priority elsewhere. In 1937 widows were given for the first time the right to inherit along with the decedent's sons, and to take their deceased husband's undivided interest in property jointly owned by the male members of the agnatic family.[6] In 1946 wives were allowed the right to sue for separate maintenance (*i.e.*, out of the joint-family home into which they had been given, willy nilly, in marriage) and for maintenance in cases of hardship, only some of which had been recognised earlier. In 1949 the wife's right to a summary order against her husband for maintenance was modified so that she might succeed even if she refused to return home, should her husband have married again. In 1947–1949 the then Bombay and Madras States deprived the Hindu husband of his right to marry again in the lifetime of the first wife irrespective of her consent, and gave spouses for the first time the right to judicial divorce: Hindu marriages are thus compulsorily monogamous. In 1955 the *Hindu Marriage Act* extended these new rights of women throughout India, enlarging at the same time the scope of choice of mate by reducing the prohibited degrees, which had been exceptionally wide, and providing a comprehensive scheme for matrimonial relief approaching a Western model. It omitted, however, to allow a divorce immediately on the grounds of adultery or cruelty. The Hindu temperament would, in 1955, not go further than to allow judicial separation on such grounds, though after two years a divorce might then be had on the ground of what amounts to a total breakdown of the marriage. In 1956 the *Hindu Succession Act* provided that wives (and mothers and even married daughters) should share on an intestacy in all a male decedent's property, both that which was separately acquired by him or the interest which he had in joint-family property. The same Act turned the former limited tenure of property available to females (who were thought previously unfit to have the absolute disposal of property in general, except for their dowries and paraphernalia) into an absolute estate—producing a temporary confusion which the reader may imagine.

The fair sex having been treated with this overdue gallantry, a problem came before the courts for the first time in the 1960s which characterises the present position of Hindu law. It became necessary to calculate the extent of a husband's interest in family property when his share passed to his heirs on his death. Should the court take into account the ancient claims of a mother or a wife to a share if the father divided joint-family property between himself and his sons, who, at Mitakshara law, had a birthright in that property along with himself? If the new law exhaustively represented the women's rights an extra share would not need to be made available to the widow by this method of calculation. If it was to be read as

[6] If F died in 1938, leaving two sons, S1 and S2, and a widow, W, F's one-third interest in the property jointly vested in F, S1, and S2 would pass without unlimited power of disposal to W. Had he died in 1936, W would have taken nothing beyond her subsisting right of maintenance.

merely altering so much of the former law as its plain words or necessary intendment required the widow was entitled to her share of the inheritance, in estimating which her own rights to a quotient must first be recognised.[7] The solution which gives her the accumulated rights is difficult to justify on strict legal grounds, but probably represents Parliament's intention.

One could go further and ask whether the *Hindu Succession Act*, the *Hindu Adoptions and Maintenance Act*, and the *Hindu Minority and Guardianship Act* (all of 1956) are 'Hindu' in any substantial sense. We have illustrated a Hindu feature in the limitations of the divorce law. The *Succession Act* retains in its order of distribution on intestacy features, such as unlimited claims by even the remotest blood kindred and the general preference of the kindred through the male line over equally near kindred through a female line, features which are explicable only against the background of Hindu notions of inheritance. It is open to argument whether an adoption by a sonless man under the *Hindu Adoptions and Maintenance Act* can give rise to rights similar to those formerly afforded to an adopted son under the old law. There are decisions going far in that direction including a recent ruling of the Supreme Court which some feel stress unduly the tendency of the traditional ideas. However, it is a demonstrably Hindu feature that a man cannot adopt unless he has no direct male lineal descendant to make offerings to deceased ancestors, and that no Hindu of either sex may adopt a child of the other unless there is at least twenty-one years' difference in age between them. Indian critics minimise the Hindu features and enlarge on the manifest departures from the Anglo-Hindu system to which they were used. The whole question is important, as India has undertaken the task of codifying all her family laws, and possibly all the ground at present covered by personal laws. The personal law of the majority community is bound to be the basis for this, and unless its nature is understood little progress can be made towards a workable 'civil code' which the Indian Constitution promised in 1950.

Interpretation is clearly as vital an art now as the rules of law themselves, and here India has a very long experience. It was argued plausibly that the traditional rules of interpretation of texts resembled the English aids to construction of statutes and documents: indeed, it would be odd if some common ground were not covered even though

[7] F dies intestate in 1957, leaving a son, S, and a widow, W. If F's share is one-third (allowing W her ancient right to a share when F separates) S and W will take one-sixth each by inheritance. If the share is one-half (ignoring W's right at that point) S and W will take one-quarter each. In the first case W will have one-third (her share under the old law) and one-sixth, and will be on an equal footing with S. In the second case W will have only one-quarter.

the material to be construed was so different. In the *dharmaśāstra* propositions of logic, of various ages, influence the exposition of the maxims of law. The maxim 'Unequal things should not be treated as equal' is often called upon. Where sexual familiarity is penalised as well as adultery it is reasonable that a lesser penalty should be imposed for offences short of adultery than those to be imposed for the latter. Likewise, should the law prescribe mutilation as the penalty for theft of property not of very high significance and should death be prescribed in other sources for the same offence, logic enabled the jurist to know that the death penalty was reserved for persistent offenders—though the text itself may not say so.

If a text tells us that land is lost to its owner when it has been in the undisputed possession of another for twenty years it will be objected not only that such possession is not listed among the causes of property (such as gift and purchase) but also that though it is urged that possession is *evidence* of property, it is plain that what *evidences* a thing cannot actually *cause* it to come into existence.

Taking isolated verses as one's guide can be misleading. The jurists insist on reading each text in its immediate context and in the light of preceding and following chapters. This at times restricts and at times develops the meaning of the bare words. Particles such as 'also' enable the reader to judge that unspoken elements were also intended by the *smriti*-writer. Words used with some particularity may be used as illustrations only.[8] The lists of offences and punishments in the criminal-law sections are long; yet where an offence not previously mentioned is found in the penance section, the jurist reasonably concludes that the offence has been prohibited, a somewhat obvious inference but a necessary one, as without the prohibition one might take a chance as to whether a penance might be called for.

Rules as to the construction of contradictory texts come from the *mīmāmsā*. Various ingenious methods of reconciliation are available in that quarter. It is an intriguing science originally an adjunct to Vedic rituals. The Vedas contain hymns and ritual instructions, and it was important to know which words were injunctive, which merely gave advice (the neglect of which might or might not have serious results), and which were merely declamation. Incongruities were smoothed out in the specialist's actual performance of rituals, but maxims of interpretation were eventually formed into a system when it was realised that the problems of using Vedic texts had counterparts

[8] The first may be illustrated by the comment upon Yājñavalkya II. 135 ('The wife, and the daughters also . . . take the property of a deceased sonless man . . .'), where the word 'also' is held to imply that a daughter's son is an heir after the daughter. The second may be illustrated by Manu VIII. 285, where it is laid down that a fine must be imposed for injuring 'trees': commentators say that 'trees' implies all plants.

in literature of a non-sacrificial nature. By the sixth century B.C. the fundamental *mīmāmsā* code by Jaimini was available, and from commentaries built on it we find that maxims originally meaningful only in sacrificial dilemmas were early used in secular situations. The jurists make constant use of them. An example would be the visualisation of the rights of an adopted son as those of a substitute which might in favourable circumstances entirely represent the principal: for all rituals involve the priest in the query whether some substitute will do either for the correct substance or the correct formula or officiant. Another would be the right to dispose of property after death; another again the effect in secular contexts of prohibitions against earning by reprobated means; or the implications of absolute title in property.

Maxims are used which had a popular origin. The maxim of the Staff and Loaf operates like our reasoning *a fortiori*. If a Brahmin, whose purity must be secured at all costs, is debarred from an act, except in a time of distress, it does not follow that castes of less ritual purity, such as the Śūdras, the servile classes, are automatically debarred. But if a Śūdra is prohibited it may well be that the castes initiated into Vedic learning are prohibited on the basis of the Staff and Loaf. If we find a stick has been gnawed upon which doughnuts are carried, and the doughnuts are gone, we can presume that what was able to gnaw the staff gnawed the doughnuts: acts of greater severity are thus prohibited where an act of lesser severity is prohibited. Less frequently used, but equally interesting, is the maxim of the Crow's Eye. It is a rule of *mīmāmsā* that no sentence may be split and no text can have more than one meaning. Jurists may argue what that meaning is, and in deriving their meaning may torture their text, but two inferences of the same type cannot be drawn from the same sentence on the same occasion or indeed on different occasions. But a word in the text may be interpreted so that it is taken with two portions of that sentence, so that with the aid of the word each in turn is meaningful. A crow has only one eye (who has seen both eyes of a crow?), and this apparently functions on both sides of its head (!): text-writers may follow this in making the occasional word do duty twice over.

The *mīmāmsā* teachers know how to classify texts exhaustively, a vital task. Injunctions, positive and negative, permission, regulation of what might be done in various ways, exceptions to prohibitions, contradictory texts raising the inference of an alternative, and purely facultative rules:[9] these are some of the types recognised. Some texts

[9] A 'facultative' rule shows how a thing you have determined to do may be done: it inferentially sanctions the doing of it in that way, but it does not enjoin that it should be done.

contain an injunction, a facultative rule, a declamation,[10] and even a reason bound up together. The *mīmāmsā*-trained jurist must know which is which and the implications of each. When a point is repeated within a continuous *smriti* composition, like Manu, he must be able to detect what is advice to the reader, emphasis, a subtle new point, or (if all else fails) mere repetition. Reasons are suspect. We are told that the Brahmin must not drink a liquor resembling whisky. At the same time we are told that if he does so he will fall into dirt or utter sacred texts unawares. If this is a reason it would follow that Brahmins who can hold their liquor or consume some antidote to intoxication may drink. The jurists explain that it is not a reason but a declamation intended to deter Brahmins from drinking, which is absolutely forbidden.

A further distinction of great importance is that between the 'seen' and the 'unseen' rule. A 'seen' rule is one which is intended for secular purposes, as that sons should inherit rather than the widow or parents or that certain offenders should be banished (a lesser penalty might be a sufficient deterrent); an 'unseen' rule is one that subserves transcendental, spiritual purposes, as that a man should not marry a girl whose patrilineal ancestors' family name agrees with his own. The first class of rule can be neglected if adequate reason appears (which the *smriti*-writer himself would be likely to recognise); but the second can never be neglected without spiritual danger and unpredictable effects.[11]

A Vedic injunction, if a plain case can be found, will overrule, or vitally affect the construction of, a contrary *smriti* text. All writers of *smritis* are presumed to have known the Veda even more thoroughly than we can. Moreover, all *smritis* must be interpreted harmoniously, for all authors were supposed to have known each others' works. What are we to do when one text says that an adopted son, when happily for his adoptive father but unhappily for himself a legitimate heir is born, takes one-third of the estate, while another says that he takes one-fourth? A possible answer is that an adopted son of high merit takes the greater, and one of lesser merit the lesser share. Differences between penances and punishments are accounted for in the same way. Each must be imposed, taking into account the character, motives, and circumstances of the offender, and the frequency or gravity of the offence.

[10] Which comments or exhorts, and so supports the injunction, *e.g.*, 'those who do not maintain them will fall from caste.' This does not necessarily lay down automatic excommunication for such failure to maintain, but is a declamation urging attention to the duty of maintenance.

[11] Ancient Hindu law excelled in classification and enumeration. The *Bhavishya-purāna* (*c.* tenth century) in a passage cited in legal digests of the early twelfth and seventeenth centuries (see Kane, *H.D.*, III, 840–1) classifies *smritis* into the five types. See above, p. 10.

The standard of such reasoning, it will be observed, was intellectual and moral, and the *dharmaśāstra* was above suspicion of partiality. Acceptance of the *dharmaśāstra* as 'true' law was a mark of prestige-bearing classes of society. It might have been otherwise if the law had been founded upon expediency. But we must clarify what part was played by convenience, for it must not be supposed that the ideals of the *dharmaśāstra* were automatically and invariably enforced; nor must it be suspected that for want of such enforcement the system was not a real system of law.

The judicial process took the teachings of the scholars into account, but no judgment could be given unless general questions of public policy had been considered. The stability of the kingdom, the security of the state, and the effects of a particular ruling upon valid local, guild, or even family customs must always be looked to. Upon this the *dharmaśāstra* itself insisted.

The British assumed that the book-law was binding upon all Hindus, unless a custom could be proved to the contrary. This made no room in so many words for consultation of custom to supplement and effectuate the bare rules of the book law. And English law naturally filled the gaps thus revealed. The personal law authorised a widow to adopt a son to her deceased husband if empowered by him; but the question whether she had been empowered was referred to the English law of powers. Again, if a member of an undivided family wanted to mortgage his interest the rights of the mortgagee had to be worked out on equitable principles: the Hindu law did not contemplate such a transaction. When the manager for an infant heir, a trustee of a religious endowment, or the manager of a joint-family estate alienated the property for purposes other than those which would bind the other interested parties, for example in speculation, the conflict was solved in a typically English way: the stranger, as a bona fide purchaser for value without notice of the defect in the alienor's powers, could retain his purchase against the 'beneficiaries,' provided he could prove that he made sufficient bona fide enquiry into the existence of the justifying cause behind the transfer. Nothing of this is in the *dharmaśāstra* in so many words, but it could be argued that such rules were latent within it. French enclaves, governed by civil-law principles, saw the development of a Franco-Hindu law with its own interpretations of the book law. The French conception of the joint family as a *communauté* is an adequate example: on a member's death the unit dissolved, a position not accepted at Anglo-Hindu law.

The methods of interpretation and attitude to norms which we find in the Sanskrit authors and later in the Anglo-Hindu law can be distinguished, but a curious agreement is maintained. The Sanskrit treatises assume that the science of righteousness *deserved* to be treated as the norm, whether or not it conformed to the practices of the people. Folk, who, it was once noted humorously, knew no more of the *dharmaśāstra* than they did of the Psalms of David were solemnly subjected by the British to a jurisprudence which took for granted their allegiance to principles of Hinduism. If communities purported to manage their affairs otherwise than as the book law contemplated, their acts were liable to be set aside, for the people were presumed to know the book law. In two areas of India the British failed to take this to a logical conclusion. In Malabar judicial recognition of matriliny and its legal manifestations saved the population from painful anomalies, and in the Punjab custom was given a high place by statute. Elsewhere the British attitude agreed in essentials with that of the *smriti*-writers. Few Englishmen had read Coke on Littleton or Blackstone, but the English law of real property was not weakened thereby. There were professional lawyers in England to advise the public, whose counterparts did not emerge in India until the second half of the nineteenth century, but the difference was not allowed to have any effect on the development of Indian law. The *smritis* were believed to embody the customs of the people, and the commentators were believed to have brought the *smriti*-law up to date. The fact that no more recent innovative indigenous textbooks had appeared was taken, somewhat hastily, as evidence that customs had become static.

Yet, throughout, the shape of the law reflected what most influential people wanted. A few *smritis* fell out of use because it was felt, by the ninth or tenth century, that this 'age' did not require them. An example would be the rule that a dead man who left no son could expect his widow to be ordered to cohabit with a close agnate so as to provide his line with a male heir. This arrangement, of great antiquity, was declared obsolete, though the jurists did not on that account totally ignore it in their treatment of the classical system. In the British period surreptitious additions and modifications were made in the course of interpretation, all of which apparently coincided with the public's actual usage. Self-acquired immoveable property was held freely alienable by a father, whose sons could have vetoed his act in pre-British times. A widow or indeed almost any female heir was disallowed from taking any inheritance as her absolute property: for, though leading medieval texts would have allowed this, influential sentiment insensibly guided the courts in a more reactionary direction. Formerly sons must pay their father's debts without limit on their means, but only when he was dead and they were majors. The British developed the rule, which is called the *pious obligation*, by confining it to joint-family property, and by forcing all sons, whether major or minor, to support to that extent all alienations by their father which were not immoral or illegal in motive or background, even in his lifetime and irrespective of whether he might otherwise have paid any ensuing 'debt' out of his separate acquisitions. This curious development is among the legacies of the British period most warmly cherished by the Supreme Court, though it is a travesty of the *dharmaśāstra's* intentions. Evidently this is to be attributed to the public's actual outlook on the subject.

In view of the overall continuity of relationship between the book law and its judicial day-to-day application it is evident that we must begin to look more closely at the *dharmaśāstra* itself. The first point to be noted is that no one expected life rigidly to be governed by the rules. India is, after all, a country in which the prestige-holding classes, especially the Brahmins, have been teachers or potential teachers and the remainder pupils or potential pupils. Surveys confirm that Indian youths are docile, altruistic, keen to receive moral instruction. A ready response greets the suggestion that our lives should demonstrate the upward curve towards universal moral and spiritual attainment. A blatantly didactic approach to life and culture is accepted, indeed expected in India. The *dharmaśāstra* contains the quintessence of 'teaching'; and discussions of partnership, master and servant, husband and wife, and the many other chapters of the substantive law would not be thought complete without moral exhortations and indications of the evil results of failing to fulfil injunctions and of performing what is prohibited, in whatever chapter of the law the prohibition occurs, spiritual or secular as well as moral. This has misled observers into supposing that Hindu law was fundamentally otherworldly and unpractical. Rather it is because scholars wanted to teach what people wanted to learn that the tone and content of the *dharmaśāstra* are as they are.

Now the ritual parts of that learning are in disfavour. The presuppositions that meritorious actions, such as gifts in charity, self-imposed penance, and pilgrimages, are essential for the well-being of society and the individual's happiness in other lives are no longer universally accepted. However, the notion that the human being has the choice whether to seek, after death, heaven and better stages of life by transmigration, or to seek a cessation from the obligation to be reborn, is still alive, and indeed lies behind much of the apparently negative reformist legislation in recent years. Some of the latter hits at caste exclusiveness and temple customs which religion had sanctioned. The system always catered for those who doubted the value of observances and the social obligations connected with them, but the emphasis has shifted away from the latter only in recent centuries. Meritorious actions are now less regarded than personal merit, as evidence of devotion to the higher, but not less Hindu, goal of cessation from worldly attachment in all time to come as well as in this present life.

But seeking after perfection, 'attainment,' after death is nonsensical if the daily routine is ignored. Well before the Christian era civilised life in India was considered to be the conscious maintenance of a self-disciplined, harmonious society, in which the castes performed their customary functions. Each household should keep its place, and each member within it should observe the roles assigned to him or her from birth. Between communities the king was the final arbiter, and he might be deposed if he failed. It was the king's responsibility to see to it that each person did his duty according to his stage of life and caste. If adherence to one's duty meant poverty the king should relieve it. Taxation, the king's wages, in theory amounted to one-sixth of the family's wealth; and he took one-sixth of the merit of ascetics and others who did not earn. The king must protect all *dharmas*, 'righteousnesses.' All castes must be enabled to perform their hereditary functions, which were believed to reflect long-inherited aptitudes and qualities of a moral and not merely a racial implication. 'Putting down the wicked,' the royal duty, was a means to that end. *Dharma* must be guaranteed by society: each individual could seek his personal goal provided his search did not impede others. Harmony in fact pressed hard upon the individual, but spiritual rewards were thought to be worth the sacrifices which family, caste, and kingdom required of him.

Everyone depends on water. Even the Himalayan snows depend on the climate, which is pitiless and unpredictable. It was supposed anciently that righteousness was natural, and the failure of the monsoon would reflect a failure of righteousness. The jurists, who shared such supersititions, founded their exhortations upon them. Some laws, such as that which required a girl to be given in marriage within three months of puberty, were evidently of a piece with laws of nature, and it was felt that at bottom many another rule was natural too, or that there was a 'true' tendency which should be observed in case of choice. Thus when various policies conflicted, that which would secure the public's confidence in its own adherence to *dharma* must have a high priority.

The king's classical education included a purely secular science called *artha-śāstra*, the science of ways and means (*artha* means secular objectives, wealth). The main textbook, attributed to a historical minister of the third century B.C., Kautalya, aims to tell rulers, in every pedantic detail, all they need to know to keep and to extend their kingdoms. The *dharmaśāstra* tells what he *ought* to do to maintain the spiritual health of the kingdom. Should he decide on the morally less commendable course, the *arthaśāstra* helps him to succeed. The four aims of man were, after all, *dharma*, *artha*, *kāma* (sensual pleasure), and *moksha* (final release from birth and living); and all four were required to make the whole man. A good and prudent king, giving each its proper balanced share, would choose the path of *dharma* if he came to a conflict between precepts of righteousness and expediency.

Maintenance of religion and learning would always be an instrument of royal policy. Brahmins of adequate knowledge and purity must be able to perform the requisite rituals. Otherwise agriculture, and therefore taxation, would fail. The law of marriage and inheritance must support purity of the home in all senses. A good law of social discipline, an appropriate law of contracts and trusts, and an effectual criminal law were all directly required by such policies. This is exactly what inspired the jurists to their comprehensive task. The family's earning must be proper, and their enjoyment secure. Against this background all the public could have the common virtues, which, though variously listed in our sources, always contain avoidance of what defiles, abstention from theft and adultery, abstention from unauthorised violence towards all creatures, obedience to elders, sweetness of speech, respect for teachers and all Brahmins, reverence for the Veda and the culture it represented, and a total abstention from oppression, *i.e.*, taking advantage of power or prestige. To assert one's rights was out of place in a society where internal discipline was strong and the king was expected to remedy all classes of complaint.

This brings us again to the question of custom. Custom was, as we have seen, at the root of the *smritis* themselves. But there could be customs repugnant to the *smriti* law, and their status was uncertain. Some customs were aberrant in that they could not be reconciled with *dharmaśāstra* presuppositions. That a *daughter* should be given in adoption for all purposes, or that illegitimate sons should share equally with the legitimate, would be repugnant to the *dharmaśāstra*, but the king was authorised to enforce them if they were indeed customs of the community in question. A custom of marrying one's sister or cohabiting with one's daughter-in-law, however, and even the apparently harmless custom of not returning possession of a field in respect of which one had a possessory mortgage when the interest received has equalled the principal, were condemned vigorously and the king was urged to enquire into them and declare them void. Customs might be eroded by a caste's gradual reaction to the *dharmaśāstra's* teaching, whereupon the king's abolition of such a custom, *e.g.*, demanding dowries at the time of marriage, would be consonant both with the spirit and the literal requirements of the *dharmaśāstra*. But what his jurisdiction was beyond such cases it is very difficult to make out. The *mīmāmsā* had the hardihood to declare all customs repugnant to the Veda and *smriti* to be void, but it is certain that kings were not advised to put this into effect as a rule.

If we place ourselves in imagination in a royal court (that is to say not in a commercial or other specialist tribunal which would follow other lines) we find the Brahmin assessor citing texts. But the actual texts, as some of their number emphasise, were not to be relied upon literally if enforcement would lead to inequitable decrees. Law without equity would be a denial of justice. Granted that the *dharmaśāstra* as construed to meet the case was free from absurdity, and that no valid custom was shown in derogation from it, a further conflict might emerge. Valid royal decrees of an administrative character stood upon a footing of equality with the book law. Indeed, they might overrule both custom and book law. But they must not purport to touch unseen matters, nor interfere with the religious life of the people in its secular manifestations. The jurists tend to make much of this. A royal order that householders should present themselves at an assembly at an hour when each should be performing his worship at home would be invalid. One bold jurist goes so far as to say that grants subject to divesting for failure to perform services are void as to the condition, and that such grants must be construed as absolute grants. His reason is that the king cannot create, by way of gift to Brahmins, a right itself repugnant to property—which involves the power of disposal at pleasure. But the correctness of the argument is open to doubt.[12] Village and guild by-laws, however, provided they were not repugnant to royal policies, and provided they did not purport to meddle in unseen matters, had an equal status with the book law, and might conceivably overrule it on occasion. A king could certainly impose an estate duty, and a marriage tax, without thereby interfering either with the law of inheritance or that of matrimony. But there were no Indian counterparts to Henry VIII: no ruler purported to be master of the religious institutions and of the doctrine.

Indeed, the king's weight must be placed behind the moral and social order. Indian Utopias were envisaged as populated by people who did not need the king's *danda* ('mace' or 'sceptre') to be applied for their correction. But in reality deterrents were much relied upon. The king's jurisdiction to punish offenders was seen as a duty to purge them for *their* benefit. He must encourage them also to perform their penance, and should not allow them to be readmitted to caste

[12] Later jurists do not follow him, and kings had been granting resumable endowments, which tended to secure the grantee's performance of his functions in scholarship, education, etc.

privileges unless their penances have been adequate. Unless he observes these rules he personally incurs the guilt of unpunished and unpurged offenders. The spirit of the system is well demonstrated by an inscription found at Uttaramerur in South India. There the rules for election to village committees provide that those who have lost caste by associating with sinners may not take part in elections until their expiation has been performed (it might take a long time); moreover, those who ate forbidden food are perpetually disqualified, even if they chose a perfectly legal but nevertheless light penance; so also even those who performed their penance for incest are perpetually excluded from voting, let alone from membership of the relevant committee. Those who had been publicly humiliated as part of their penance, and those who had forged documents could vote, but not stand for election.

Public opinion, the receptacle of transcendental and mundane ambitions, was the final arbiter: in this sense *dharma* was king even over kings. Public opinion has its own ways, alongside those of law. The *dharmaśāstra* believed in marriage as the gift of a virgin. Only in this way could the husband fulfil his obligations to perform, as a complete person, his *dharma*, and obtain offspring which would pay his debts and continue the line. Widow-remarriage was thus a convenience about which the *dharmaśāstra* affected to know nothing. In many castes widow-remarriage was practised, and the law did not brand the offspring as illegitimate, they were *de facto* members of the family, and as such taken care of by custom. In recent centuries lower castes have been imitating Brahmin ethics, and have been eschewing the remarriage of widows. Meanwhile the state, in 1850, allowed widow-remarriage to castes which the *dharmaśāstra* had previously excluded from this facility. The same castes are by no means obliged by law to marry virgin brides (naturally); but they are taking up the custom of marrying off their daughters at puberty, though the statutes against child marriages nominally penalise those that engage in them—the reason being that prestige-bearing circles have claimed these recruits by imitation, statutes or no statutes. The missionary career of the *dharmaśāstra* goes on, and the statutes alluded to are very mercifully applied in practice. The traditional law claims converts from the lower end of the social scale while it seems to lose adherents at the other.

But this loss may be superficial. The self-contained and delicately balanced society came, as we have seen, under foreign rule, and for its former leaders were substituted others whose prestige did not stem from a regard for the ancient culture. The opinions of London began to rule in Bombay and Madras. The natural intellectual aristocracy could no longer teach what the majority wanted. The energy that used to be spent on learning the Hindu scriptures was diverted to Shakespeare, J. S. Mill, and the textbooks of Anglo-American jurisprudence. Even the joint family began to feel the draught. Members wanted to keep their earnings without sharing them, and, if they should die joint owners with their relations without having separated (out of respect for their elders), they wanted their shares to be capable of being bequeathed to legatees of their own choice. Young people wanted to marry on their own initiative and not at their parents' pleasure, which had often been corruptly, if not always unsuitably, indulged. Polygamous unions, which used to cure a husband's regrets, began to affront romantically minded and morally awakened Hindus. Women ceased to be a 'means of achieving *dharma* and progeny,' and became persons in their own right.

Rigidity of caste, which in its positive aspects had promoted social discipline (so long as it was not abused by caste heads who gave way to faction), prevented leaders of society from even dining together, and this began to be seen as a bar to political unity. A system of personal law which recognised caste distinctions began to seem more of a nuisance than an inspiration to concentration, humility, and achievement. The religious emphasis was thus consciously detached from the aspect of works and their alleged occult value in after lives. The path of faith, which had always refreshed the underprivileged to whom the works of the 'twice-born' had been forbidden, came into its own. Self-government brought with it a determination to apply democratic principles.

Unrepealed parts of the Hindu law which had been sedulously retained out of regard for religious scruples were now reviewed. In the law of adoption religion had been the shield behind which widows had been allowed to embarrass, indeed harass, their husband's relatives—by adopting, with retrospective effect to the time of their husband's death (perhaps seventy years before). The adopted son, as the dead husband's heir would protect his adoptive mother. The Privy Council allowed religion and logic more scope than even the litigating public accepted, and this error had to go. The widow, in her own right, is now secure, as we have seen, and the occasion for harassment having gone, the anomaly was readily abolished in 1956. But the religious ceremonies for the deceased husband and his ancestors may still be performed if the widow chooses to adopt both under the *dharmaśāstra* and under the statute, and if the family are religious they will give this adopted son the share that he would have had under the old law—though whether they are obliged to do so is doubtful.

The British saw no reason why the father of an only son should not give him in adoption, if he wanted to, without the boy's mother's consent; he could also appoint guardians without asking her opinion, even superseding her herself. These antique rules have also been abolished by the legislation of 1956.

The Hindu legal system has thus the parti-coloured character of a system in a transitional stage of adjustment to modernity. The *dharmaśāstra* lives on in penance (which holds its own on a voluntary basis in those areas where excommunication is forbidden) and in ritual contexts: as when a house is to be dedicated or a sick man wants the evils of unexpiated sins purified by ceremonies for which he pays. This is, of course, not law. In religious endowments the basic principles known to the *dharmaśāstra* are safeguarded: an untouchable nowadays can enter a temple belonging to ritually pure castes, but he cannot come nearer to the image than may any non-ministrant of the deity, and the age-old ritual must be observed as long as the sect itself endures. This position *is* legally protected. Marriages follow the ancient precepts; people seldom marry out of their castes or, worst of all, with the bride belonging to the formerly superior caste; similarly, the genealogists adhere to the *dharmaśāstra* when they record marriages and births, and the family priests follow it when arranging the sacraments of initiation, marriage, etc. But the law allows the individual to contract a valid marriage in a 'reformed' manner, even with a non-Hindu if the intended spouses go before a registrar under the *Special Marriage Act*, and if priests and genealogists ignore the union for all purposes only orthodox old ladies will now be seen to care much.

This is an ideal compromise. The law does not fly in the face of faith. Parties who wish to follow their cultural traditions may do so. Personal holiness is not frustrated. It is up to the individual whether he avails himself of the new juridical regime.

The joint family as an economic unit is still, no doubt rightly, largely governed by the Anglo-Hindu law. The rights of fictitious members, such as adopted sons, concubines and illegitimate sons, survive as they existed centuries ago, only marginally affected by the reforms; but this seems a transitional feature, for cosmopolitan concepts of the family are gaining ground as the law seems to expect. The statutes which affect devolution of property on death do not make exceptions for those relations whom the high moral tone of the day does not favour; but the adopted son is placed on a par with the natural-born legitimate son.

The modern Hindu law of guardianship does not differ vitally from the previous law, except in that less discretion is allowed to strangers to act in minors' interests—it is assumed that a court may be consulted in any emergency. As we have already seen, the old principles may be adhered to in marriage and adoption, but greater freedom is allowed to those who need it, and humanitarian principles are given greater weight. Individuals' needs are now placed above the stern call to discipline. The law of maintenance renews the recognition of a wide sphere of dependants surrounding the hypothetical breadwinner, but it attempts to organise the order of priority under which various funds and sources are to be approached. The basic Hindu value of compassion and living for others dominates the picture still.

Modern remedies are indeed available. A wife deserted by her husband can, after a decent interval, obtain a divorce virtually on that ground; a woman treated cruelly by her husband's parents can similarly be freed (if she wishes) from them and from him, though she will have a poor chance of being married again if her society is strict. The law is relaxed in favour of compassion, for previously she had no resort but to run away, without a future. The ancient Hindu belief that marriage is a union for life for all purposes, spiritual and secular, is untouched. Those who believe in it may regulate their lives accordingly. The doctrine that marriage is a sacrament has stood the test of millennia, but is no longer an excuse for the husband to treat his wife with inhumanity. The litigiousness of the people is, however, a cross to be borne and must be remembered when we tend to be satisfied at India's joining the Anglo-American juridical family. She will educate herself slowly into a more realistic and responsible attitude towards her own legal system. Here as elsewhere the educational ideals of the *dharmaśāstra* retain some scope.

Mismanagement of temples and peculation in monasteries never hindered the faithful from pursuing their belief in piety and self-sacrifice, and the modern law of India, with its stricter control of public endowments, does nothing to hinder it now. The emerging framework suits ancient notions, which it appears at times to affront but in fact supports and furthers. In private law a man may in his last illness wish that his property should be spent in part for religious work conductive to his soul's benefit. The new law of succession does not give the estate to the heir whom the *dharmaśāstra* would have chosen, as best fitted to make the offerings to the dead. But the decedent may himself provide by will that such an heir shall take a proportion, or, subject to the rights of dependants, even the whole; or the actual heirs may carry out their religious obligations and employ a priest to perform the ceremonies. In the field of dowry legislation the spirit of the *dharmaśāstra* has at length triumphed, in that considerations for agreeing to a marriage are prohibited and penalised; but this will not prevent relations from endowing their daughter in a style in keeping with the ancient injunctions to 'purify' the lineage by alliance with a sought-after bridegroom.

We have devoted space to considering the effects of reforms upon religious belief and practice. This is relevant because the Hindu law from its commencement took religion and superstitious sanctions as the allies of jurisprudence, while recognising that no actual judgment could ignore public opinion or public policy. Hindus at large believed in *dharma*, with its political, social, charitable, and ritual elements. An individual's doubts or eccentricity of belief, even amounting to nihilism, would not affect the common spiritual complexion of the community which guaranteed that kind of freedom. Principles based upon religion never seemed to deny the force of purely secular needs, and thus their prestige was assured. A conflict between religion and the state never arose, and the consequence remains that every organ of government believes itself under a permanent obligation to enforce, by adjustments, every individual's duty to show compassion, responsibility, and loyalty as these have been defined in the course of centuries. The codification of Hindu law in India furthers this concept, and to that extent is not a radical departure from the Hindu law still in force in other parts of the world. If further modifications lead to a more decisive step it is reasonable that India should be followed in other jurisdictions, rather than that expatriate Hindus should be swallowed up in an amorphous, undifferentiated state legal system.

BIBLIOGRAPHY

A comprehensive survey of the sources of the traditional Hindu law, with comments on the Indian legislation which has amended it is to be found in the encyclopedic work:

P. V. Kane, *History of Dharmaśāstra*, 5 vols. in 7 parts (Poona, Bhandarkar Institute, 1930–62).

A shorter work for those who read French summarises the story up to the British period, relying upon Kane (among others), but having a movement and conciseness which Kane lacks:

R. Lingat, *Les Sources du Droit dans le Système Traditionnel de l'Inde* (Paris/The Hague, Mouton, 1967).

Several of the important ancient Hindu legal texts are translated in the *Sacred Books of the East* series originally published by the Clarendon Press (Oxford) and recently reprinted in Benares:

The Laws of Manu (vol. 25); *Āpastamba* and *Gautama* (vol. 2); *Vasishtha* and *Baudhāyana* (vol. 14); *Nārada* and *Brihaspati* (vol. 33); *Vishnu* (vol. 7).

The medieval writers, whose works are more important from the point of view of the application of law, are collected (so far as they had been translated by the date of publication) in:

S. S. Setlur, *A Complete Collection of Hindu Law Books on Inheritance* (Madras, 1911); while a somewhat more complete collection may be seen in the rarer and more cumbersome work of J. C. Ghose, *Principles of Hindu Law*, 3rd ed., 3 vols. (Calcutta, 1917).

A useful short survey of the system relying on the *smritis* alone is:

N. C. Sen-Gupta, *Evolution of Ancient India Law*, 2nd ed. (Calcutta/London, 1962).

The following works, though out of date in many respects, are still of great value:

P. Sen, *The General Principles of Hindu Jurisprudence* (Calcutta, 1918).

K. L. Sarkar, *The Mimansa Rules of Interpretation as applied to Hindu Law* (Calcutta, 1909).

J. Jolly, *Hindu Law and Custom* (Calcutta, 1928).

J. D. M. Derrett, 'The concept of Law according to Medhātithi, a pre-Islamic Indian jurist,' in W. Hoenerbach, ed., *Der Orient in der Forschung* (*Festschrift O. Spies*) (Wiesbaden, 1967), pp. 18–41, is a study showing objectively how the *dharmaśāstra* operated as the chief component (but not always the source of the rule) in the Hindu law in practice.

Among the practitioners' books on the current system of law the following is the most suitable for a newcomer:

N. R. Raghavachariar, *Hindu Law, Principles and Precedents*, 5th ed. (Madras, Madras Law Journal Office, 1965).

A more condensed introduction for the law student is:

J. D. M. Derrett, *Introduction to Modern Hindu Law* (Oxford University Press, Bombay, 1963).

A series of studies on aspects of religion and law in India from early times to the present day, including the impact of European administration, is:

J. D. M. Derrett, *Religion, Law and the State in India* (London, Faber and Faber, 1968).

For the critical balance in India between the ideals of the secular State and traditional values see:

D. E. Smith, *India as a Secular State* (Princeton University Press, 1963) and by the same editor, *South Asian Politics and Religion* (Princeton University Press, 1966).

CHINESE LAW

H. McAleavy

THOMAS DE QUINCEY confided to his journal in May 1818:

> 'I have often thought that if I were compelled to forgo England and to live in China, I should go mad. The mere antiquity of Asiatic things, of their institutions, etc., is so impressive that the vast age of the race and name overpowers the sense of youth in the individual. A young Chinese seems to me an antediluvian man renewed. In China, I am terrified by the modes of life, by the manners, and the barriers of utter abhorrence and want of sympathy, placed between us by feelings deeper than I can analyze. I would sooner live with lunatics, or brute animals.'[1]

This notion of the ineffable antiquity of Chinese civilisation is so deeply rooted in western minds, exciting even today in many people the same aversion as it did in De Quincey a century and a half ago, that it is worth pointing out at the beginning of this essay that compared with the ancient cultures of Egypt and Mesopotamia, China is a newcomer in the world. Her past cannot be traced archaeologically with any confidence beyond the second millennium before Christ, while her historical records proper do not begin until the eighth century B.C. On the other hand, though she cannot claim any special seniority in age, we must concede her a remarkable degree of cultural self-sufficiency. The social institutions which, as described to Europe by the Jesuit missionaries, compelled the admiration of Voltaire and other leaders of the Enlightenment and which persisted over much of China until the Communist victory of 1949 owed almost nothing to foreign influences, but derived their pedigree from beliefs and customs already discernible among the primitive farmers along the banks of the Yellow River four thousand years ago.

This great waterway has played in China a role nearly as important as that of the Nile and the Euphrates farther west. Yet there is one striking difference. The culture that sprang up in Northern China could not be described with accuracy as simply belonging to the Yellow River area. There were a number of local centres, situated

[1] T. de Quincey, *Confessions of an English Opium Eater, together with Selections from the Autobiography* (London, 1950), p. 333. For a needed corrective of this point of view see Joseph Needham's witty 'Dialogue between Asia and Europe' in R. Iyer, *The Glass Curtain* (1965), pp. 279 *et seq. Ed.*

at places where various tributaries of the Yellow River entered the main stream. True, these communities recognised their mutual similarities: in contrast to the nomads of the northern steppes, or the tribes occupying what are now the Chinese provinces south of the Yangtze, they formed in their own eyes a domain of civilisation surrounded by barbarism, and they listened with pleasure to legends of a golden age when their forefathers had lived in harmony as one people under the care of preternaturally wise and benevolent rulers. Yet their common origin, and resemblance in speech and manners, did not prevent them from waging incessant wars against one another. It was in such circumstances of disunity that the pattern of Chinese civilisation emerged into the light of history. Indeed, a period peculiarly fertile in the development of ideas, between the fifth and the third centuries B.C., is officially designated the Epoch of Warring States.

It is not surprising that together with the art of war, theories of government should have occupied the most intelligent minds at such a time. Nor were these speculations purely of academic value. Rulers were always on the look-out for advice upon how to manage their affairs in the most advantageous way possible, and more than one philosopher was given a pressing invitation to become a counsellor of state. But of all the pursuers of wisdom whose works have come down to us, one name stands out supreme, that of K'ung Fu-tzu, 'Master K'ung,' or 'Confucius' as seventeenth-century Jesuits latinised the Chinese syllables. He lived between 551 and 479 B.C., and owed his celebrity not so much to his originality—he himself very truthfully declared that he was a transmitter, not a creator, of ideas—as to the extraordinary way he personified the genius of his race. We ought therefore at this point to glance for a moment at some of the beliefs which formed the intellectual background of his time.

Among these, the one destined to have the widest future influence was the common-sense calculation that the best provision a man could make for his declining years was to beget sons to support him when his own strength should prove insufficient to wrest a livelihood from the soil. Then, as far as he was capable of speculating upon the world around him, the ancient Chinese saw that his existence depended upon his cultivation of the land according to the rhythm of the seasons. Behind the phenomena of nature he detected the presence of divine beings whose goodwill he sought to gain by prayers and offerings. He pondered in the mystery of death and thought that perhaps the spirits of his ancestors were among the denizens of this kingdom of shadows, and could be sustained and made happy by ritual sacrifices.

So far, these ideas were not noticeably different from those of many other primitive societies. There was, however, one respect in which the Chinese were already manifesting an attitude peculiar to themselves. They regarded mankind as being so organically a part of the system of the universe that not only did human society depend in the final resort on natural forces but that these forces in their turn were themselves affected by human conduct. Any action by man which was not consonant with the natural order tended to disrupt the cosmic rhythm, and if serious or widespread enough could result in calamities of the gravest sort. The sexual instinct, for instance, naturally leads to procreation: children naturally are subject to parental authority. Homosexuality, therefore, or parricide are abominations which, if occurring with any frequency, will upset the harmony of the seasons and very likely bring drought or floods to the land.

These beliefs, by his day already firmly established, were taken up and developed by Confucius. He collected and recast a body of canonical literature consisting largely of historical records and traditional ballads, to which in due course were added his own opinions, especially his sayings as written down by his disciples (known to English readers as the *Analects*).[2]

In the process of digesting this material into a coherent philosophy, Confucius performed one operation in particular which profoundly modified the quality of Chinese intellectual life. He eliminated theology altogether, declining utterly to express any views on such matters as the immortality of the soul, or the existence of a personal god. Filial piety and its extension to the veneration of dead ancestors were the corner-stones of his social system, but it was left to every man's private judgment whether or not to believe that the forebears to whom he was so scrupulous in paying his respects and at whose shrine he reported the important transactions of his career really survived as conscious personalities. In other words, the phrase 'ancestor-worship' commonly employed in the west to designate Confucian practice, is highly inappropriate and misleading.

If Confucius ignored the next world, in compensation he attached the most serious importance to man's duties in this. It was a problem which engaged the attention of several of the petty chieftains, and we read that two principalities had by the sixth century B.C. promulgated embryo penal codes. But this attempt to promote virtue by fear was alien to Confucius's style of thinking. For him, the essential problem was to induce men to perform their correct social functions spontaneously, through education and example. This was especially

[2] The numerous translations include Arthur Waley's *The Analects of Confucius*, 5th imp., London and New York, 1964.

the province of a ruler, and the most effective method of instruction was the polishing of manners by a scrupulous observance of etiquette and the cultivation of such refining arts as music. Of course not all people would be equally receptive to such influences: there would, still, be need for an ultimate threat of chastisement against the refractory, but in a properly regulated community penalties of such a kind would scarcely ever be used.

For more than two centuries after Confucius's death it seemed that his opinions were unable to withstand the pressure of events. The number of principalities steadily decreased as smaller units were swallowed up by stronger neighbours, until in the year 221 B.C. one kingdom, known as Ch'in, had overrun all its rivals and united them into one great empire to which the outside world began to apply the name 'China.' The victory was achieved by the construction of a ruthless machinery of government for which the blueprints were devised not by idealists pining for cosmic harmony but by men whose theories have earned for them the name of 'Fa Chia' or 'Legalists' and who taught that the commands of a ruler rigidly enforced were the only source of law that deserved to be taken seriously. In fact, to the prince of Ch'in, who assumed the title of 'First Emperor,' the partisans of Confucius, with their implied appeals to a higher authority, seemed a pernicious threat to his newly established throne, and we learn that large numbers of them were put to death while their books were burned. The severity defeated its own purpose by provoking a rebellion which in the space of a few years had swept the tyrannical regime from the land. Yet the national unity so recently created was not lost. Of the insurgent leaders who fought over the ruins of the Ch'in state, one imposed his authority by victory in the field and founded the dynasty of Han, which endured for four centuries down to A.D. 220. Thenceforward, unity under a central government was to be the normal condition of the Chinese world, not, however, without interruption. In the course of time, administration would become weary and inefficient, a ruling dynasty would fall, and the country would be plunged into chaos, out of which a fresh leader would emerge to found a new dynasty, and the process would be repeated.

Early in the Han dynasty the legalist philosophy lost the day to the followers of Confucius, and from then on the doctrines of the latter supplied the theory of the Chinese state. What Confucius had longed for, but had not lived to see, had at length come to pass, and the whole of civilised mankind was gathered under one roof. As regards the barbarians, there was some dispute among the learned whether properly speaking these could be termed human beings at all, but even the most liberal minds recognised the essential disparity of

Chinese and non-Chinese in the scheme of things, and could not imagine diplomatic intercourse with foreigners other than the reception of envoys from abroad bearing tribute to the Son of Heaven. This title, in the sense in which it was applied to the Emperor, requires a little explanation. Heaven (the same word also means the sky), though capable of bearing the meaning of a personal deity, was ordinarily taken to denote impersonal Nature, which had conferred on the monarch a Mandate to rule, simply by permitting the founder of the dynasty to triumph over his rivals in the struggle for the throne. The commission was then handed down from father to son, on the condition that each recipient fulfilled his role adequately. For an unworthy holder, or at least a series of unworthy holders, would inevitably cause the loss of the Mandate, which would pass through rebellion and chaos into the hands of someone better fitted to exercise such a function, and thus a new ruling house would come to power. While on the throne, the Emperor was surrounded by every mark of the most profound respect, yet his commands deserved obedience only in so far as they were declaratory of the natural order. When, as might occur under a bad ruler, an imperial decree was issued in flagrant violation of the principle it was a subject's highest duty to remonstrate, not to obey. Meanwhile, the sovereign in his task of administration was assisted by the wisest heads in the country. Civil servants—'mandarins' as westerners called them—were recruited by public examinations open to all males irrespective of their wealth and social position, with the exception of the children of parents in a few professions regarded as infamous, such as prostitution or the stage, and although since education was private the sons of the rich had a decided advantage in the competition, yet enough poor men rose to the top to justify the claim that careers were open to talent.

Imperial China, then, for two thousand years down to the abdication of the last Emperor in 1912 was governed according to Confucian principles. Yet, as has been shown, the initial unification of the country under the victorious Ch'in in 221 B.C. owed a great deal to the anti-Confucian notions of the Legalists, who laid the foundations of Ch'in power by exalting the will of the sovereign into the primary source of law, and in spite of the ultimate triumph of the followers of Confucius, the debt due to their rivals was acknowledged by the Han and all subsequent dynasties in the enacting of penal and administrative codes, and by the severe chastisement decreed against those who infringed these statutes. The legal history of China is therefore to a large extent made up of the interaction of these two divergent tendencies.

In the first place the Confucian success is evidenced by the fact that in all the voluminous collections of imperial legislation there is nothing bearing the faintest resemblance to a civil code. The lawmaker assumes that the institutions of marriage, adoption, and so forth are already in existence and known or at least knowable, whether from custom deriving its source from the instincts of man or by the teachings of the sages. The codes of law promulgated in various of the Warring States, up to and including the legislation of the victorious Ch'in, have long since been lost, but we can surmise their nature from the headings which have come down to us, and it is clear that no topic of what we should call civil law was touched upon. It was not until 200 B.C., on the first promulgation of a Han code, that we find a section on the household which, though primarily designed to facilitate census-taking and taxation, provided penalties against abuses of marriage. But even the Han laws, as indeed those of several subsequent dynasties, have been transmitted to us in a most fragmentary condition, and it is only from the seventh century A.D. with the T'ang dynasty that we find ourselves in possession of a relatively complete text of a code. This fact alone, in a country where records of the past were preserved with such care—the political and economic history of the Han and the other pre-T'ang ruling houses forms part of the unbroken series of dynastic histories—may itself serve to illustrate the slight esteem felt by Confucian scholars for legal texts.

Although our knowledge of Chinese legislation before the seventh century A.D. is incomplete, enough material remains for us to be satisfied that the Chinese historians are correct in holding that the T'ang code followed closely the model of its predecessors, while the T'ang laws in their turn are patently in essentials one and the same system with those of the last of the imperial dynasties down to the opening years of the twentieth century. This system was composed of criminal and administrative law, though the T'ang and later codes followed and developed the example of the Han in recognising certain customary rules of private law by decreeing penalties against those who infringed them. This legislation, however, was directed towards the protection of institutions such as marriage and succession, of which the matter was considered grave enough to form part of the natural order and which could not be contravened without danger to the community. But many transactions of daily life could not be so regarded. As far as the cosmic rhythm was concerned, for instance, it scarcely mattered—so long as good faith was kept—what rules were created by custom to govern business contracts. In consequence, topics of commercial law were conspicuously lacking in the imperial code.

The great size of China would lead one to believe that there must be a profound divergence of custom between one part of the country and another, and indeed the Chinese themselves have from the earliest times constantly remarked upon the variations of their local habits. Yet in this as in other respects foreigners would be well advised to be on their guard against overemphasis. It is the unity rather than the diversity of Chinese culture which should engage the attention. The stories we are so often told of a babel-like confusion of dialects, to mention only one subject of misunderstanding, are a grotesque distortion of the truth. To be sure, along the southern coast from Canton to Shanghai there are regional forms of speech differing from one another and from standard Chinese quite as much as English does from Dutch. Everywhere else we find dialect variations of the degree occurring in English or French, which, of course, means that villagers talking among themselves may be almost incomprehensible to a stranger, although the latter has no difficulty in making himself understood and in understanding what is said to him. To this must be added the fact that the written characters are identical throughout the country and the same books read from the banks of the Amur to the frontier of Vietnam.

The traditional system of education was another important element of unification. At its heart lay the state examination, success in which gave entry to a privileged class of literati and with luck to a career in government employment, the great goal of every ambitious man. No modern civil service occupies a place which even faintly suggests the prestige of the old Chinese mandarinate. The subject of examination was limited severely to the exposition of the Confucian classics, and all schooling, even the most elementary revolved around these standard texts, which the introduction of printing as early as the ninth century A.D. ensured would be distributed with an ease impossible at that time for the literary productions of any other country in the world. Those fortunate enough to be chosen as instruments of the imperial rule were invariably sent to posts outside their native province, to forestall the emergence of local autonomous regimes, and as in any case candidates for the highest degrees were obliged to attend in person in the capital, there was a great deal of coming and going among the educated class, which tended to advance the standardisation of culture. Since the essential features of social organisation were laid down either in the Confucian canon or the commentaries thereto, even though these works could not be said to possess the force of law, it is easy to understand that there was spread across the country in the course of the centuries a solid substratum of beliefs upon which a superstructure of social institutions could be firmly erected. Furthermore, even when, as happened on occasion, some dogma, too important to be ignored but yet in the circumstances too inconvenient to be adhered to rigorously, cried out to be interpreted casuistically the same devices or fictions were resorted to from one end of the land to the other.

At this point it seems desirable to illustrate what has been said by a common example. The ancient Chinese, intent as always upon discerning patterns for human conduct among the phenomena of nature, decided that the distinction between the sexes could be traced through the whole realm even of inanimate matter. Just as mankind sprang from the union of male and female parents, so all things came into being from the conjunction of Heaven (or the Sky) and Earth, and the male and female principles permeated all creation, as evidenced by Day and Night, Light and Darkness. As a unit of time, a day was made up of two periods, one of light, one of darkness, so the unit of parenthood was a couple, one man, one woman. The usual word for wife, *ch'i*, resembled in sound another word meaning 'equal.' From all this it was plain that a man might have only one wife at a time, and that both partners were of equal dignity. The male being the active and dominating element, parental powers over children were during the husband's life primarily exercised by him, but after his death they passed to the widow. There was never in China anything like the *patria potestas* of Roman law. The word 'father' never occurs by itself in any legal text: the phrase is always *fu-mu*, or 'father and mother.' This honourable status was reserved for the wife alone. A concubine differed not only in degree but in kind, and was a subordinate member of the family, not sharing the parental niche side by side with the husband in the manner of a wife.[3]

Any confusion of this pattern was regarded as a grave interference with the natural order, which as a matter of public policy must be checked by the state. All the extant codes forbid bigamy in the most explicit terms, which show little change from T'ang times onwards. The latest code (that of the Ch'ing dynasty, 1644–1912) states: 'Whoever having a wife shall marry another, shall receive ninety blows and (the purported second wife) shall be sent back to her family.'[4]

This prohibition was entirely consonant with the general custom of the people, except in one special set of circumstances. The Chinese attached enormous consequence to the provision of ritual successors to keep alive the memory of parents after their death. Where there was no natural son, the room was filled by adoption. But the rule was that the person adopted must belong to the same clan and be

[3] For a more detailed analysis, see H. McAleavy: 'Certain Aspects of Chinese customary law in the light of Japanese scholarship,' *Bulletin of the School of Oriental and African Studies*, 17 (1955), pp. 535–547.

[4] See B. Boulais, *Manuel du code chinois*, art. 521 (Shanghai, 1924).

a generation junior to the person succeeded to. If of a pair of brothers *A* was childless while *B* had two or more sons, there was a compelling moral obligation for one of the latter to be given to *A* in adoption. But what if *B* had only one son? Normally a man could take only one succession, and of course the claims of his own parents overrode those of all others. Yet if *A* were the elder, *B* would seem to be guilty of a dereliction of duty by keeping his son entirely to himself. In such circumstances, therefore, the custom grew up of permitting *B*'s son to take both successions. Very likely, *A* and *B* had already effected a partition of joint-family property in order to create each his own separate family. At least such a step would be foreseeable in the future, and it was felt necessary that *B*'s son should be equipped with two spouses, so that in due course he could emerge as the head of two households, namely as the heir of his own father, and as the adopted successor of his uncle.

The law of the state, however, as declared in the code, insisted that only one of the women could be a legitimate wife. Obviously, therefore, the second partner could be no more than a concubine. Yet this was unsatisfactory in several ways. As the purpose was to establish two distinct lines of descent, it would be invidious for either of them to have a humbler origin, from a concubine, than the other. More important still, if the husband died his powers would be exercised by the one legitimate widow, and the property of the adoptive lineage might be confused for purposes of management with that of the natural family. To avoid these embarrassments, the custom grew up of regarding an adopted son, in such a case, as being endowed with a double personality, on the one hand as the appointed successor of *A*, on the other as the natural heir of *B*, and permitting him to marry a legitimate wife in each role.[5]

Although this device had a long history behind it, it seems that the state did not take cognisance of the irregularity until the eighteenth century, when an imperial decree permitted an only son, while retaining the succession to his own father, to be adopted by a childless uncle, provided that the latter was the father's elder brother or had some other special claim to the privilege, such as distinction in the public service. Even so, not a word was said about a second wife, and the code continued not only to prohibit bigamy but to forbid the union of a man and a woman, formed on such terms, to remain in being even as concubinage. At last in the year 1821, in the course of a criminal trial in the northern province of Shantung, where a second 'wife' of this kind had been killed by her father-in-law, it became

[5] The *dvyāmushyāyana* ('double belonging') adopted son of Hindu law was very similar to this. Since 1956 it is doubtful whether the institution survives in India. *Ed.*

necessary to establish once and for all precisely what was the relationship between the parties, since this determined the degree of homicide. The question was referred to the Board of Rites at Peking, which declared that 'the taking of two wives for the purpose of begetting children for two lines of succession need not be considered as a case of bigamy calling for the separation of the parties. Yet according to the Rites, a man cannot have two legitimate wives, and so the more recently taken of the spouses must be regarded as a concubine.'[6]

The rule thus stated in 1821 was never formally questioned throughout the remaining ninety years of the Empire, and indeed even after the collapse of the imperial regime in 1912 it was reaffirmed under the early Republic by the Peking Supreme Court. With the promulgation of the Nationalist Civil Code in the 1930s, and the withdrawal of legal recognition of concubinage, the institution might be thought to have suffered a mortal blow, since the second 'wife' could no longer claim to be acknowledged as any sort of spouse whatsoever. Yet the undoubted fact is that all the legislation, whether imperial or republican, was entirely without effect on the domestic habits of the Chinese people, and that in cases of multiple succession two or even on occasion three 'wives' were taken without any regard for the clearly expressed law of the land. In 1948, only twelve months before the Communist victory, a man, of old-fashioned manners, no doubt, but clearly of considerable education and social standing wrote to a Shanghai magazine to express his astonishment on discovering, after living with two 'wives' for ten years in the country and then migrating with them into the city, that the municipal authorities would not list both the ladies as wives in the register of households.[7] In Hong Kong, although there, too, the second 'wife' is apparently treated by the courts as merely a concubine, there is no doubt that the custom of bigamy in cases of double succession is every bit as flourishing as it used to be in pre-Communist China.[8]

It would be easy to understand if this conflict between custom and statute law had come about in recent times, as a result of the introduction of westernised legislation by a modernising republic government. In fact, as has been shown, the clash occurred long before the west had impinged upon the traditional Chinese world, and the legislation not so much set at defiance as totally ignored was that of the Confucian state.

It has seemed necessary to discuss this topic at length in order to

[6] *Taiwan shihō* (Tokyo, 1911), Vol. II, Pt. 2, p. 266.

[7] See H. McAleavy, 'Some aspects of marriage and divorce in Communist China,' in J. N. D. Anderson (ed.): *Family Law in Asia and Africa* (London, Allen and Unwin, 1968).

[8] *Chinese Law and Custom in Hong Kong* (Hong Kong, 1953), p. 237; *Chinese Marriages in Hong Kong* (Hong Kong, 1960), p. 71.

clarify one most important proposition, which is too often lost sight of by western observers, namely, that to ascertain the effective rules of traditional Chinese law in what we should term private or civil matters, one must exclude statute in favour of custom.

The Confucian state was well content that its subjects should settle their private disputes between themselves without recourse to its laws. In most cases the mere fact of appealing to a magistrate, even where the appeal had right on its side, stamped a man as a trouble-maker. In the seventeenth century one of the greatest of Chinese rulers, the Emperor K'ang Hsi, went so far as to declare that 'law-suits would tend to increase to a frightful amount, if people were not afraid of the tribunals, and if they felt confident of always finding in them ready and perfect justice. As man is apt to delude himself concerning his own interests, contests would then be interminable, and the half of the Empire would not suffice to settle the lawsuits of the other half. I desire therefore that those who have recourse to the tribunals should be treated without any pity, and in such a manner that they shall be disgusted with law, and tremble to appear before a magistrate.'[9] In fact, because of the lack of civil procedure, a litigant could invoke the help of the state only by accusing the other party of a crime, as for instance of fraud in the non-payment of a debt, and even if his resentment was so strong that he was willing to incur the odium of taking so drastic a step, he had to bear in mind that if he failed to establish his case he himself would be punished for wrongful accusation.

So unwelcoming were the courts towards litigants, that they often gave the appearance of being reluctant to interfere, even where the wrong complained of contained a criminal element. In the early eighteenth century the city of Canton was scandalised by a feud between two prominent families, who were connected by marriage. The vendetta in the long run led to arson and murder, and culminated in a sensational criminal trial, but the incident I wish to refer to here, taken from an account by a journalist written about sixty years ago, happened while the affair was still in its early stages and had not yet passed the stage of minor harassment. One of the families decided that a good way to hurt the other was to steal a crop of sugar-cane from the latter's plantation in the country, and hired a gang of ruffians to carry out the depredation. These were seen in the act by a steward in the employment of the second family, and as he was hopelessly outnumbered, he ran and told the head of the local constabulary, who lived some distance away. When, after much grumbling, this official had collected a *posse* of subordinates and gone with the steward to the scene of the outrage, the perpetrators had

[9] S. van der Sprenkel, *Legal Institutions in Manchu China* (London, 1962), p. 77.

disappeared, leaving the plantation completely denuded of its crop.

The plot in question was one of a number of similar plantations, belonging to various owners, on adjacent ground, but the damage had been confined to it alone, and in all the rest the sugar-cane was flourishing undisturbed.

'This is very strange, isn't it?' said the policeman. 'Why should your land be singled out in this way? Are you quite sure your master doesn't owe somebody money which he hasn't repaid? Perhaps one of his creditors has decided to help himself?'

'No, I'm certain it can't be anything of that sort,' said the steward. 'Mind you, I know my master has enemies, and this must be some of their work.'

'Enemies, eh?' exclaimed the policeman. 'You said nothing about enemies just now. All you told me was that a gang of ruffians had come to plunder your sugar-cane. Now you start talking about enemies! You know you really must learn to watch what you say!'

What is one to deduce from this passage? If the crop had been taken solely for motives of thievery, then clearly in the policeman's eyes the steward would have been justified in calling upon the public authority to help. But if the takers of the crop could allege, even remotely, what we should call 'a claim of right,' then the steward was somehow to blame for bringing the law into the matter at all. This was especially so if the taking was done in order to recover a debt. Even if it was merely to satisfy a grudge, the existence of the grudge was sufficient to turn the theft into an incident in a dispute which ought to be settled by neighbourly arbitration. Of course this is stating with too great a simplicity what in reality was an exceedingly complicated question. The Chinese state, for instance, frowned upon any attempt at self-help by creditors, and there was no doubt that the taking of the sugar-cane was a crime. Nevertheless, the steward had not done the proper thing in bringing a criminal charge.

As regards the junior members of a family, an extensive jurisdiction was conceded to the parental authority. Only in the gravest matters, such as treason, could a son or daughter denounce a parent to the magistrate. Any attempt by a child to invoke the protection of the state against parental ill-treatment was itself a most enormous crime, striking as it did at filial piety, that corner-stone of the social structure, and was punishable by death. In theory, parents did not have the right themselves to put a child to death: this, as well as lesser penalties, would be inflicted by the state at the parents' request. But the death of a child as a result of parental chastisement incurred no blame, and a cursory reading of Chinese newspapers of the last years of the Empire reveals numerous instances where unfilial sons or daughters were even drowned or buried alive with apparent impunity by their indignant families.

Yet this parental authority, though the state would do nothing to restrain it at a child's plea, did have limitation. A father as family head was the manager, not the owner, of the family property. It was usually found that a buyer of land would not feel his title safe unless the adult sons of the vendor had joined in the conveyance. Nor could a father frustrate a son's expectations by disposing of the family property by will. And in practice, where an improvident father was squandering the estate, senior members of the clan would often intervene in the interests of the children.

The clan in fact was a most important source of private law. In that agrarian society, when a family split up on partition it commonly happened that the new families thus created were bound together by economic as well as sentimental links. If, for example, two brothers after their parents' death decided, as they usually did, each to set up on his own the rule was that the property was equally divided. But very often certain assets could not be treated in this way. A buffalo, say, or a set of agricultural tools would obviously be required by both parties, and would accordingly be held in common. The clan, then, formed by the fragmentation of a family tended from the start to have clan property, and in south China in particular this could be very extensive, for there (more than in the north) whole villages were frequently inhabited by members of one clan, and land would be dedicated to the upkeep of temples, schools, and other institutions of clan welfare: indeed, the clan would assume many of the functions of local government. The largest and wealthiest clans often organised their own defence forces for the protection of their property against bandits or predatory neighbours. We learn from the famous eighteenth-century novel *The Dream of the Red Chamber* that it was standard practice for a magistrate to keep a list of those clans within his jurisdiction whose importance make it inexpedient for them to be interfered with, and to pass on the list to his successor. In the south especially we hear of occasions where magistrates would look on helplessly while feuding clans settled their difference by miniature warfare, or at the most would tender their good offices as neutral referees. In the middle of the nineteenth century the great landowners of central China, whose interests were threatened by the peasant uprising known to history as the Taiping Rebellion, finding that the imperial government in Peking was impotent to restore order, decided to help themselves, and using these small private forces as a nucleus built up from their tenantry formidable armies to which the western powers were glad to extend assistance. The future General Gordon of Khartoum first rose to fame as

'Chinese Gordon' when he was seconded as military adviser to one of these armies operating in the hinterland of Shanghai. When by this means the Taiping Rebellion was suppressed in 1864 the local forces were incorporated into the armies of the state, but in fact had greater loyalty to the grandees who had recruited them than to the central government. The seed of disunity, thus planted, bore fruit after the collapse of the imperial system in the shape of the warlords, who during the early Republic disputed between themselves the plunder of the country.

Decisions concerning clan affairs were made by the clans council, consisting of the senior clansmen. This body, however, was by no means an assembly of equals, since all its members stood in graduated relationships towards one another corresponding to their generation and age, and this fact alone sufficed to ensure that the principle of 'one man one vote' was never so much as thought of.

As marriage was generally arranged by parents, it was in some respects more of an alliance between families than a mere contract between two persons. The settlement of matrimonial disputes, therefore, usually called for agreement between the respective family-heads, with the assistance of the go-betweens, whose participation was a necessity in any betrothal or wedding, and who could give evidence regarding the circumstances of the union. In the case of marriages between members of wealthy families, these go-betweens would usually themselves be prominent local personalities whose status added weight to their opinions, and who in consequence were well accustomed to being invoked as peace-makers. It was a cardinal principle in this sort of arbitration that neither party should be granted an outright victory. Considerations of 'face' as well as the desire of appeasement invariably recommended a compromise, no matter how slight the grounds for such an arrangement might be by any western standard.

Yet another important source of law was to be found in the guilds which regulated the affairs of various trades and professions. These rules were fixed by the members of the guild in council, but here also, as in other Chinese assemblies, there was no suggestion of decision by majority vote until in the present century certain associations of modern-style businessmen with foreign ideas began to be formed in Shanghai and a few other cities.

From what has been said, it may be surmised that the legislative and judicial functions of the traditional Chinese state were in a relatively undeveloped condition. Such a conclusion, however, would be unwarranted. True, there were extensive areas of social behaviour into which the Emperor and his officials did not seek to intrude. In particular, even the most vigorous imperial administration never effectively asserted a claim to the monopoly of force within its dominions. None the less, the Chinese *corpus iuris* is a remarkable achievement, and one which has had a wide influence outside the frontiers of its own country.

Statute law derived its formal validity from its promulgation as the will of the Emperor. To be sure, if this will conflicted with the order of nature, disobedience was justified, but the justification would be acknowledged only by posterity, or after the overthrow of the tyrannical regime, and pending such a revolution the imperial command was binding on the officers of state. The form in which the commands were expressed had a lengthy pedigree, going back indeed some centuries before the first unification of the Empire in 221 B.C., but the earliest dynastic code extant in sufficient detail, and the one which fixed the pattern of future legislation, was that of the T'ang dynasty (seventh century A.D.). This was composed of two sections. One of these was a body of statutes called *lü*, which imposed penalties for the commission of certain acts. The other was a collection of positive ordinances called *ling*. The subject matter in both comprised public law, the *lü* amounting to a criminal code, the *ling*, although disobedience to them also incurred punishment, being essentially an administrative code. As has been already mentioned, what in the West is called private law was touched upon only indirectly. This in itself forms a marked contrast to the development in Europe, where, for instance, the great compilations of Roman jurisprudence are concerned primarily with the institutions of private law. Indeed, Far Eastern scholars of comparative law declare that already before the Christian era China, in the domain of criminal law, must have reached a state not attained in Europe until the sixteenth century. Since of all statute law the criminal code made the chief impact on society, it is worthwhile to look at it in a little detail, as it is represented by the code of the last, or Ch'ing dynasty (1644–1912).

The nucleus of it was the *lü*, most of which were identical with those of the T'ang dynasty promulgated in the seventh century. Many of them had an even earlier origin, and as they had been enforced by intervening dynasties, it has been said not altogether unfairly that they may be called the fundamental and unchanging part of the criminal law. Even so, their unchangeability was merely relative. In fact, their number varied slightly not merely from one dynasty to the next, but even in the course of the same dynasty. Thus, for example, the first edition of the Ch'ing criminal code, published in 1646, contained 457 *lü*, which by 1740 had been reduced to 436. They were arranged under the six Boards, or departments of state in Peking, concerned with Civil Office, Revenue, Ceremonies, War, Punishments, and Works. The Board of Revenue handled such matters as the registration of families for taxation purposes, and therefore it was in the section assigned to this Board that were found such *lü* as the following: 'Whoever already having a principal wife, shall purport to marry another of the same rank, shall be given ninety strokes, and the parties shall be separated'; 'Whenever two persons of the same surname shall purport to contract a marriage, the authorisers and the male and female parties shall each be given sixty strokes and the couple separated.'[10]

It happened occasionally that the *lü*, for all the deference paid to their immutabiity, were felt to have outlived their usefulness. Now and then this situation was remedied by dropping the *lü* in question from subsequent editions of the code. One instance of this was a *lü* of the Ming dynasty (1368–1644) which prohibited the taking of concubines by ordinary citizens, except by men who had reached the age of forty without having a son. To judge from Ming literature this rule was totally ineffectual, and the Ch'ing code, from 1946 onwards though in general adhering closely to the Ming *lü*, quietly omitted it. More often, however, the difficult *lü* was permitted to remain in the book, but was qualified by the addition of a supplementary statute called a *li*, which was not considered to be so sacrosanct as the *lü*, and to have a temporary nature. By the nineteenth century these supplementary statutes had become about four times as numerous as the *lü* they were designed to qualify, and amounted to some 1800 items. They had their origin in imperial decrees, in rescripts (where the Emperor endorsed a memorial submitted to the throne by a mandarin whether as an individual or as a member of a government office) and in the decisions of the six Boards, especially those of the Board of Punishments. It was from the staff of this last organisation that were chosen the officials who handled the editing of the supplementary statutes, which from the eighteenth century were issued every five years. Since these decisions frequently ratified the judgment of lower courts, we can see that such judgments constituted an important ingredient in the imperial legislation.

The supplementary statutes were principally designed to modify the *lü* by increasing or lessening the penalties assigned to a particular crime by the latter, in consideration of special circumstances. Some of them, however, had the role of attaching criminal punishment to actions not otherwise provided against, by using methods of analogy to assimilate the actions in question to crimes specified as such by some *lü*. However subordinate the supplementary statutes might be in theory, in practice their legal validity was in every respect equivalent to that of the *lü*, and a subsequent *li*, so far as it went, prevailed over a pre-existent *lü*. Indeed, from the 18th century the official title

[10] Boulais, *op. cit.*, arts. 521, 582.

of the criminal code was Ta Ch'ing Lü Li, or the Lü and the Li of the Great Ch'ing (Dynasty).

Complete editions of the code contained three sets of commentaries. One, called official, was printed in small characters in the body of the text, of which it was construed as a constituent part, having the full force of law. There was another commentary which was simply a paraphrase of the text, while at the top of the page ran a collection of decisions and other illustrative matter, not having the force of law but serving merely as a useful guide to magistrates.

To make all this clearer, here are examples. First of all, let us take a *li* which simply modified a *lü*. We have quoted above the *lü* which declared that when a man already married to a principal wife purported to marry another wife of equal status corporal punishment was incurred and the couple were to be separated. But we have seen that when an only son, who was in duty bound to succeed to his own parents, wished at the same time to become the adopted successor of a childless uncle it was the custom for him to marry two principal wives in order to sustain the double role. Yet according to the *lü*, not only was the status of the second wife unacknowledged by the law, the mere cohabitation of such a couple was impermissible. Then, as has been mentioned earlier, a decision of the Board of Rites in 1821 held that in these special circumstances, although the second spouse could be considered merely as a concubine, it was unnecessary to break up the union. This decision, incorporated as a *li* into the code, granted a welcome impunity to many such households, who in fact, as has been shown, continued to ignore the inconvenient reference to concubinage.[11]

Next, we may give an instance of an analogical *li*. Fornication between a man and a girl, according to the strict law, formed an impediment to a subsequent marriage between the couple. What if a betrothed pair, before the actual wedding, anticipated their nuptial privilege? Betrothal was in certain respects a bond almost as stable as marriage itself. It was quite possible that the girl might already be living with the groom's family. In any case, to enforce the law would result in intolerable hardship. A *li* was drafted to the effect that in such a situation the *lü* to be applied was not that concerning fornication but the one which prescribed sixty blows for disobedience to parental authority. The marriage therefore was saved.[12]

Finally, an example of an official commentary: the *lü* quoted above forbidding marriage between parties of the same surname reflected the Chinese abhorrence at the idea of incest between descendants of a common male ancestor. Yet educated people were aware that the possession of the same surname did not invariably mean that such

[11] See p. 114, n. 6 above.

[12] Boulais, *op. cit.*, art. 553.

a relationship existed, and the paucity of family names in China sometimes made the prohibition a real hardship. The following note was subjoined to the text of the law: 'the main question, in case of people of the same surname, is whether they are actually of the same clan. If they are not of the same clan, then (the magistrate) should decide according to the circumstances. He need not stick to the letter of the law.'[13] Curiously enough, this liberal interpretation had little or no effect on popular behaviour.[14] Not only did the prejudice against such marriages remain as strong as ever—indeed, it still exists today long after the legal prohibition has been removed—but it was extended to cover surnames resembling each other in sound or writing, or to which tradition attributed ancient enmity or some other relationship as a barrier to intermarriage.

To apply this corpus of law there was no judicial system separate from the executive branch of government. The basic administrative unit was the district, of which in the nineteenth century there existed about fifteen hundred, with an average population of two hundred thousand each. Each district was governed by a magistrate, who must, as we have seen, not be a native of the province in which the district was situated. It was he who was responsible for the administration of justice within the district, and all criminal cases had to come before him in the first instance. With minor offences, for which the punishment was only a beating of a less severe kind, sentence could be pronounced and carried out on the spot, subject to the prisoner's right of appeal to a higher court in the case of more serious crimes, the district magistrate had to listen to evidence, and then submit a report to the court of second instance, that of the prefecture, which consisted of a number of districts. In the report the district magistrate specified the article of the criminal code which he believed to be applicable, and recommended what he considered to be an appropriate judgment, but the actual result was up to the decision of the higher authority. The prefectural court had power to impose and execute sentence (again subject to appeal) for offences not involving loss of life where punishment did not exceed temporary banishment. Other cases had to be referred, in the same way, to higher courts—usually a couple more till the provincial governor was reached. Capital offences were sentenced by the Emperor himself, after discussion by a committee of leading mandarins from the Board of Punishments and other bodies.

During the last hundred years there has grown up in the west a sort of 'black legend' about the Chinese penal system which lingers in

[13] *Taiwan shihō*, Vol. II, Pt. 2, p. 267.

[14] Modern Hindu law, having escaped by statute from a very similar predicament (above, p. 88), is still ahead of public usage in this regard. *Ed.*

people's minds even today. From the brief description just given, it will be seen that quite apart from the right of appeal, serious charges were automatically subject to a whole series of revisionary examinations, and that the death penalty could be imposed only after deliberation by the highest authority in the land. Methods of punishment were, essentially, flogging, transportation, death by strangulation or beheading. When we bear in mind that until the French Revolution burglars and highwaymen were broken on the wheel in so highly civilised a country as France we can understand why it was not until the nineteenth century that Christian Europe began to feel itself superior in humanity. Even the grimmest penalty of all, death by slicing—the so-called 'death of a thousand cuts'—which was prescribed for specially heinous crimes, was in the opinion of a member of the English Bar less atrocious than the hanging, drawing, and quartering inflicted upon traitors in Britain till comparatively recent times.[15]

But if the sanctions imposed by the Chinese code were no worse in point of cruelty than those commonly employed in Europe before the nineteenth century, it must be admitted that the conduct of criminal trials by the courts themselves was a disgrace to Chinese justice. It has already been mentioned that state policy, as expressed by an edict of one of the greatest of Chinese rulers, the Emperor K'ang Hsi, in the seventeenth century, enjoined upon magistrates the necessity of making their tribunals places without pity and nobody could have accused the officials of remissness in this duty.

Although the courts were purposely unwelcoming to would-be litigants, everyone had a right to petition the magistrate for justice, and there was a general obligation to report crimes. The magistrate was bound to conduct an enquiry, for which purpose the most convincing evidence was thought to be the confession either of guilt by the accused or of malice by the petitioner. Torture was therefore freely resorted to, and the literature is full of instances where a prisoner or a witness dies under the rigours of such an inquisition. Even if matters did not go so far, everything was done to strike terror into the persons questioned, who were compelled to kneel in front of the magistrate's table while attendants harassed them with menacing cries and gestures.

One striking consequence of Confucian agnosticism upon judicial procedure was the absence in the state courts of any form of trial by ordeal or of anything corresponding to an oath. In contrast, both of these were frequently employed by the people when administering justice according to their own customary rules. We read, for instance,

[15] E. Alabaster, *Notes and Commentaries on Chinese Criminal Law* (London, 1899), p. 58.

in the twentieth century of parties to a dispute being compelled to put their hands into a rack containing a snake and to grope about until they had touched the reptile, after which the merit of their case was estimated by whether they were bitten or not, or by the comparative severity of the wound. Another method of ordeal was to try and snatch a coin from a jar of scalding oil. As for oaths, popular custom was acquainted with a wide range of formulas. Sometimes the person swearing would slaughter a chicken, while calling down a similar fate on his own head if he should be lying; or he would smash a piece of crockery with the same intention. This latter practice, carried abroad by Cantonese laundrymen and waiters, is accepted in England and elsewhere as a Chinese form of oath, though it was—and is—totally unknown to any court of the Chinese state. Of course, the law had to take account of the fact that the mass of the population was influenced by superstition. Thus decapitation was treated as a severer penalty than strangulation, though the latter—a treble garrotting, with the revival of the victim during the intervals—was to foreign notions infinitely the more unpleasant, because of the popular belief that the severence of the head from the trunk would destroy the possibility of the spirit's survival of death. And the Confucian doctrine of the connection between human conduct and the rhythm of nature was observed in the general rule that executions should not take place in spring and summer, when the life-force was in the ascendant, but in autumn when the year itself was declining, it would, however, be exceedingly difficult to indicate any way in which Chinese state law was influenced by the organised supernatural religions, that is to say Buddhism or Taoism, except in so far as the government tried to restrict the number of men and women taking monastic vows, and to control church affairs. Persons claiming to practise witchcraft were punished, not as satanists but for disturbing public order!

The constant re-editing of the Criminal code, from the eighteenth century onwards, with the incorporation of new supplementary statutes and the adding of commentaries, might lead us to suppose that even before the importation of western knowledge traditional China possessed a reasonably developed science of jurisprudence. Nothing, however, could be farther from the truth. In the first place, the intellectual formation of the mandarinate was entirely literary. Superficially, there seems a good deal in common between the traditional Chinese schooling and the cultivation of the Greek and Latin classics, until the other day the basis of western education for centuries. But whereas among us even the most devoted classicist would attempt to justify the system by declaring that a man would be all the better at law or any other profession, from an acquaintance with

Homer or Cicero, his Chinese counterpart would despise such an argument. The Confucianist indeed had an aversion towards specialist or technical education, and loved to quote the Master's saying that 'the accomplished scholar is not a utensil.'[16]

When the gentleman amateur did find himself obliged to function as a magistrate it was necessary for him to assign every case that came before him to its proper section of the code. Yet the code formed no part of a gentleman's reading, as gentlemen were only too anxious to point out. The late Dr. van Gulik, who by his creation of Judge Dee has done more than anybody else to introduce a knowledge of the traditional Chinese criminal law to the west, informs us that in the old Chinese courts 'Copies of the code and other books of legal reference are conspicuous by their absence' on the magistrate's table.[17] The explanation was that the drudgery of becoming familiar with the letter of the law was relegated to a subordinate race of clerks. These men, who handed down their craft from father to son, hailed for the most part from the city of Shaohsing, about two hundred miles south of Shanghai, which oddly enough is famous for a happier product, for it gives the Chinese world the most delectable of rice wines. The 'Shaohsing clerks' formed a numerous but compact trade union. They were paid by the magistrates who employed them and often became indispensable to their masters, who carried them along in their own ascent on the ladder of promotion. Even so, there was a sharp social distinction between these lawyers and the mandarinate proper. They did not fit themselves for their profession by studying the Chinese equivalent of Justinian's *Institutes*, for the sufficient reason that no such book had ever been written. Most of their knowledge was gained by being apprenticed to what Blackstone so well describes as 'the trash of an office.' Over the years, manuals had come into existence to lighten the drudgery, but these at the best were no more than handy abridgments of the code, or undigested collections of decisions. Nor could the skill thus acquired be put at the service of private clients, for the giving of legal advice to the public was regarded as an encouragement of litigation, and was a crime. The consequence was that although many of the clerks and even certain mandarins did show unmistakable signs of what we should call a legal cast of mind, it remains true, in the words of the late Professor Escarra that in China 'there has not existed, until our own day, a real "science of law" in our sense of the term.'[18]

Before turning to look at the effect on Chinese law of the collision

[16] See R. Levenson, *Confucian China and its Modern Fate*, Vol. I, Chap. 2 (Berkeley and London, 1958).

[17] R. H. van Gulik, *T'ang-yin-pi-shih* (Leiden, 1956), p. 53.

[18] G. Escarra, *Le droit chinois* (Peking–Paris, 1936), p. 359.

with the western world from the 1840s onward, a word ought to be said about the legal influence China exerted on her neighbours. Of these the northern peoples, such as the Mongols and the Tungus, presented from the earliest times a danger, against which one of the historic functions of the Chinese State was to provide defence. Yet the Great Wall, completed by the First Emperor in the third century B.C., was effective only when manned by the troops of a vigorous dynasty. The collapse of the Han regime, in the third century A.D., was the signal for a series of invasions of the northern provinces by barbarians from beyond the wall, some of whom settled and founded dynasties in the territories they occupied, while purely Chinese regimes held the southern regions. But when the T'ang Dynasty united the Empire in the seventh century it could be seen that Chinese culture had triumphed, and Confucian legal institutions were uncontaminated. For a hundred years, in the thirteenth and fourteenth centuries, the whole country was under Mongol rule, and this time the conquerors did promulgate statutes which sought to introduce modifications into such topics as the law of succession. When in the middle of the fourteenth century the invaders were expelled by the native house of Ming their attempted innovations remained simply as dead texts, having had not the slightest influence on the old customs. The Manchus, who ruled the land from 1644 to 1912, made no attempt to alter the traditional Chinese law, and although during their tenure of power they endeavoured to preserve their racial identity by forbidding intermarriage with their subjects, they very soon lost their own language and culture and are now indistinguishable from the Chinese masses into which they have merged.

Chinese law was exported to her neighbours in proportion as they adopted the Chinese written language. The Mongols, Tibetans, and Burmese never did this, while the Vietnamese and the Koreans prided themselves on their assimilation of Chinese culture. Vietnam for a thousand years to the ninth century A.D. was an integral part of the Chinese Empire, and even after it gained its autonomy not only was a tributary of the Dragon Throne, but retained the Chinese written language for official purposes and followed Chinese models in all its institutions. To be sure, in the fifteenth century the Vietnamese Le Dynasty promulgated its own code, but here also the influence of T'ang China was paramount, and although some non-Chinese characteristics may be discerned, many of the divergencies from Chinese statute law have arisen because the legislator has followed Chinese custom instead. The last native Vietnamese Dynasty of Nguyen, at the beginning of the nineteenth century, promulgated a code which was apart from a few unimportant provisions a word-for-word replica of the Ch'ing code of contemporary China. Korea, too, until its absorption by the Japanese Empire in the early twentieth century was in every sense a cultural colony of China. As for Japan, although the sea prevented her from coming at any time under Chinese political control, throughout history China was the great source of her arts and sciences, and the T'ang code in particular exerted a great influence on her legal development. It is a curious fact that after the Meiji Restoration in 1867, when Japan was taking her first steps towards modernisation, she turned again for a moment towards her old mentor, and in 1873 promulgated a body of laws based on the Ch'ing code. The experiment was still-born, and almost at once was abandoned in favour of western models.

In conclusion, it remains to trace briefly the fortunes of Chinese law during the last hundred years. The Opium War with Britain ended in 1842 with the Treaty of Nanking, the first of the so-called Unequal Treaties which in the course of the nineteenth century turned China into what Mao Tse-tung terms with justice a 'semi-colony.' Yet it took an amazingly long time for even the most intelligent Chinese to grasp the immediacy of the danger which threatened their country. By the 1860s the government recognised that western military techniques were worth imitating, but not for another forty years was it seen that China had anything to learn in the sphere of law and government. Meanwhile the traditional civil service was for the ambitious still the supreme avenue to success, and only occasional students tried to advance their career by acquiring foreign knowledge at missionary schools or abroad. It was not until the early years of the twentieth century that the abolition of the old civil service examination opened the gates to modern education. In 1912 a wave of national revolution swept away the imperial system.

One consequence of the Unequal Treaties had been the granting to foreign residents of the privilege of extraterritoriality. Indeed, from what has been said about the condition of Chinese legal administration, it will be easily understood why westerners should have been reluctant to entrust themselves to it and insisted on being amenable only to the law of their own countries. It will also be obvious that extraterritoriality was looked upon by patriotic Chinese as a peculiarly odious stigma, which must be erased as soon as possible. To this end it was necessary to equip the country with a modern system of law. The first tentative steps in this direction were being taken in the last years of the Empire, but the coming of the Republic was followed almost at once by the chaos of the warlord period, and it was not until the Nationalist Revolution of 1926–1928 had established a new government at Nanking that the task of legislation could begin. Between 1928 and 1935 a complete system of modern law was promulgated, patterned for the most part on the codes of Switzerland,

Germany, and France, though in the civil code the sections dealing with the family and succession retained a good deal of the traditional institutions adapted to modern conditions.

It is however, only fair to say that this formidable achievement was almost entirely a dead letter, owing to the administrative impotence of the Nanking government. Even before the outbreak of the Sino-Japanese War in 1937, the central authority controlled only the provinces of the Lower Yangtze Valley. Elsewhere, former warlords, now provincial governors, managed their territories in their own way. A sizeable area was always occupied by the Communists, who in 1931 proclaimed a Chinese Soviet Republic. In the same year the Japanese detached Manchuria from the rest of the country, and the separation lasted till 1945. Of the havoc wrought by the Japanese invasion of 1937 it is unnecessary to speak. In a word, the Nationalist codes were a façade, behind which 95 per cent. of the people continued to regulate their lives by the customs of their forefathers.

In September 1949, on the eve of the establishment of the People's Government, the Communists proclaimed the abrogation of all Nationalist laws. During the eighteen years since then no new codes have appeared to take the place of the abolished ones. The *Marriage Law* of 1950, which effectively checked concubinage and parental tyranny, and made the intervention of the state necessary for marriage and divorce, together with the *Agrarian Law* of the same year, which liquidated the landlord-class, brought a drastic change to Chinese society, while the Constitution of 1954 moulded the organs of government. But already the Constitution seems to be out of date in some respects, and the Chinese leaders have declared that they are in no hurry to promulgate, for instance, a civil code and prematurely fix property-relationships which are still in a fluid state. Meanwhile, apart from the recognition of 'progressive' customs, there is a considerable amount of *ad hoc* regulations, most of them until recently based on Soviet models.

In face of the scarcity of authentic information, it is impossible to say to what extent the old customary law still survives in mainland China. One can, however, see that in certain ways it has prepared the country for the road it has chosen to follow. The cardinal principle of the Confucian system was that society is built upon the notion not of rights but of duties, and although prior to 1949 this doctrine was impugned by 'progressives' of every hue, it accords admirably with Maoism in action, and indeed with the ideology of the Cultural Revolution. The Confucian aversion to litigation found an echo, before 1949, in the Communist courts' refusal to hear civil cases until arbitration had been attempted, and although this is no longer the rule, there is the strongest pressure to submit to arbitration first, and in China now law is studied only as a subsidiary branch of administration. Legal knowledge is no more essential for judicial office than it was in Ch'ing times. Lawyers in private practice have almost disappeared. Defence 'counsel' are usually laymen.

Although the Confucian system was intended to govern an agrarian society, and had certain prejudices against the mining of mineral resources and other such violations of nature necessary for industrial development, these impediments to modernisation were not very serious, and were more than counterbalanced by the absence of anything resembling a caste system or other religious obstacles in the way of national unity.

Overseas, the Nationalist codes are to a far greater extent the effective law of Formosa than they ever were of mainland China. More important still in matters of the family is the influence of the old customary law in Hong Kong and among the Chinese in south-east Asia. True, legislation in Singapore and elsewhere is attempting to modify some of its features, but the Chinese are a supremely unlitigious people, and it may be confidently predicted that for many years they will manage their family affairs in their own way without benefit of courts or lawyers.[19]

BIBLIOGRAPHY

J. Escarra, *Le droit chinois* (Peking–Paris, 1936), is the leading western authority: good on philosophical background, but weak on substantive law.

S. van der Sprenkel, *Legal Institutions in Manchu China* (London, 1962), is a sound work of scholarship.

G. Boulais, S. J., *Manuel du code chinois* (Shanghai, 1924), is a handy abridgment of the Ch'ing code in Chinese with French translation.

G. T. Staunton, *Ta Tsing Leu Lee, being the Fundamental Laws and a Selection from the Supplementary Statutes of the Penal Code of China* (London, 1810), though incomplete, and now hopelessly out of date in point of scholarship, is constantly referred to by the Colonial Courts in Hong Kong.

P. L. F. Philastre, *Le code annamite*, 2nd ed. (Paris, 1909), is a complete translation of the code of the last Vietnamese dynasty, promulgated in the early nineteenth century. As this was almost a word-for-word copy from the Chinese, the work forms in effect the only complete version of the Ch'ing Dynasty code in a European language.

T'ung-tsu Ch'ü, *Law and Society in Traditional China*, 2nd ed. (Paris–The Hague, 1965), is an indispensable source of information.

[19] M. Freedman, *Chinese Family and Marriage in Singapore* (London, H.M.S.O., 1957).

E. Alabaster, *Notes and Commentaries on Chinese Criminal Law* (London, 1899), is still the principal foreign work on the Ch'ing Dynasty code.

P. Hoang, *Notions techniques sur la propriété en Chine* (Shanghai, 1897); *Le mariage chinois au point de vue légal*, 2nd ed. (Shanghai, 1915): two useful studies by a Chinese Catholic priest who was well acquainted with the laws of his own country.

These works trace legal developments under the Republic:

M. H. van der Valk, *Conservatism in Modern Chinese Family Law* (Leiden, 1956); M. J. Meijer, *The Introduction of Modern Criminal Law in China* (Batavia, 1950).

G. W. Keeton, *The Development of Extraterritoriality in China*, 2 vols. (London, 1928), is a detailed history.

M. Freedman, *Chinese Family and Marriage in Singapore* (London, H.M.S.O., 1957), is a masterly survey.

The law of Communist China and also the law of the Imperial and Republican periods are dealt with in:

Fu-Shun Lin, ed., *Chinese Law, Past and Present. A Bibliography of Enactments and Commentaries in English Text* (New York, East Asia Institute, Columbia University, 1966).

AFRICAN LAW

A. N. Allott

AFRICAN LAW has many points of contact with the other legal systems dealt with in this book. Like Jewish, Islamic, and Hindu law, for instance, it is, though not a religious law in a strict sense, yet a system predicated upon a particular set of supernatural beliefs and ritual practices. Like Chinese law, its main source of rules has been ancestral custom. But equally there are profound differences which strike the observer: of these the most notable are that this is the law of preliterate societies, and that it is not (perhaps in consequence of this) a jurist's law. Most important of all, it is not (and here it differs radically from all the other systems represented here) a single system, even one with variant schools, but rather a family of systems which share no traceable common parent.

It would have been possible, in view of this, to have selected a single system of African customary law for closer examination; but there are good reasons for treating African customary laws as forming a coherent unit for comparative study. Not the least of these reasons is that the literature on African law ranges widely over the African continent and its peoples; the writings of one scholar supplement those of another in building up a comprehensive view of Africa and its laws. But, more fundamentally, African laws reveal sufficient similarity in procedure, principles, institutions, and techniques for a common account to be given of them. The variations, some minimal, some major, which may be detected between different African systems do not obscure, but rather illuminate, the reasons for and the advantages of each system in its own environment.

The legal scientist thus finds in Africa the possibility (so often denied to him elsewhere) of investigating the consequences of a variation in legal structure where other elements in the social situation remain constant. Society A recognises exclusively matrilineal succession, for instance; its neighbour, society B, comparable in all respects except this, recognises patrilineal succession; the effect of this difference on parental authority, the structure of the corporate family, or the rights of an inheritor can be readily compared. Such a situation, for example, prevails among some of the peoples of southern Ghana, and among different Ibo-speaking peoples of south-eastern Nigeria.

Many of the similarities of customary laws in tropical Africa are due not so much to any genetic relationship between the inhabitants or of cultural influence between one society and the next as to uniformity of response to the challenge of a shared environment. There are also similarities implicit in the social system. Of these the most obvious is the absence of writing, and hence the absence of all written legislation, law reports, and juristic analyses. A purely oral legislated law is possible; but, in practice, unwritten law tends to consist mainly of customary law. African legal systems share, then, the common characteristic that they are all unwritten and mainly customary in origin.

This is not the whole of the story. There are a limited number of legal possibilities from which particular systems have selected; and some themes (*e.g.*, the role of the family in marriage and the tenure of property, the arbitral element in adjudication) recur in most if not all African laws. Between the laws of people who share a common origin or culture the resemblances are naturally much more pronounced. And lastly we must not forget that African laws, though a distinct species, form part of the wider genus of customary laws which has subsisted throughout the world, both in time and space. The study of 'ethno-jurisprudence,' if we may so term it, takes in the customary laws of the ancient Greeks and Germans and Anglo-Saxons, as well as those of the Amerindians, Indonesians, and Polynesians of our days. Here again the significant resemblances outweigh the differences; and here again the study of African law can offer much by way of illumination to the student of European, American, or Asian laws.

Let us now pick out and illustrate some of the insights and comparisons which the study of African law may afford. The first which comes to mind is of interest to the historical jurist, the scholar who is concerned to trace the processes by which legal systems, and legal institutions and ideas, evolve over time, and change from one form or state to another in response to new demands or new influences. The picture commonly built up of the universal pattern of legal development is from one where the society was small, based on kinship, technologically backward, and dominated by the hopes and fears of the other world just as much as by the rigours of the present, to one which is large, complex, equipped with an advanced technology, and controlled by secular or materialistic preoccupations. The laws have, on this view, correspondingly developed: unwritten customary laws based on religious belief and sanctioned by religious practices give way, it is said, to legislated laws administered and studied by professional lawyers, where the sanctions now rest on the enhanced power of the state machine rather than on fear of the supernatural or the strong arm of the complainant.

Our knowledge of the customary laws of antiquity is meagre, despite the clues which may be gleaned from Tacitus and Homer. African customary laws, existing in our present age and accessible to profound study by anthropologists and others, appear to be available to fill the gap. This is perfectly true: the study of contemporary African laws can supplement, on the role of customary laws in the evolution of law, the deficiencies or challenge the presumptions of Maine, Vinogradoff, and Diamond (none of whom wrote with any personal or reliable secondary knowledge of the legal institutions of Africa). But there is a real risk in this procedure. Modern Bushmen, and *a fortiori* modern or recent Baganda, Ashanti, or Barotse, are not ancient Britons, Germans, or Greeks; still less are they representative of palaeolithic or neolithic man in prehistoric times. So to argue backwards from African laws of the last two centuries to what law was like before the Indo-Europeans colonised Europe is a suspect undertaking.

Speculative thought has dominated historical jurisprudence. From a few ambiguous clues provided by classical Roman law, eked out by reference to Hindu and Scandinavian sources, Maine was willing[1] to infer a general historical law of the disintegration of the family and the movement of 'progressive societies from status to contract.' The evidence from African customary laws is much fuller. It enables us to say whether such laws hold for these simpler societies in the nineteenth and twentieth centuries. Relatively hard facts (though the interpretation of some of them is hotly contested) thus take the place of inference and speculation.

African customary laws were not book-law. There were no legal texts or manuscripts, no statements of claim formulated on pieces of paper, no summons or writ of execution, no conveyances in writing, no learned commentaries by doctors of law. These facts inescapably determined the style of the law, the relationship of the law both to those who administered it and those who were subject to it, and the processes of legal development. Minute textual criticism of Acts of Parliament, learned debate in journals about the meaning of a section or the scope of a judicial decision, procedural arguments about the appropriate forum or form of action, did not arise. A broader, more ambitious and humane approach dominated the law, namely to render essential justice in the particular case in conformity with the general principles and the appropriate patterns of behaviour recognised by custom for each relationship or transaction.

To say that there were no law books is not to say that there were no well-recognised principles or rules of law, or no specialists in legal theory and procedure. The African evidence thus contradicts

[1] *Ancient Law* (London, 1861), Chap. V.

Maine's speculation (p. 7) that 'Law has scarcely reached the footing of custom: it is rather a habit.' In some respects African law could be highly formal (especially with the routines for the creation of a marriage, the transfer of property, or the disposal of an estate). Every adult member of the community might be expected to know the generally accepted principles of law which obtained there, but legal specialists were also recognised in many societies, persons who by reason either of their training (which was often hereditary) or of their frequent involvement in legal disputes were esteemed to know more of the law and its implications than the ordinary citizen.

Nor are such legal experts confined to the more politically advanced societies, those with a strong central administrative structure and highly organised courts; the simpler segmentary societies where kinship or local residence was the basis of government also admit of local specialisation. Thus the Kikuyu of Kenya recognised the *muthamaki* (leader, counsellor) as chief spokesman and judge in legal matters. As the *muthamaki* gained experience and developed his natural talents for wise advice and judgment, so he would come to be regarded as a 'leader in law' (*muthamaki wa chira*), his reputation would extend over a wider and wider area, and he would be called in constantly to settle cases or advise in discussions and quarrels.[2] Similarly, among the Arusha of Tanzania, every lineage and age-group would have its own spokesman or counsellor (*olaigwenani*) who would act as advocate, counsellor, and arbiter in disputes in which his group was involved.[3]

The chiefly societies, too, were familiar with this notion, though in their case the legal experts were not so much advisers to or spokesmen of particular families as part of the machinery of justice and administration controlled by the chief. The Chief's court among the Tswana of Botswana, for instance, was presided over by the Chief, advised by counsellors and 'remembrancers' (*bagakolodi*, or men expert in the law).[4] And the central figure in Ashanti administration is the *okyeame*, the 'linguist' or spokesman of the Chief, who is the repository of customary law, the presiding officer in the traditional court, and chief prosecutor in the customary criminal procedure.[5]

The fact that the law and procedure were oral naturally led to simplicity and directness in its formulation. Rules and principles were expressed in everyday language which the ordinary citizen could understand. Technical legal terms were known and employed;

[2] H. E. Lambert, *Kikuyu social and political institutions* (London, 1956), pp. 100 *et seq.*

[3] P. H. Gulliver, *Social control in an African society* (London, 1963), pp. 47 *et seq.* and 101 *et seq.*

[4] I. Schapera, *A handbook of Tswana law and custom*, 2nd ed. (London, 1959), p. 282.

[5] R. S. Rattray, *Ashanti law and constitution* (London, 1929), Ch. xxxvi.

but these formed no barrier between the legal expert and the litigant. The very processes of adjudication and the promulgation of new statutes contributed to this popularisation of the law. Thus among the Tswana new laws were deliberated and enacted at a *pitso*, or general assembly of all the adult males of the tribe. In theory, every man could attend and take part in its deliberations; and there was a similar right to attend and participate in a case before the court of a local chief. Not every African law went as far as that of the Tswana in permitting popular participation in law-making and adjudication; but the general drift is clear. The law is not an arcane mystery but a matter of public concern. Maine's suggestion (at p. 11) that in 'the epoch of Customary Law' knowledge of the laws was the exclusive monopoly of an aristocracy or 'juristical oligarchy' which were 'universally the depositaries and administrators of law' is completely contrary to most African judicial practice: African customary law was not and is not known only to a privileged minority.

The customary law was expressed in simple language. Citizens could take part in its making and administration. Yet another factor which contributed to the popularisation of the law was that legal processes were generally localised rather than remote. Wherever there was a community, be it a village or extended family unit, there was machinery of greater or less formality for the public settling of disputes. Every man thus had a court of some kind on his doorstep (perhaps one should say on the threshold of his hut!). To adjudicate or arbitrate in disputes is in traditional African society an essential appurtenance of office, so that not only the chief or village headman but the lineage elder and the father of a restricted family would be expected to settle cases which arose between those subject to their authority.

Many of the questions which modern jurists or law-reformers pose are almost meaningless when directed at traditional African law. The attempt, for example, to separate legal norms from those which are merely of moral obligation presupposes (if we neglect moral norms whose breach affects only the individual) a state of society in which there can be a serious lack of correspondence between what ordinary members of the community feel to be a proper way of behaving towards each other and what the official organs of the society say should happen. African traditional law was not like this. The law expressed the common moral code of the people; if the code changed, the law would automatically change as well. Similarly with religious beliefs and practices. There was no conflict or opposition between the religion of the community (a religion which was the shared system of beliefs of all those in the community—a state religion, if one likes) and its legal institutions. The religious beliefs permeated the whole of the secular world: the family structure was often organised around the cult of the ancestors, with whom the living head of the family acted as the official channel of communication; and this substratum was brought out—to take but one example—in the ideology of the family property system, in which the ancestors might be viewed (as in many of the peoples of West Africa) as in a sense co-proprietors with the living members of the family. What was punished as crime was often what society treated as sins or breaches of taboo; thus the Ashanti, as Rattray tells us in his classic work,[6] criminally punished 'things hateful to the tribe' because——

> 'These acts were looked upon as sins of which the central authority was bound to take immediate official notice, lest certain supernatural powers, to whom the deeds were regarded as peculiarly offensive, should wreak their vengeance upon those whose paramount duty it was to protect their interests and to punish breaches of immemorial law or custom.'

We must not over-labour the point: new religious cults could spread in African society (as Islam and Christianity were to spread later on); the law could not punish many breaches of morality or compel everyone to act morally; much of the law was completely secular in tone. But the general point remains: African society enjoyed an integrated culture, or set of institutions and beliefs, in which the law occupied a central position. This integrated society was grossly disrupted (as we shall see) by the incursion of European political rule, western commerce, and foreign religions. The attempt to restore a measure of integration in contemporary African society is one of the more interesting aspects of modern legislative action.

African communities were generally small in scale. There was naturally an enormous variation in the populations of different autonomous units (from the fifty or so in a Bushman band to the half-million or so people living under the suzerainty of the King of Ashanti); but the typical African hierarchical system of government meant that even in the largest empires most governmental functions were carried out in a restricted local community, and usually by a functionary who lived in and came from that community.

The fact that government and the processes of law and dispute-settlement were mostly confined within a community of limited area and population lent a distinctive character to African law. Face-to-face contacts, both between potential disputants and between a disputant and one who might later judge his case, were frequent.

[6] *Op. cit.*, p. 294. [One may compare the position in ancient India, and pre-nineteenth-century Britain, under which an offence might be punished in one court as a sin and in another as a crime. *Ed.*]

Neighbours knew each other, for better or ill. Relationships between parties in dispute often extended far beyond the issue which had brought them to quarrel before a court.

In the result, many of the cherished principles or assumptions of modern western law found no place in Africa. The judge was not a remote member of an official order, but the man in the next hut. The English fiction of judicial ignorance would have been severely strained in African customary processes. Not only did the local judge or arbitrator often know most, if not all, of the facts of a dispute before ever it came officially to his notice, but he would also probably be aware of the previous history of the relationship between the contestants; he would know that X was always quarrelling, that Y beat his wife, that Z was a stranger who only came to the community a few years ago; and so on.

Equally it would be much more difficult for the litigant to pull the wool over the eyes of a court consisting of his neighbours who knew him well. The gap between legal truth and actual fact was thus diminished. Rules of evidence were less formalistic and restrictive than those of English law or those of Islamic law.[7]

During the latter part of the nineteenth and first part of the twentieth centuries there were superimposed, swiftly and overwhelmingly, upon the traditional customary laws of Africa, highly organised legal systems developed in an utterly different environment, motivated by different objectives, following procedures far removed from those of African law, and backed up by the administrative systems and military and police forces of the colonising powers.

There have been many previous occasions upon which conquerors have tried to extend their own legal systems, as well as their political power, to territories of a different legal culture. One recalls the extension of Roman law over the Roman empire, and the coming of the Normans to Anglo-Saxon England. The Norman conquest, and the subsequent development of an Anglo-Norman law, has often been cited as offering a close historical parallel to the evolution of law in modern Africa; it has been suggested, for instance, that legal development in Africa will follow a similar trend to that which occurred in medieval England with the emergence of an English 'common law.'

But these parallels can mislead: Anglo-Saxon England was as cultured as Normandy; the conquered society was neither illiterate nor uncivilised in its upper echelons. There was thus no culture gap; there was no religious gap either. Indigenous Africa, on the other hand, was worlds apart from Britain, France, Italy, Belgium, Germany, and Holland as regards language, literacy, technology,

[7] See above, pp. 67–68.

religion, and systems of government. This enormous gap between conquerors and conquered is almost without parallel. Naturally one would have expected the indigenous laws to crumble and wither away under such an impact, just as the previously viable indigenous technology, art, education, religion, and economic systems gave way or were displaced by the products of European civilisation. But this did not happen: customary laws largely held their ground.

The first reason was that in the early stages European colonial intervention in African institutions was limited both for financial and man-power reasons to establishing the minimal framework of peace and order. Grave social abuses, such as slavery and barbaric modes of punishment, were quickly suppressed; but the rest of the law (and of the customs which underlay it) was allowed to continue. Gradually effective administration spread over the newly acquired territories, and the governments tried more seriously and effectively than before to shape African society (through improvements in agriculture, enhancement of the legal and social status of women, the spread of educational facilities, and so on).

But the notion that the appropriate policy to follow was one of respect for existing indigenous institutions was by then firmly entrenched in the political philosophy and the legal systems of the colonial administrations (especially those of the British and the Belgians). In British colonial thinking this approach was systematised in the writings of Lord Lugard and Sir Donald Cameron, and the policy of 'Indirect Rule' which they both advocated and applied in such territories as Nigeria and Tanganyika. Indirect Rule meant in particular the preservation of local government by traditional chiefs and elders following their own customs and procedures. The native courts of such rulers were officially recognised by the British colonial administrations and became the lowest grade in the judicial system. Often the supervision of these native courts was kept away from the professional judges and magistrates (who, it was feared, might subvert the traditional laws and try to force them into conformity with the technicalities of English law) and entrusted instead to administrative officers who could take a friendlier and less formal view of customary law.

This policy, which one might have thought would have earned commendation as showing a proper respect by the alien rulers for the traditions of their subjects, has recently been criticised as being equivalent to setting up 'anthropological zoos': just as the wild-life was preserved in game-reserves, so the traditional institutions were artificially preserved in the 'native reserves.' Whatever the merits of each view (and here the political philosophy of the critic predetermines his response), historically the policy of Indirect Rule (and its analogues in other European colonies) demonstrates that not every conqueror has automatically assumed his institutions to be superior and fit for immediate and total application in his conquered territories, and explains in part the survival of African indigenous institutions to the present day.

The parallelism that was thus created between indigenous customary laws and imported European laws has provoked a dialogue, and often competition or conflict, between them. As time has gone on, each law has penetrated more deeply into the other: European legal ideas have infiltrated into customary law by legislative act, by judicial decision, and by imitation; while customary laws have been applied by the western-type courts and have modified or displaced some of the rules and principles of the western laws.

Many examples could be given of these processes at work. We must restrict ourselves to two. In many West African customary laws interests in land are largely controlled by corporate lineages, each of whose members usually enjoys both a common right to benefit from the joint assets of the lineage and a particular individual right to exploit for his own benefit a piece of land or other property, subject to family control. The customary laws know nothing of elaborate and artificial conceptions of juristic personality, but nevertheless the sentiment of 'jointness' in customary families is strong, and these groups are felt to be separate entities in the law. The western lawyer faced with such entities is puzzled how to classify and treat them; English-trained judges, for example, have at different times sought an analogy with the relationships of partnership, trustee and beneficiary, principal and agent, corporations aggregate, corporations sole, and unincorporated associations, and have in each instance reinterpreted the African institution accordingly. A judicial customary law has thus emerged, with strong English overtones. It is this new hybrid institution of the family which is recognised by statute, is made capable of taking part in legal proceedings, and may be registered as proprietor of family land.

But the customary laws have had their revenge. English notions of legitimacy, marriage, the status of a wife, or rights over children have in some of the countries been modified—and sometimes eliminated—in favour of customary notions. Thus a 'child' in Nigeria may include—for the purposes of applying an English Act of Parliament received into Nigeria—not only the legitimate child of a person duly married by a monogamous marriage but a child howsoever procreated if the appropriate local customary law says that it is right to treat such a child as a child of its parent for this purpose.

Comparative lawyers who spend much of their time on library comparisons of two legal systems which obtain in different countries or at different periods have the opportunity in contemporary Africa of seeing what happens when two or more fundamentally different legal systems are thrown together. Can a translation be made of the legal institutions of one system in terms of the institutions of the other? Is it possible to put together an amalgam of principles and rules from different systems and make a coherent functioning whole out of them? What do we mean when we say that a given institution in one society is similar to or dissimilar from that in another? All these questions not only can be answered but must be answered, in the day-to-day administration of justice in Africa today. Africa, then, is a comparative-law laboratory, in which the processes of legal comparison and conflict can be seen in action.

This raises the exciting possibility that not only can we learn more about the processes of legal development from the African experience, but legal systems in other parts of the world may well be enriched by drawing on some of the insights and alternative approaches afforded by African law.

African laws are described, as we have already seen, as 'customary.' Ask a traditional expert in the customary law, an elder or councillor, for example, where his law comes from, and he will tell you that it traces back to the immemorial customs of the tribe. It is 'the law of the ancestors,' 'the law of long ago.' Many outside observers—judges, anthropologists, administrators—have taken the same for granted. It would seem to follow that customary law must be inflexible in its structure and incapable of deviating from the routines and principles handed down from the dead and now given a quasi-religious status.

There is clearly support for such an analysis. Many of the routines —for transferring land, for appointing a chief, for negotiating a marriage—are customary and traditional. It is difficult to innovate in these domains. But if one attends a customary court or examines the trend of legal development over the last hundred years the impression one derives is not that of unthinking adherence to immutable principle but precisely the reverse. The style of African adjudication is flexible; the principles are there, but so general are many of them in content that it is a moot point how to apply them to a given circumstance. Often the principles themselves form no more than a starting-point for negotiation between the contending parties as to the most suitable settlement of their quarrel, or a court may allow a deviation from the rule in the interests of a lasting harmony between the disputants.

The history of African law argues the same way. Enormous changes have taken place in customary law, both before and after the advent of colonial rule. Many of these changes have emerged from the heart of the traditional system in response to changing needs (*e.g.*, population pressure on the land leading to recognition of sale of land among the Kikuyu or Ibo) or a changed assessment of a role or status (the chief allowed to retain his private property among the Akan of Ghana, whereas formerly all of this would have merged with his official property when he assumed his office). The process by which individual farmers enclosed and appropriated what was formerly community grazing land among some of the cattle-keeping societies of Kenya is particularly interesting in this connection.

Philip and Iona Mayer have described the process for one such group, the Gusii of western Kenya, during the period 1925–1950.[8] The British administrators left the Gusii to develop their land law along their own traditional lines; but such development was not on an authoritarian basis, as the Gusii traditionally lacked all centralised political authority. Development of the land law was largely in judicial hands, *i.e.*, those of the new native tribunals set up by the British and consisting mainly of the elders (*etureti*) traditionally skilled in the law and in settling disputes. Land shortage led to increasing competition, and a growing number of land disputes between Gusii families competing for this scarce resource.

> 'It was within this framework,' say the Mayers, 'that the new land law emerged. As the old communal agrarian system was in process of disruption, families and individuals quarrelled over land more and more frequently. At times local *etureti* elders tried to reconcile the disputes without the guidance of legal rules; at other times they applied rules proper to a more familiar type of quarrel, that is, over bridewealth rights.' [9]

Under the traditional system of land tenure, areas of land were controlled by particular clans or neighbourhoods. The members of each local land-controlling community usually shared a common field, which was marked out in individual plots in the form of elongated strips. Mostly cultivators returned to their old plots each season, but some would open up new plots in vacant land, which might lead to conflicts, either with neighbouring clans or with other individual exploiters. Individual interests thus depended partly on clan title and partly on individual acquisition or appropriation of previously unoccupied land. The clan pastures, which adjoined the cultivated section, were theoretically open to the whole clan community, but in practice tended to be marked out into separate areas.

With the cessation of inter-clan fighting and the growth of population under the British, a new land law began to emerge. The scattered

[8] 'Land law in the making,' in *African Law: Adaptation and Development*, ed. Hilda and Leo Kuper (Berkeley and Los Angeles, 1965), pp. 51–78.

[9] *Op. cit.*, p. 56.

plots were consolidated into family farms, and the old common pastures disappeared, to be replaced by individualised pastures adjacent to each homestead. Individual boundaries gradually became firmer and more legally defensible as a newly established cultivation or building was unchallenged by other farmers. There was a rush to establish individual holdings on the former clan bush land.

By the late 1940s, say the Mayers, what was originally extra-legal had become accepted: 'the legal and social concepts of estate ownership had become partly, but not fully standardised.' Vague boundaries might be demarcated by specially planted hedges. A large number of disputed boundaries were settled by the statutory native tribunals (which, although new bodies, were successors to traditional ones). Wherever a particular boundary might be thus fixed, the important fact was that a boundary was now fixed where none had been before. The initial impetus to settle a boundary came from the wish of the competing families to have a protected possession of their estates, and of the administrative and judicial authorities to ensure that tranquillity was restored. The largely spontaneous development of the Gusii customary land law thus anticipated and mirrored what was to become the official governmental programme of land consolidation by substituting defined, consolidated, registered holdings for the previous scattered and community-based tenures under customary law.

But custom and tradition are by no means the only sources of law. Someone—often a chief or a judge—must have decided at some stage what the rule should be in a novel case presented to him: the result was the establishment of a precedent or the enacting of a law. Schapera has described this process at work among the Tswana of southern Africa:[10] in this centralised society

> '. . . chiefs have from time immemorial had the power to change the law, either by abolishing or amending an existing usage or by establishing a new rule of conduct. Within relatively recent times legislation of this kind has become fairly common, owing mainly to the new conditions created by the impact of Western civilisation. . . .
>
> Although seldom recorded in writing, which itself is of course an innovation in Tswana life, such laws are usually well known to the people. . . .'

Schapera goes on to show that the new laws are widely publicised, that they present no special complications of wording or content, and that they mainly consist of straightforward prohibitions or

[10] 'The sources of law in Tswana tribal courts: legislation and precedent,' [1957] J. of African Law 150.

injunctions. Generally the project for a new law is formulated by the chief and his councillors, and then put to a general assembly of the male members of the tribe for enactment. One of the most celebrated of such laws was that made by Kgama, the famous chief of the Ngwato tribe of the Tswana, abolishing for his people the custom of *bogadi* (or bride-price); this he did under Christian missionary influence.

Overt legislation of this sort was not confined to the centralised, chiefly, societies: Lambert reports that among the Kikuyu of Kenya:[11]

> 'Legislation is a function of the senior lodge or the senior rank of the elder's lodge. . . .
>
> Laws and specific orders are usually proclaimed at public meetings by *athamaki* or *agambi* [judicial counsellors] of the ruling generation or set. . . .'

Traditional Kikuyu government was by a ruling generation or age-set, which handed over administrative and judicial power after a set period to the next succeeding generation. In a way reminiscent of the Roman praetor's edict, statutes lost their authority at the going out of power of the generation which made them;[12] and the elders of the incoming generation usually publicly re-enacted, with variations or additions, the laws handed over to them.

Precedent again is a major source of law. One might have thought that the absence of law reports and advocates would have prevented this; but this is not the case. The customary law was imperceptibly built up by the *ad hoc* decisions of judges and arbitrators, assented to both by the parties and by their fellows in the community who were bystanders at the proceedings. Sometimes, but not often, the memory of a particular decision might endure, and a principle would be cited as depending on the ruling of such-and-such a judge; but mostly this was not so. The remembrancers of the Tswana traditional courts were available to cite precedents when possible; and among the Kikuyu:[13]

> 'case-law is a potent factor in the assessment of individual decrees. A *muthamaki* or *mugambi* depends for his judicial reputation very largely on his knowledge of the principles on which the judgements in previous cases have been based, and this, though theoretically it only strengthens or reiterates early principles of common law and custom, in practice tends to codify the detailed findings in celebrated cases into precedents which acquire the force of law.'

[11] H. E. Lambert, *op. cit.*, pp. 120, 131 *et seq.*

[12] Above, pp. 8–9.

[13] Lambert, *op. cit.*, p. 120.

Equity is not a source of law in African customary practice: the antithesis of law and fairness is not one which an African judge would or could make, since he would feel that the legal system, as operated by him, already made provision for doing justice as between the parties. Clearly there are occasions when African law produced what would appear, to the outside observer or to the accused or losing party, as an unfair result. The traditional law contains many presumptions of fact and law—such as that a statement by a married woman when giving birth to a child that it is the child of a man not her husband is conclusive evidence of adultery against that man—which can cause hardship or a miscarriage of justice; and many of the sanctions of the law were automatic in their operation and applied irrespective of personal fault. But there is no separate body of equitable principles to which appeal could be made to rectify such weaknesses. On the other hand, a judge or arbitrator in civil proceedings was often given a wide mandate to do justice between the parties, even if a rule of law or a right obtained under it might have to be waived. The desire to promote the final reconciliation of contending parties was often of overriding importance in African adjudication; strict rules of law might have to yield to this objective. Adjudication is in effect guided negotiations for a settlement in chiefless societies like the Arusha of Tanzania; in arbitral proceedings the norms of the law—

> 'are guides, and not absolute principles to be rigidly followed. They provide the initial basis for discussion, and they are manipulated during negotiations as seems most advantageous to each disputant.'[14]

Legal fictions are few and far between in African law. The African institution of 'ghost-marriage' appears to be based on a central fiction, namely that a dead man can father a child by a woman to whom he has never been physically united; but no one pretends in such an instance that the facts are other than they are, nor is there evidence to show that this institution is designed to cloak a change in the underlying law.

Argument by analogy, on the other hand, is of the essence of African adjudication. Such a style of argument is particularly necessary in the present era, when new problems, institutions, and objects have to be dealt with under the old customary laws. African courts have never shown any hesitation or reluctance in such cases. New forms of property—lorries, cash, houses—are deemed to fall under the same property law as the old—huts, cattle, land, spears. A young man from the Bemba of Zambia going to perform his

[14] Gulliver, *op. cit.*, p. 234.

bride-service for his father-in-law may work in his father-in-law's fields, or nowadays perhaps help him in his business.

The role of religious beliefs and practices in African law has already been referred to. Here we may briefly mention some of the main areas in which such beliefs are of significance:

In the law of procedure oaths (self-imprecations) were used both as guarantees of veracity and also as means of settling cases where evidence was lacking or conflicted; divination and ordeals were also used on occasion. But resort to such irrational means of decision was exceptional.

In the law of crimes many wrongs had a religious basis. The person of the chief was sacred in many societies; to touch it or to damage the chief's *persona* (as by illegal interference with his property or wives) was a breach of taboo and at the same time a crime. Incest was repressed for religious reasons, as were a number of other sexual offences. There was a long list of taboos, breach of any of which required expiation, cleansing, and sometimes punishment. (Among the more fascinating taboos reported from old Ashanti by Rattray were the prohibitions against wearing the hair long or whistling in towns!)

In the law of the family religious and ritual requirements had to be met. The ancestors had to be consulted before important transactions and decisions.

The law of land was shot through with religious observance. The Akan of Ghana, for example, have a particular day of the week (Thursday or Friday) when it is strictly taboo to go to the farm. The traditional land authority responsible for overseeing the use and transfer of land is often a land priest in origin.

If we turn from the substantive rules of law to the procedures for the settlement of disputes we find the key to understanding African customary law. At the heart of African adjudication lies the notion of reconciliation or the restoration of harmony. The job of a court or an arbitrator is less to find the facts, state the rules of law, and apply them to the facts than to set right a wrong in such a way as to restore harmony within the disturbed community. Harmony will not be restored unless the parties are satisfied that justice has been done. The complainant will accordingly want to see that the legal rules, including those which specify the appropriate recompense for a given wrong, are applied by the court. But the party at fault must be brought to see how his behaviour has fallen short of the standard set for his particular role as involved in the dispute, and he must come to accept that the decision of the court is a fair one. On his side he wants an assurance that once he has admitted his error and made recompense for it he will be re-integrated into the community.[15]

[15] This exactly agrees with a traditional Indian view of litigation, above, pp. 96–97. *Ed.*

These are the objectives which a customary court will set itself. Only in this way will the judgment receive the endorsement of the community as a whole. Mutual acceptance of a judgment and subsequent reconciliation are the only guarantee, in view of defective enforcement procedures, that a judgment will be duly executed.[16] The general tenor of conciliatory procedures is described for the Arusha by Gulliver:[17]

> 'It is perhaps significant that the Arusha have no word that can be translated as "justice," nor does any such concept appear in their ideology. It is an irrelevant consideration. They are prepared to agree to something which is as near to their claims as possible in the particular context of the strengths and weaknesses of the two parties to the negotiations. Further, they believe that undue insistence on one's "rights" under these norms may well conflict with obtaining an effective settlement, and with establishing or maintaining otherwise satisfactory relations.'

This reconciliatory function appears in more formal adjudication too, both in the chiefly and the chiefless societies. But it is of paramount importance in the societies with no strong central authority, in civil cases, and in cases where the parties in dispute are already in some relationship with each other, as kinsmen, neighbours, landlord and tenant, and so on. In criminal cases and in civil disputes between unconnected persons reconciliation will be of less or no significance.[18]

There are other modes of adjudication found in various African societies. The most important are the imposition of authority, as where a chief or head of family (*i.e.*, lineage) decrees the way in which a breach of norm is to be rectified; and the appeal to the supernatural, through oaths, ordeals, and divination; but reconciliation is the most characteristic. The reason for this is not far to seek: in a small closed community an unsettled dispute or a grievance is a running sore which weakens the integrity of the group. Survival depends on co-operation, co-operation on mutual good will. These are threatened by every dispute.

The involvement of society in the settling of disputes is also a common theme. Often a court case gives the judges an opportunity to moralise, to lecture the litigants on their duties and their failings, to remind them and all present of the basic *mores* of the society. Litigation, or rather adjudication, thus has a socially educative role.

[16] This, too, agrees with the Indian position prior to European dominion there. *Ed.*

[17] *Op. cit.*, p. 242.

[18] This is evidently one reason why in extended, complex societies like a modern state the emphasis has drifted from reconciliation and the restoration of harmony to the application of abstract rules of law. *Ed.*

It is often said, especially at the present time, that Africans are naturally and typically litigious, ready to resort to law at the slightest opportunity, and to pursue their case, whether well-founded or no, through every channel of appeal. Certainly, judicial statistics from various African countries (such as Ghana and Nigeria) appear to bear out this assessment; but if we seek for an explanation of this litigiousness it is partially to be found in the traditional availability of courts of law. The judicial arena was not something strange and forbidding; it was rather like a football pitch, to which everyone might resort for entertainment and excitement and to challenge.

So far we have assumed that legal norms in African law obtain between individuals, as in modern western law, and that disputes arise and are settled between individuals—*A.* v. *B.*, *Smith* v. *Jones.* But it is now time to see whether this assumption is justified.

Many western writers have argued that African law is essentially a law of groups and communities. This alleged characteristic expresses itself in several distinct ways. Firstly, it is asserted that the individual in African society had no separate legal existence, that he only achieved recognition by the law in and through his simultaneous membership of a variety of groups and communities. Full legal personality, on this view, was restricted to such groups or to those who officially headed them, the chiefs, headmen, and heads of lineages or households. Secondly, an individual, it is said, could only gain a right to make use of the productive assets of his community on a subordinate or dependent title: the 'real' title to such assets was vested either in the 'tribe' or political unit, or in his extended family or lineage. Individual and absolute ownership of land and other property was thus unknown.

And thirdly, it has been suggested that litigation in African law was characteristically and solely between groups, and not between individuals. Even where one individual injured another, the matter would be taken over by their respective kinship groups or family heads; so that every dispute would be an inter-family rather than an inter-personal one.

As with so many generalisations, there is some truth in these. African laws were undoubtedly dominated to a degree unmatched in modern individualist legal systems by group and community rights and powers. But African laws *did* accord legal capacity to individuals to hold interests in property, to negotiate with each other, and to appear as principals in litigation. These rights and powers were often conditioned by the prior rights of the communities of which their holders formed part—but the same is true, it can be argued, of modern laws.

Individuals possessed legal personality, then, though the capacity of various minority classes within the population—women, slaves, unemancipated minor members of a family, strangers—was less ample. It is an almost universal characteristic of African laws that a man's entitlement to occupy and use land depends on his membership of an appropriate land-controlling group or community (often of several of these simultaneously): such a group may be the tribe or maximal political unit (thus effectively excluding non-citizens), or a lineage or household (thus excluding those who are not kin). But the individual's title, once he has acquired it in this way, may be almost as unrestricted as that recognised in many western laws.

As for litigation, the evidence from small-scale segmentary societies such as the Nuer of the Southern Sudan supports the view that customary proceedings were between groups. Where a homicide occurred (and this is quoted as the typical inter-group wrong), a state of feud would instantly follow between the groups concerned. As Howell tells us:[19]

> 'In the past there was no conception of individual punishment inflicted on the person of the killer. . . . The two parties concerned in a feud are referred to as *ji ran*, which means "the people of the man" (*i.e.*, the deceased). These are the people who will seek vengeance on the *ji thunge*, "the people of the compensation," who are the kinsmen of the killer and will be called upon to pay *thung* or compensation.'

A more common pattern, however, was that observed by the chiefly Tswana.[20] In criminal cases it is generally the actual malefactor who must answer for his misbehaviour at the chief's or headman's court. In civil cases an attempt is often made by the family-groups of complainant and defendant to settle a dispute out of court. If this fails, the matter is brought to court. The plaintiff first lodges his complaint with his own headman, generally through a senior relative. The headman or his representative transmits the complaint to the head of defendant's family, who in turn reports the matter to his own headman; it is in the court of the latter that the case will be heard.

What has happened here, then, is that there is considerable family involvement in the processes of dispute-settlement; each family may (or may not) support its litigating member before, during, and after the hearing (as by helping to meet any fine or compensation awarded); but the primary liability remains that of the individuals concerned, and they are the principal parties.

We may conclude that African laws, with their strong organisation

[19] P. P. Howell, *A Manual of Nuer Law* (London, 1954), pp. 40, 42.
[20] Schapera, *op. cit.*, pp. 283 *et seq.*

of tribe, family, locality, age-grades, societies, and other associations, undoubtedly emphasise the corporate and collective, at the expense of the individual element in social life and law; but the difference from western society is no more than one of degree, and there is, as in western society, a dialogue or tension between the collective and the individual principles in which now one, now the other, prevails.

Maine's remark, therefore, that '. . . Ancient Law, . . . knows next to nothing of Individuals. It is concerned not with Individuals, but with Families, not with single human beings, but groups' (p. 250) would seem to be of somewhat limited application to African law.

It is mainly, though not entirely, as a result of the observation of this strong community life that some writers (following Maine among others) have argued that legal relations in traditional African society were status relations; that is, that the legal obligations to which an individual was subjected flowed not from the particular exercises of his freedom of choice and action but from the roles or relationships in which he found himself, as father, child, subject, husband, wife, tenant, and so on. Individual contracts—other than those of a formalised character, such as marriage and property transfers—were on this view non-existent or of minimal importance. This assessment of African laws appears to validate Maine's most celebrated dictum (already cited above) that 'the movement of the progressive societies has hitherto been a movement *from status to contract.*'[21]

Freedom of legal choice and action in African customary laws was undoubtedly restricted by comparison with modern English law. But in so saying there are three points to bear in mind:

(i) We must beware of comparing the *practice* of African law (as described by observational anthropologists) with the *theory* of English law (as put by legal writers): if we compare freedom of legal choice in practice in modern England the comparison might be much less striking.

(ii) There was, of course, freedom in African law to choose whether to enter into a legal relationship of a certain sort or not. Not all obligations were imposed *a priori* by the law. A man might choose whether to marry or not to marry, whom to marry, and often how much he would pay by way of bride-price; a farmer might decide which piece of land to appropriate, whether to realise the exchange-value of his land by tenancy, gage, or sale, whom to sell to and for what price; and so on.

(iii) There were, lastly, many agreements and promises to which the law would give effect. Many of these agreements were either formless or had only so much form as was necessary to publicise their existence in view of the absence of written records, as with the

[21] *Op. cit.*, p. 165.

very interesting giving of drink as a thank-offering in Akan law. The ceremonious giving, receipt, and sharing of the drink confirm the agreement and make it notorious. Scholarly investigation which is now proceeding is revealing more and more of these enforceable customary agreements. The whole of the dispute-settling process in many societies rested on a basis of agreement, as we have already seen. Trade was widespread, even in pre-colonial times, in many parts of Africa. Contracts of agistment,[22] tenancy, service, manufacture, and many others are encountered in the laws of many of the indigenous tribes. There is therefore little support from African law for Maine's observations that there are practically no contracts in 'early' society, that those which are found are between family and family or chieftain and chieftain, and that[23] '. . . the transaction is one of the same nature, and attended by as many formalities, as the alienation of property, and the disregard of one iota of the performance is fatal to the obligation.'

We may now pursue some of the basic themes which we have already noted, the postulates of African law, as they express themselves in the different facets of the substantive law. These might be put as follows:

1. A man belongs by nature to a variety of human communities, territorial and familial. Membership gives him the right to draw on the resources of the community for support, economic and moral; but it creates a countervailing obligation to respect the underlying and continuing needs of the rest of the community, which implies that the community should have the paramount power to control the way in which individual access to resources may be exercised.

2. A man is entitled to the fruits of his own labour.

3. Human society consists of categories of persons who occupy different statuses. Differentiation of rights and obligations as between chief and subject, parent and child, man and woman, etc., is a concomitant of such inequality.

4. Those who transgress the *mores* of society must be punished, whether such *mores* are established by custom, religious belief, or positive enactment.

5. Where a dispute breaks out between fellow-members of a community, it is vital that it be resolved, and resolved in such a way that the future harmony of the community is restored.

The law of the family is the central and most typical branch of the customary law, which exemplifies all the postulates mentioned above. Everyone in customary law belongs to a kinship or family group; but this simple statement conceals a considerable variation both in

[22] Taking in cattle to remain and feed, pasture, at a certain rate.
[23] *Op. cit.*, p. 302.

the size and composition of the 'family,' and in the degree of corporate or collective action which such a family undertakes. Among the types of kinship grouping found in African societies are the corporate lineage or 'clan,' whose members all share a common descent in a single line, male or female (often segmented into a number of sub-lineages), the extended family based on a lineage segment but including other persons connected by marriage, and the household based on a parental or grandparental (or in some places fraternal) family. In societies with developed lineage structures a person may simultaneously belong to a whole hierarchy of such family groupings.

All customary families tend to have a head, designated either by automatic assumption or transmission of office or by election by the other responsible members of the family. The legal functions of the head of family or head of household are crucial in the operation of the laws of property, succession, marriage, and domestic relations generally. Those who are not heads of families may have—and retain throughout life or until they become heads of family themselves—a subordinate or dependent legal status.

These family units often function as corporate legal entities, in the sense that the members co-operate closely together in the exploitation of the family-controlled lands, and that they are viewed as units in their dealings with the outside world (whether what is involved is participation in a dispute or the alienation of property). As such corporate units, families were often jointly and vicariously responsible for their members' torts and breaches of contract, though this responsibility might be moral rather than legal. If a family rejected responsibility for an erring member's wrong, however, this meant in the old days a simultaneous rejection of the member generally, his being cut off from the family; expulsion of a member would often have had as consequence the exposure of the ex-member to enslavement or other maltreatment without the protection for him which membership of a family would otherwise bring.[24]

It was in the law of property that family membership and family control were most significant. An individual's access to natural resources generally depended either on a grant or allocation from a lineage or household head, or—where he acquired by his own exertions or in his own right—on the assistance that his dependants or other relatives might give him in clearing the ground, building a hut or house, looking after cattle, and so on. The continued existence of a lineage or household was expressed in and rested on the continuity of

[24] *Cf.* excommunication still used in parts of India and Britain till Hanoverian times; outlawry (Holdsworth, *Hist.* iii, 604) abolished in civil actions (Legge, 1779) in *1879. Ed.*

the family fund, be it (as in the pastoral societies) cattle or other beasts, or (as in the agricultural societies) land for farming.

This family fund, built up by the individual exertions of the family members over time, might in some societies be transmitted as a unit to the succeeding generation on the death of the present holder or controller; whereas in others the law of succession envisaged a continual subdivision, fragmentation, and rearrangement of the family holdings at each death.

Families were not the only type of grouping with a claim to control over the exploitation of natural resources; territorial and political units, such as 'tribes' and village communities, also exercised land control powers in many societies. So pronounced was this land control that in many centralised peoples, such as the Baganda of East Africa, it was claimed that all the land occupied by the tribe 'belonged to' the supreme chief or ruler; and for many other areas it has been asserted by writers that land was essentially controlled by village communities (as with the Fante of Ghana).[25]

Often occupation and use of land were subjected to concurrent control by a hierarchy of such authorities, political and familial. Beneath such a weight of control, one might feel the individual occupier would be entirely submerged, and would have no defined, separate, or durable rights. This is by no means the case. The extent of individual interests in land varied greatly from one place to the next, but most customary laws observed the principle that a man was entitled to the fruits of his own labour (one of our basic postulates cited above). Thus, if a man cleared the virgin bush this would give him the right to exclude others from using the same piece of land; if a man planted the land with annual or perennial crops or erected a hut, then the crops or hut would be his, and no one else could deprive him of them except for due cause.

But the community aspect of the property law would also make itself felt at every stage. The land which the individual farmed might well have been obtained by allocation from the community or family pool. Often the individual citizen would be expected to contribute first fruits or other perquisites to his political superiors, and to maintain his family (whether he was in a superordinate or subordinate position in respect to it) by contributions from his crops and land. And if the individual tried to alienate his land to an outsider he would probably find that this was either not legally possible or only allowed with the sanction of the chief or the family head (or both).

Does African law recognise marriage as we know it in the western world, the sort of relationship defined as 'Christian marriage' in the

[25] *Cf.* J. M. Sarbah's analysis in his *Fanti Customary Laws*, 2nd ed. (London, 1904) and *Fanti National Constitution* (London, 1906).

law of England—'the voluntary union for life of one man and one woman to the exclusion of all others'; or do relationships between the sexes proceed on an entirely different basis? Early observers of African customary laws, for instance, noted the institutions of polygamy and bride-price, and concluded that marriage in African law was utterly repugnant to western notions, and was no more than an unequal transaction whereby a bride was sold by one man (the father of the girl) to another (her husband).

African customary marriage is and was everywhere polygamous (more precisely, polygynous); that is, a man might simultaneously have more than one wife (though a similar option was denied to the woman). The status of the wives of a polygamist was not, however, reduced in consequence: unlike in some other legal systems, each was a lawfully wedded wife and not a mere concubine, and often a husband is specifically required by law to accord equal treatment to each of his wives.[26]

As for 'bride-price', no legal institution has, perhaps, been more misunderstood. The very name misleads, since what is paid over by the husband-to-be (or often by his father or family on his behalf) to the father or guardian of his future wife is not a price by which the husband acquires dominium and the right of disposal over his wife. She is not his property, even if she may be in a subordinate position, and he has no power to transfer her to another man. The bride-price usually consisted, in the pastoral societies, of cattle; elsewhere hoes, cloth, and other chattels or beasts might be given. Money is being substituted more and more these days for these payments in kind. It should be noted that bride-price in African law is in this respect unlike Islamic dower or dowry under English or other European laws, as there are different payers and recipients, and the payments serve different legal purposes.

The 'bride-price' serves several legal purposes in African law. To begin with, its ceremonial transfer from husband's to wife's people is a public record and expression of the coming into being of a new matrimonial relationship. It is thus both evidence of a solemn transaction and also the validating act by which it is concluded. Secondly, it marks the formal creation (or, more often, confirmation) of the husband's marital power over the wife, giving him exclusive access to the wife, making it the legal wrong of adultery for another man to have relations with her, and in many societies giving him a claim over her services in home and field. And lastly, especially in the patrilineal societies, it gives the husband parental power over the children born to his wife. The issue of the bride are not only under her husband's legal control but are by the payment of 'bride-price'

[26] For the Islamic counterpart see above, p. 75.

legally affiliated to him. This is why some writers have asserted, in a vivid slogan, that 'bride-price is child-price.'[27]

There are two other aspects of African customary marriage which deserve mention here: first, there is the major involvement of the families of the spouses in the making, maintenance, and dissolution of the union; and secondly, there is the tendency in customary law to treat marriage as a process rather than an event: in other words, as a relationship which gradually develops and is legally strengthened over time, rather than a once-and-for-all occurrence with no possibility of future legal development.

These two aspects are linked together. Regular marriage in African law might customarily begin with the betrothal by her father or guardian of an infant girl to a young boy or man. Each side is represented by the family of the spouse-to-be during the elaborate negotiations which lead up to the actual handing over of the bride. The bride-price is typically transferred from the one family group to another, either in a single lump sum or by a series of instalments. During the marriage each family (through its representatives) keeps an eye on the behaviour of the married pair; if there is matrimonial strife they may jointly intervene to reconcile the spouses. If the dispute is irreconcilable African law typically provides that the marriage may be dissolved by or at a joint meeting of the two families. If the marriage remains in being till the death of one of the spouses many customary laws allow for its extension by the replacement of the defunct spouse by one of his or her relatives through the institutions of levirate, widow-inheritance, and sororate.[28]

It is for these reasons that African marriage has been described as an alliance or association between two families as much as a union between two spouses. These principles also help one to understand why marriage in many customary laws is viewed as a subordinate or minor relationship in comparison with the family (lineage) relationship: in other words, marriage is transitory, the family is permanent.

The continuation and readjustment of legal rights and duties over time is assured by the law of succession. There are several features here which are widely found in African law, and which either link up or contrast sharply with legal systems elsewhere.

First there is the role of succession law in underwriting the family

[27] See above, p. 13, n. 2.

[28] '*Levirate*.' A legal arrangement by which a marriage is prolonged after the death of the husband, whose place is taken by his brother or other close male relative. Children procreated by the substitute husband are legally affiliated, not to him, but to the deceased husband.

'*Sororate*.' A similar arrangement for prolonging a marriage after the death of the wife (and sometimes also *inter vivos*, where the wife proves infertile). Her place is taken by her sister or other close female relative. Children born of the substitute wife may be assigned rank within the family as if they were children of the original wife.

structure. At the death of a man his self-acquired property falls into the family pool, and may thereafter either be maintained as a corporate fund subject to family control or redistributed among his 'heirs.' In West African laws, such as those of the Akan of Ghana, the former solution is adopted; but in the customary laws of, for instance, the Southern Bantu the death of the head of a kraal or household leads to the primary division of his estate between the various 'houses' (each consisting of a wife and her children by him). Each house then holds jointly under the control of the eldest son in that house, the household as a whole being now under the control of the eldest son of the deceased father by his senior wife.

This connection of succession and the family is also expressed through the power which the family has in many societies to determine who is to succeed, or the exact shares which each will take in a divisory scheme of succession. The will or wish of deceased as to how his property is to be divided is generally subject to family approval. The notion of a binding will or testament which can take effect regardless of the survivors' wishes is completely foreign to African ideas, and succession is generally intestate. There are ways in which an individual can influence the mode of distribution of his estate—by designating his heir, ear-marking property in his lifetime, death-bed declaration, etc.—but none of these corresponds to an effective will under English law.

African customary succession was generally onerous, in that the successor or successors succeeded to debts and liabilities as well as to assets, even when the former exceeded the latter. Thus a successor might be required to take over his predecessor's responsibility for maintaining his widow and children, or to meet debts or other legal claims which the deceased had incurred.

African succession was not restricted to tangible property, but might include succession to rights and duties over persons (widows, children, other relatives, and dependants). For this reason some customary laws include wives and children as part of the 'estate.'

What is the future of these African laws to be? Paradoxically the study of them has never been so advanced as at present, when the laws themselves, and the societies which produced them, are undergoing profound and irreversible changes. Clearly the old societies are disappearing for good: it is not possible to turn back the legal clock, however much some present-day African rulers would like to restore the legal and moral aspects of the past, more particularly the emphasis on community control and family co-operation, and the freedom from technicalities of the African law as compared with modern English or other European laws.

Africa as a whole is now entering a period of major legal reform, whose main purpose is to adjust the legal systems to contemporary economic and social realities. Unification and codification of the laws will be the end-product of this reformist movement; but there is a possibility that the new African legal systems will retain some of the better and more suitable features of the old laws, although the old institutions will emerge in a completely transformed state, both as regards form and content. One of the most extreme examples of the modern transmogrification of African customary law is provided by the new *Ethiopian Civil Code*, 1960, which in theory abolishes all customary law, but preserves something of their spirit, *e.g.*, in the machinery for dissolving statutory marriages and in the arrangements for recording community interests in land.

Just as the old English forms of action and the previous predominance of equity have each lent a distinctive character to modern English law, it is likely that African customary laws will leave their impress on the African codes of tomorrow; but if this is to happen, then more intensive legal study of the customary laws, and their analysis in the light of comparative legal insights, is urgently required so as to facilitate that harmonisation of western and African legal ideas which is the declared aim of contemporary African law-givers.

BIBLIOGRAPHY

A. N. Allott, *Essays in African Law* (London, 1960).

M. Gluckman, *The Judicial Process among the Barotse of Northern Rhodesia* (Manchester, 1956); *The Ideas in Barotse Jurisprudence* (New Haven–London, 1965).

P. H. Gulliver, *Social Control in an African Society* (London, 1963).

P. P. Howell, *A Manual of Nuer Law* (London, 1954).

H. and L. Kuper (eds.), *African Law: Adaptation and Development* (Berkeley and Los Angeles, 1965).

H. E. Lambert, *Kikuyu Social and Political Institutions* (London, 1956).

R. S. Rattray, *Ashanti Law and Constitution* (London, 1929).

J. M. Sarbah, *Fanti Customary Laws*, 2nd edn. (London, 1904).

I. Schapera, *A Handbook of Tswana Law and Custom*, 2nd edn. (London, 1959).

ENGLISH LAW

A. K. R. Kiralfy

MOST OF THE WORLD is governed in some form by either the civil law or the common law, the latter of Norman-English growth. The Normans, like the Romans, were tough soldiers, great architects, and inspired lawyers. Roman law enjoyed three periods of expansion: in the days of the Empire, at the time of the reception of Roman law by the Renaissance states, and in the form of the French Civil Code which was the model for so much of modern European and South American law. English law spread over the face of much of the earth as part of the expansion of the British Empire, and, as the recession of imperial power has generally been a peaceful process, unlike the overthrow of the Roman empire by races with alien traditions, systems based on English law are still in force in the Old Empire and much of the New. Even where the imperial tie was cut by war, as in the American War of Independence, judges with English training continued to administer justice with little visible change. The Custom of Paris was preserved to regulate civil relations in New France, when it became part of British North America, and Quebec Province in Canada still retains the former French law. In the same way that law was in force in the Louisiana Territory when acquired by the young United States, and is the basis of the law of the modern State of Louisiana. Otherwise the law of Canada and the United States as well as that of Australia and New Zealand is English common law. It has even been held to apply in States like Florida which were under Spanish rule at the time of British colonisation in America. Much English law, civil, criminal, and commercial, is also still in force in India and Africa. Naturally it is subject to change by local legislation. English law has not, however, been received simply as such anywhere. As a practical system, with its own special sources, techniques of interpretation, and traditions, it only works effectively with judges and lawyers trained in it. It is peculiarly intractable if transplanted into any country with differing legal background, and requires a simultaneous transfusion of English legal training and professional institutions. The flexibility of its principles has made it adaptable to different geographical conditions, and the general uniformity of its application in many countries is due to a general desire to preserve its heritage and for one jurisdiction to benefit from the experience of others.

Although modern continental lawyers are fond of regarding the common law of England as the 'law nobody knows,' it is in fact a European survival from the Middle Ages. Our law formed part of a broad belt of medieval legal systems covering much of north-western Europe, and based on customs of Nordic peoples influenced by Romanised institutions and practices. The Anglo-Saxon law before 1066 was naturally more purely Germanic, but this had little continuing influence. The Norman Conquest introduced a new political establishment which continued to apply ideas current in north-western France at that time. The royal court was only the highest stratum of a society administered by smaller landowners and their entourages of petty local assemblies of citizens. The unique feature of the Norman Conquest, though not immediately achieved, was the practical replacement of a great mosaic of oral local customs by a single system of law worked out by legal experts, the 'common law,' the law common to all England. Such expertise could only be a professional attainment. The history of the first two centuries after the Conquest is a history of the substitution of professional lawyers and judges for patrons and civil servants. King Edward I, whose reign (1274–1307) marked an era in legal progress, is often termed the 'English Justinian,' and though he came at the beginning rather than at the end of a development, he has some claim to that title. Of course, a lawyer of his time would find it difficult to recognise the English law of today, but the thread can be traced without a break back to his day.

Sir Henry Maine regarded the Romans and the Normans as the great masters of legal progress, and later ages and fresh skies have added little to the fundamentals of English common law, a tribute to Norman legal genius. It was thanks to the earlier union of legal and other functions that our judges still enjoy such unusual prestige in England; as high counsellors of state they originally ranked close to the sovereign and only gradually came to concentrate on the routine of the administration of justice. Our judiciary has only twice come under suspicion, once in medieval times, when some corrupt judges were dismissed, and once under King James II when the bench was packed with judges complaisant to the king's unpopular claims to power. It may be due to this latter event that they lost their aspiration to equality with the legislative and executive branches of government, an aspiration which had led most lawyers into the Parliamentary faction, and which, if it had been satisfied, would have given the courts a decisive constitutional function. Some of the judicial aura also accompanies the Bar, from which alone judges are selected, and which also enjoys a deservedly high reputation for independence, integrity, and ability.

Every legal system essentially corresponds to practical demands, but the English common law is particularly responsive to the pressures of daily life through its lack of any broad rigid framework. It is a truism to say that it is a pragmatic system, like most Anglo-Saxon institutions, rather than an abstract, intellectually satisfying artifact. Dislike of 'theory' is not based on a reluctance to understand and accept the reasons for one's own actions, but rather on an instinctive distrust of the broad generalisation which is felt to force subtle and complicated relationships on to a Procrustean bed of over-simplification. The English legal system is also generally described as 'inductive' (as contrasted with the 'deductive' systems), *i.e.*, gradually arriving at a rule from a consideration of numerous particular instances, as contrasted with the subsumption of situations under one or other of a limited number of unchanging and sometimes unchangeable prescriptions. Such contrasts must not be exaggerated, for lawyers are lawyers the world over, codes are elastically worded, and some principle underlies every detached English precedent. Experience in the Canadian Supreme Court demonstrates that there is a remarkable similarity in result between the application of the Anglophonic common law decisions and the Francophonic code's provisions. Still, the English system seems to enjoy some greater flexibility, for which it suffers a corresponding lack of logic and symmetry.

The great American jurist, Holmes, has said that the life of the law is not logic but experience. This is bred in the bone in English law. A bench of medieval judges once sneered at a barrister for using the 'sophisticated reasons' of the philosophers at the ancient English universities. Law was taught, till the eighteenth century, only in legal practice at the Inns of Court, a workaday 'tough' law in Maitland's view. Inherent in this law is the distrust of philosophical analysis which still survives. When the problems of causation in the English law of tort reached the limits of refinement we wisely, if belatedly, introduced the old Roman rule of apportionment of loss according to the respective faults of the parties. In a case where the same article was left by will to different persons in successive paragraphs the courts ended by dividing its value, with Solomonic wisdom, rather than follow old arguments as to which gift was the 'last' will of the testator, whose will came into force as a whole when he died. Such theoretical problems as accession and specification which fascinated the Roman jurists, *e.g.*, the fate of a poem written on another's parchment or a wine made with another's grapes, have been neatly avoided by stark and simple rules in favour of one claimant or another. Certainty is, to quote another cliché of our law, more important than justice (whatever that might be). It must be admitted that in this field our law causes more hardship than the Roman, as where one man builds a house on another's land and it becomes the other's property. But our courts are ingenious in finding ways to circumvent this result in practice wherever possible. Our law of contract is marked by a simple 'keep your word' which eliminates all subjective elements like the party's fault (as with the Roman *culpa in contrahendo*[1]) by concentrating on the sense of the agreement, and pays little attention to changes of circumstances save in very exceptional cases.

Whereas Roman law flowered under pagan auspices, English common law is the product of a Christian culture. Yet the doctrines of religion have had remarkably little influence on our post-Conquest law. This is partly due to the separation of church and state under the Normans and lay officialdom's jealousy of the church, and partly to the rude feudal origins of our law. Our early judges were in holy orders and our early Chancellors were bishops; yet this has left little mark either on law or equity. Such ecclesiastical jurisdiction as there was followed rather from the practical administrative functions of the clergy, such as the recording of marriages and the probate of wills, than from their spiritual role. Of course, heresy and apostasy were serious crimes in the Middle Ages, and religious persecution was flagrant in the Renaissance struggle between the faiths, but such crimes found their place in the general body of law, and had also a political flavouring. Some concepts of canon law were defiantly rejected by English lawyers, such as the legitimation of children by the subsequent marriage of their parents, feudal dignity being preferred to Christian charity. The attempt by church courts to anticipate our law of simple contract by enforcing plighted faith was also frustrated by the jealous common lawyers, who themselves began to offer remedies in the same situation much later. There are religious echoes in occasional judicial pronouncements—Lord Chancellor Nottingham described the perpetual tying up of property titles as contrary to the law of God, and Chief Justice Coleridge condemned shipwrecked seamen for eating a comrade, for whom, so Christianity requires, they ought rather to have sacrificed themselves, but these cases would undoubtedly have ended in the same way in any event.

As a result of laws passed in modern times in favour of religious toleration, the point has now been reached where the law even grants certain privileges to the non-Christian; it is a crime to wound the religious feelings of believers in other religions, charitable foundations

[1] Buckland and McNair, *Roman Law and Common Law*, 2nd edn., p. 238.

may be established to promote other faiths, and it is no longer an offence to make propaganda against Christianity. Of course, it is difficult to estimate how far the observance of Christianity and familiarity with Christian principles have coloured legal developments, but a comparison of its rules with those developed in pre-Christian Rome suggests that this influence has been remarkably small. The English legal terms for court sessions were indeed fixed in accordance with the ecclesiastical calendar, to leave certain seasons free from civil strife; and though no common-law judgment can be given on a Sunday, ministerial acts and judgments in Chancery may be validly passed on that day, because Jesus approved of doing good on the Sabbath;[2] but these very rare exceptions tend to prove the main contention.

Economic theory has had little conscious effect on English law. The judges appear always to have assumed that freedom of contract, of competition, and of transfer of property are beneficial to the community, so that the courts presumably proceed from some 'inarticulate major premise' of freedom of enterprise. Many statutes have worked changes in this connection, *e.g.*, in favour of tenants of dwellings who refuse to leave them on the expiration of their leases. The under-privileged contractor is often prevented from 'contracting out' of terms implied by law for his protection. Whereas between the wars restrictive trade practices were upheld as for the general good, recent legislation has aimed to suppress them. Judges in the new Restrictive Practices Court have expert lay assessors to advise them on economic matters, but the decision as to where the 'public interest' lies is left to the court with little legislative guidance, so that a new economic common law is being built up on rather uncertain foundations.

It is often emphasised that one cannot legislate morality and that courts are courts of law and not of morals. Yet there is probably a very large if undemarcated contribution made by ethical ideas to our law. Here the elastic concepts based on the reactions of the 'reasonable man' are often the vehicles of moral ideas, but of moral ideas fairly applicable to the everyday practical problems of an imperfect world and not those of a Utopia. It may truthfully be claimed that our law has become increasingly more moral with the advance of civilisation, quicker to protect the weak and foolish, quicker to sacrifice form and technicality in favour of fairness and good sense. Fictions and implications are readily used by our courts to adjust the law to the requirements of morality without altering its basic and familiar principles. There will probably always remain some residual dictates of personal morality which law cannot effectively

[2] A decision of 1967 to this effect relied on *Mackalley's Case*, itself decided in 1611.

enforce and which might indeed be weakened by any attempt at compulsion.[3]

A view which is not now widely supported would regard law as a necessary evil, the least law as the best law. But in any case our law starts with the assumption that all things are lawful, all transactions duly formal, and all persons innocent of wrong-doing. Every transaction is given its intended effects unless it violates paramount considerations of the legal order. A grant is to be construed most liberally against the grantor, and a will is to be interpreted in order to dispose effectively of as much as possible of the testator's estate. Our law of evidence assumes that the possessor is the owner, that cohabitating couples are married, and that rights long enjoyed have a lawful origin. Naturally, recent years have seen the growth of a more paternalistic state, interfering more and more in individual activities, prescribing more and more regulations, organising and controlling more and more trades and professions. The titles and contracts of individuals are often the victims. Courts and lawyers in England have not, however, modified their traditional approach to interference with private rights, which has produced an imbalance in modern statutory interpretation, to such an extent that the judges seem at times set on frustrating the obvious intentions of the legislature.

One of the remarkable effects of our past legal permissiveness has been the strong lay contribution to the law: the layman devises a transaction or creates a relationship, his legal advisers clothe it in legal form, and the court, in case of dispute, passes judgment on its validity. The layman does not wait for judicial approval before he acts, nor is anyone concerned with the tidy place to be filled by his conduct in the legal pattern. When a reported case is published it is often found that the validity of some dealing had long been assumed. Thus, to take only two recent conspicuous examples, when a court held in 1956 that a right of adjoining landowners to use a pleasure garden was a good right appurtenant to the ownership of their land, they were upholding a right created in full legal form as long ago as 1855 in the teeth of *dicta* in previous decisions and textbooks, and when in 1957 payment of money was held to be a valid condition of enjoyment of a right of way the covenant for payment thus enforced was found to have been signed in 1851. Premature formalisation would hamper the exercise of such freedom of manoeuvre and

[3] Supererogation is a notion based historically (and perhaps erroneously) on the Parable of the Good Samaritan but analogous to the Jewish concept of 'keeping within the border of the law' (see p. 38), *i.e.*, keeping within the fringe of righteousness which protects the law itself from infringement. Supererogation is a sign that to be content only with obedience to law is to fall short of perfection: *The Gospel According to St. Matthew*, xix. 16–21, especially verse 21 ('If thou wouldest be *perfect*, go, sell that thou hast, and give to the poor, and thou shalt have treasure in heaven: and come, follow me!'). *Luke* xvii. 10: 'We are useless servants: *we have only done our duty*!'

deprive the law of its usefulness to the citizen. Instead, his legal advisers may be called on to use greater imagination in formulating new relations out of court than his learned counsel in defending well-recognised rights before the court.

English common law constitutes a classic system of case law or judge-made law. This means that under the Anglo-American system courts have played, and continue to play, a leading part in creating new law, besides claiming the authority to give binding pronouncements on the true interpretation of statutes passed by legislatures. The judges have made a virtue of necessity, since there was no adequate or uniform body of law applicable in England after the Norman Conquest. The Anglo-Saxon customs lost their practical effect, while the customs brought with them by the invading host from Normandy, Anjou, and other places did not precisely fit the new conditions across the Channel. Differences in law between the English and the original Norman territories of the dynasty were quite early recognised by the courts. When it is added that no really new legislation was to be passed in England for about two centuries after the Conquest the magnitude of the judges' task can be appreciated. They worked on the basis of current feudal practices and underlying assumptions, concentrating in earlier decades on the all-important law of land title, with which public political power was identified, and from which wealth was derived, the owners living on deliveries of goods or payment of cash by the actual tillers of the soil. The sophistication of this part of our law was to set the tone for its general development, deciding intricate disputes between haughty and belligerent feudal lords on such terms as to satisfy the parties that right had been done.

Legal rules tend proverbially to lead their own lives. They form patterns of conviction which do not always correspond to the circumstances of their origin. In this way the common law soon passed beyond the grasp of everyday men and became the preserve of professional judges. The natural reason of the layman gave way to the 'artificial reason' of the law, which required training for its comprehension. It would, however, have been unacceptable for judges to claim juristic authority, on the lines of the Roman and Islamic schools. They therefore had recourse to the idea of custom as the basis of law; they were expounding what the invariable practice of courts was in the cases they decided. The result was the inception of the typical doctrine of 'binding precedent.' By following each other's decisions, wherever not obviously defective, judge-made law imitated the uniformity of custom and the unchanging character of the words of statute law. Precedent was evolved as a curb on possible overweening acts of judges, and began to make the common law predictable for litigants. The practice, common in Tudor and Stuart times, whereby 'all the judges of England' solemnly settled a knotty point in consultation, must have helped in the same direction. The fiction that judges 'declared' a supposedly pre-existing law in fact gave them wide legislative powers without personal responsibility for the results. By the fourteenth century decided cases were treated as at least evidence of the law, and collections of decisions were being compiled and circulated.

Although parallel courts would tend to follow one another's decisions, they might not always agree on the statement of the law in question, and conflicts might arise. The very possibility of appealing to higher courts to overrule a decision meant that trial courts could not claim infallibility. This led to the growth of the modern distinction between cases strictly binding on lower courts, being laid down by superior jurisdictions, and cases accepted as correct but liable to be overruled if an appeal were taken. This is expressed in the form of the 'hierarchy of courts,' with higher courts binding lower courts only. In modern times appeals are much more frequent than in former centuries and the proportion of binding principles is higher. On the other hand, it is usually possible to 'distinguish' a former decision on some difference in the circumstances, so that the law even now is left in some uncertainty on many issues. The tendency is to observe such rules as exist, until some litigant has the hardihood to take his case to the highest court in the hope of producing a surprise reversal of the rules, which not infrequently happens.

The use of the fiction that courts 'declare' rather than create law has another disadvantage, that law is made retrospectively. The law is applied perhaps to the relations of the parties to a dispute at the moment of judgment and when it is too late to do anything about it. Nor is it any protection for a party that he took eminent legal advice before he acted. It is a tribute to the grounding of our law in justice and its consonance with generally accepted ideas that this seldom inflicts much hardship. The party forced to pay damages has generally done something clearly 'wrong.' Where parties are likely to make arrangements in advance to regulate their affairs with confidence, as in transactions with property, the courts proceed carefully and responsibly. They are especially careful not to overrule long-accepted decisions which parties obviously used for their guidance. Criminal law, in particular, has been put into statutory form so as to obviate much of the danger of surprise, and this branch of the law is always interpreted most favourably to the accused.

Constitutional niceties have always been observed in England by treating the courts as subservient to the legislature, in the sense that Parliament may (as it often does) pass a law to alter the law laid down by a court. Where Parliament does not intervene it may not unfairly be said that it adopts the rule of case-law and provisionally ratifies it. Now that the legislature holds frequent sessions and passes a great volume of legislation annually there is less difficulty in correcting unpopular developments in judge-made law, provided Parliamentary time is available. Hence the one-way system of precedent, under which courts can never fully retrace their steps, is workable. In 1966 the Lord Chancellor asserted a claim that the highest court, the House of Lords, might reverse its own previous decisions in exceptional circumstances. This lays claim to legislative power, as the old 'declaratory theory' of the common law will not stretch so far. It may be justified by the view that certain basic legal problems are best decided by a number of the most skilled lawyers in the land in the House of Lords sitting judicially, rather than by a programme of legislation which may be party-political in inspiration and debated in an almost empty chamber in these days when lawyers have ceased to predominate as members of Parliament. The distinction between 'lawyers' law,' which is the proper subject for the courts, and 'social law,' which rests on policy rather than justice, is fairly clear. Courts are fitted to maintain and improve the traditional common-law system, and Parliament is best fitted to superimpose on it special, often temporary, legislation.

Since the judges were supposed to be enunciating an existing body of customary law, no immediate steps were taken to publish court rulings. The great English medieval jurist Bracton pointed out in the middle of the thirteenth century that English judges could develop the law by their decisions, whereas Justinian forbade Roman judges to do this. But reporting of cases was in its infancy and continued for centuries to operate on an informal and unsystematic basis. The great series of *Year Books* which spans the period from Edward I to Henry VIII (d. 1547) varies considerably in style and information. Scholars are still undecided as to their authorship, and it may be that they began like lecture notes of individual law students and gradually developed into more uniform and responsible reports. They did at least circulate contemporaneously, as did the great reports of Chief Justice Coke in the early seventeenth century, but many reports in Tudor and Stuart times were only posthumously published, and there was a period when the young barrister had no access to recent cases, being reduced to citing old principles and urging value judgments, to which the bench replied by referring to cases in their experience which had not yet seen the general light of day.

A new epoch began with the publication of the *Term Reports* from 1785, and the modern pattern of citation was established, under which relevant previous decisions are traced by the researches of the barristers who argue the cases, and then presented for consideration by the judges. Pressure of work makes it difficult for the trial judge to undertake research into his cases, but his previous legal training and experience at the Bar enable him to avoid serious errors and actively to control the legal argument before him. It is extremely rare for the English supreme court to deliver an erroneous judgment through omission to consider the authorities or handle them properly. In the House of Lords the importance of the cases and the reduced pressure of litigation often lead to personal research by members of the court into the law to be applied, and they may refer to cases not cited by counsel, *e.g.*, analogous decisions in Canada, Australia, and the United States.

The existence of numerous up-to-date textbooks and encyclopaedias of law makes it relatively easy for the English lawyer to find the relevant authorities on any problem. In the United States the enormous bulk of reported cases from various states, all of them entitled to be cited in any court, has led to an unofficial Restatement of the Law, which is inevitably not merely an encyclopaedia but an original work, in which many solutions are proposed for questions on which differing state precedents exist. There has also been a codification of common law in the state of California which works well, and many branches of common law have been codified for use in India and Africa. As a result, discussion of a possible codification of English law is now no longer heretical. The reasons for the lack of codification have been various. Many foreign codes owe their origin to the necessity of resolving conflicts between local customs by means of a general enactment, as was the case with the *Code Napoléon*, which replaced numerous provincial customary systems in France. The general enactment, however, is no mere collage of separate rules but a new beginning with a new basic theory. It incorporates ideas about the nature of law and its objectives as seen at the time. It has an internal consistency, proceeding from the general to the particular, aiming at the broadest generality throughout, *e.g.*, having common principles of legal personality or capacity for all cases, having fundamentals of the law of obligations which are paramount in every situation in that part of the law, and so on. Codes flourish where academic lawyers enjoy authority and are prepared to draft systematic legislation.

English law was precociously unified at the Conquest; Saxon customs became obsolete with a few exceptions, and the courts set their faces against local customs generally, by subjecting them to rigorous tests of proof and reasonableness. Thus one of the main driving forces for codification, the desire for unification of the national law, was missing. The 'tough law' of the Inns of Court in London, bodies of legal practitioners, assumed the authority in

England enjoyed by the law professors abroad, with a resultant stress on the practical and useful rather than the logical and philosophical. No need was felt for overall doctrines or theories, with the result that legal topics and subdivisions of topics grew up in tight compartments. The law luxuriated in sophisticated detailed rules to meet infinitely various situations but at a very low level of abstraction. Convincing solutions of pressing disputes were preferred to abstract and internally elegant worlds of legal norms. Given a highly skilled bench and Bar, a relatively isolated geography, and an uninterrupted legal development of nine centuries, the English system is admitted, even by continental jurists, to work well, though some of them, worried by its unwritten and uncodified character, doubt whether it is other than just a stream of cases. The predictability of English law, in fact, appears to be at least as great as that of codified law, for its rules are highly detailed, and the doctrine of binding precedent keeps them from abrupt change. The broad terms of many codes allow far more play to the initiative of judges, and the absence of the idea of predecent allows many conflicting rulings to co-exist and create uncertainty abroad, which our system obviates. If a general codification of English law ever takes place it will be due to different considerations, *viz.*, a desire to make a more fundamental change in the law, to shake off the dust of centuries and make a new start, aided by thorough research into the consequences of the present system and its disadvantages. In this event it is most unlikely that we shall draw our inspiration from existing Codes or their philosophies. The language and techniques of the present law will probably be preserved, and the practice of following precedents if relaxed will not be eliminated.

We have seen that academic jurists enjoy little authority in English law. There is no distinct stream of academic doctrine as a source of law. A few old treatises are accepted as records of the state of the law at the time, where no more direct statutory or judicial authority can be discovered. Most of the great treatises, like those of Coke and Blackstone in the seventeenth and eighteenth centuries respectively, are the works of judges, not jurists, and are valued for their fidelity to the basic sources of law, and not for any independent or critical approach to them, still less to any assumption of power to overrule them. This is not to say that academic works possess no influence, especially today, when very many lawyers first study law at the universities. Their experience of a more critical approach certainly stays with them, and may contribute to the more general recognition by judges and practising lawyers that the law may usefully be reformed. In some fields academic influence is stronger, *e.g.*, in private international law the basis of the law rests on juristic commentaries.

Academic lawyers can deal particularly well with this, for England, somewhat uncommon situation. It is a field developed by foreign lawyers and it has no long tradition in England. In the course of time the wealth of case-law will no doubt make the study of academic opinions nugatory. The American experience has been historically different. Blackstone's *Commentaries on the Laws of England* (1765–1769) provided a useful compendium of common law at the time of the American Revolution and enjoyed more authority in America than in England, where the process of legal development went on unchecked. They also served as a common basis for the separate sovereign legal systems of the new states and set a fashion in commentaries. The leading American commentaries, those of Kent and Story, were, like those of Coke and Blackstone, the work of eminent judges, not academic lawyers. They were used throughout the states and incorporated much continental European law on topics like commercial law which had not been as yet fully developed in England at the time of the American Revolution. Elaborate treatises by great legal scholars take into account the embarrassing wealth of case law which now exists in America and bring it into some kind of order.

How great has been the influence of foreign law on English law itself? Except during the actual Roman occupation, of which some legal traces exist, Roman law has had relatively little effect on the main stream of English development. But combined with canon law (itself penetrated by Roman-law ideas) and mercantile law of continental origin, it has probably had more influence than is sometimes admitted. The remedies of injunction and specific performance in English equity procedure are cases in point. The English entail of land was originally inspired by a rescript of Justinian on a private litigation in Constantinople, and the law of rights of way and water present too many similarities to Roman law for these to be accidental. The tort and crime of defamation of character were influenced by Roman law through the Court of Star Chamber, and Roman sources were referred to as authorities by it.

Roman law has, for historical reasons, had most effect on the law now administered by the Probate, Divorce, and Admiralty Division of the English High Court. Probate is an official recognition of the validity of a will of property in the abstract, unlike typical common-law proceedings, which are concerned with disputes, and the law of evidence in probate proceedings is lax and quite unlike the strict common-law system. Divorce law knows the institution of the Queen's Proctor, an official clearly related to the French *Procureur du Roi* and more modern equivalents who intervene in private disputes in the name of society. Decrees of divorce also have a general effect on status and not merely a personal effect between parties.

Admiralty law, based on Romanised Greek rules, is a world of its own; judges sit not with juries but with assessors, general decrees (*in rem*) are passed, and the Roman apportionment of damages between the parties, *e.g.*, in collision-damage cases, was always practised in this court, although not generally introduced into English procedure in other courts until 1945. The law of Prize is similarly indebted to foreign practice.

It may be mentioned that the English Crown established special courts to deal with cases involving Jews and set up a system of registration of debts owed to Jewish creditors (1194) which may have influenced the later systems of registration of title deeds and bills of sale. The Edwardian legislation of 1285 which assisted urban creditors to recover debts from land was probably an outgrowth of the privileges and special system of registration of Jewish 'starra' as they were called.[4] The expulsion of the Jews from England by Edward I in 1290 prevented any continuing influence being exerted except indirectly through European mercantile law.

Modern European law has had less direct effect on English law, except in commercial law, where banking, insurance, agency, negotiability, and other important institutions are of Italian origin, and to some extent in the general principles of contract, where Pothier's views have sometimes been followed. Foreign law is sometimes the indirect basis of reforms in English law. The modern statutory protection of a man's dependants from being 'cut off' by a will in favour of strangers is clearly influenced by the Roman *querela inofficiosi testamenti*, the classical English doctrine having favoured complete freedom of testation. The Law Commission today are interested in comparative law with a view to law-reform and further research into the solutions of various legal problems under foreign systems of law, especially in countries with similar institutions and traditions to our own, such as the Commonwealth, American, and Scandinavian nations.

Although English law was ceremoniously described as the custom of the realm, the role of custom in modern times is small. The jealous ambitions of the royal court led to a general enforcement of rules laid down at the centre, and in a tightly knit, highly industrialised country with good communications local rural customs were obviously an anachronism. Urban customs were more suggestive, but the royal courts profited by their example and embodied their advanced ideas into the developing fabric of the common law itself.

The English approach to statute law is paradoxical. The volume

[4] The singular *starrum* represents the Hebrew *shetar*, 'a contract,' M. Lincoln, *The Starra* (Oxford University Press, 1939). For the work of J. J. Rabinowitz (relevant here) see the bibliography to Chapter 2 above. *Ed.*

of such law is very great, and a perusal of a typical law report shows that more of the courts' time is spent deciding cases on statutory provisions than on other rules. Yet statute law has never provided a systematic body of rules governing everyday relations, save possibly the *Copyright Acts* and in some enactments like the *Bills of Exchange Act* which merely state the results already arrived at in decided cases. The Parliamentary draftsman knows the existing law, written and unwritten, and adapts his project of law to fit into this mass, with the appropriate modifying effect. He does not construct a separate or parallel system. Hence much of our legislation is difficult to comprehend without background knowledge. The results, however effective in practice, are not such as to inspire us with much affection for this type of law. Sir Edward Coke described statutes as 'raging tyrants' and the common law as a 'nursing mother.' By this he meant that the common law was carefully built up with full consideration of its possible effects, whereas statutes could be passed in the heat of the moment to deal with a pressing problem and without being justified in principle.

Until the fourteenth century English judges belonged (as mentioned above) to the *élite* which exercised legislative, executive, and judicial powers, and interpreted statutes liberally and in accordance with the known intention of the king and Council. This was encouraged by the declaratory character of many early statutes, which merely authoritatively confirmed or made more precise existing unwritten law. But as statutes became more truly innovatory, as the judges came to be a judiciary in the strict sense, and, perhaps, as a result of their loss of the prestige in the judicial scandal we have already referred to, so the court's approach to statute became extremely literal. Judges feared the charge of usurpation of legislative power and at the same time resented the growth of statute law above their heads and gave it as little scope as possible. There are a number of instances in which the courts seem to have defeated the clear words of a statute, *e.g.*, by interpreting a modern provision that a loan contract should be 'void' as if it were merely voidable. Draftsmen were accordingly compelled to adopt very precise wording to prevent this, so that a vicious circle resulted, the dry and unenlightening language of the statute giving ever less guidance as to its interpretation.

English law was able to reach maturity early, and thus to dispense with any necessity to receive any older legal system. The royal courts were able to concentrate on matters of interest to the Norman dynasties, mainly land titles, leaving minor disputes to the still active local courts. Gradually the royal courts extended their remedies and jurisdiction and absorbed the whole of the law. Early common law was marked by feudalism and formalism. Typical litigation concerned the question of priority of seisin (or freehold possession) of land or disputes among rival heirs to land. The economy was such that the results of lawsuits affected the life of the nation. Serious crimes were proceeded against as much because the convict lost his lands to his feudal superiors as for the sake of punishment. The typical tort (or civil wrong) was a violent raid by one landowner on his neighbour's livestock or produce. Such contracts as came before the royal courts generally concerned agreements about land transfer or for the erection of buildings. The freeholder who owned land by free services to his superior could alone vote at elections and sit on juries. Hence common law was largely a law of property rather than obligations, and a law of a special kind of property, land. This descended in special ways on death, differing from the succession to goods. Land could be 'settled' on successive owners for long periods. It could be 'entailed' in the direct male line of descent so as to provide the means for the upkeep of a peerage.

This rather rigid 'Gothic' system was alleviated in the course of time by having to adjust itself to the pressure of rival internal systems, that of the Chancery court held by the Lord Chancellor for the time being, the Court of Star Chamber, the Admiralty court, and others. The Chancery was the product of the Renaissance; it attached less magic to land and dispensed with undue formalities. It may almost be termed a capitalist court, dealing in money claims and funds and influenced by commercial and canon law. The Star Chamber, as we have seen, used Roman law in fields such as libel and forgery, and the fall of the court brought all these matters into the common-law courts by default. The Admiralty court dealt with matters of foreign trade on a basis of European mercantile custom. By drastically limiting the Admiralty jurisdiction, the common lawyers assumed power over shipping, marine insurance, and many other commercial matters, and accepted mercantile custom as a living source of common law, the traditional common-law rules being too cumbrous and unsuitable for merchants' cases.

This continuity of English law is probably unique. Although altered in many details, our law of property is still basically medieval, as is our law of tort. Our law of contract is much the same as it was in Tudor times, if anything more strict in some respects, as in the insistence on a new consideration for a promise to be binding. We still prosecute for the same crimes, under the same names, as in medieval times, though current law reform is beginning to set a new style. Thus a court was required only a few years ago to decide whether a foreigner living abroad was 'within the Queen's peace' so as to make his killing murder, and our law has been plagued by the restriction of the crime of theft to cases involving the physical movement of some article. English legal history also often follows recurrent patterns.

Thus one of the objects of persons settling land in medieval times was to separate the outward legal ownership from the beneficial ownership, by vesting the legal title in trustees and thereby give them the administration of the property without its enjoyment. In 1535 the *Statute of Uses* put an end to this division. Yet the device of the modern 'active trust' enabled that statute to be circumvented. In 1882 another statute sought to vest the legal title in the beneficial owner and reunite both capacities in the same person. Yet here again, by means of the 'trust for sale' a method exists of keeping the two titles separate today. The medieval system of conveyancing insisted on public transfers of land before the eyes of the neighbourhood. Landowners who wished for privacy managed to transfer land informally, relying on the Chancery to enforce the transaction on conscientious grounds in case of dispute. A statute of 1536 required all such informal agreements to be registered. This requirement was evaded by landowners by the device of leasing the land to the purchaser, which at that time required no ceremony, and then releasing the landlord's title by private deed. By 1845 public transfers had fallen into disuse. Conveyancing is still private today; title must be registered under the 1925 legislation, but the register itself cannot be inspected without an authorisation by the registered proprietor. In medieval times pieces of land were held by various tenures, *e.g.*, provision of food or military service. The coming of a money economy dissolved these duties, which were commuted into fixed sums. Yet the 1947 planning legislation in a sense re-feudalised land by requiring each parcel to continue to be used only for the purpose it had on the 'appointed day' under the Act, unless official permission for a 'material change of use' was obtained. General zoning is also likely to dictate the future use of as yet undeveloped land under these statutes.

A system like the English system, as we have described it, might seem to risk premature rigidity. This is prevented by a number of built-in devices which preserve the general framework but allow wide freedom of movement within it. Our private law conforms in many ways to a 'natural law with variable content.' The key word is 'reason'; this is ultimately a question of fact, and thus adaptable to changing conditions. The usual example of liability in tort today is the failure by a defendant to take reasonable care to avoid a reasonably foreseeable injury to the plaintiff. Standards of care and foresight change with technological advances and riper experience. Again, an occupier of land may use 'reasonable force' to eject an intruder, a prosecution may only be launched for 'reasonable cause,' and a term in a contract may be void if it operates in 'unreasonable restraint of trade.' The courts are also prone to imply terms in contracts on the basis of what the judges think right rather than what the parties may or may not have intended. Such implications will vary from age to age. At one time all terms of a contract had to be expressly stipulated, but it is not uncommon to make a contract for goods or services without fixing a price, so that a 'reasonable price' is recoverable. Similarly, contracts must generally be performed within a 'reasonable time' if no date is specified.

The test of actionability in defamation is equally flexible. A man who publishes a false statement is only liable for defamation if the statement was such as to bring the plaintiff into hatred, ridicule, or contempt, and damage his career. Clearly this will depend on contemporary *mores*. Our libel law was at least partly developed as a substitute for the practice of duelling over affronts to one's honour. Imputations which at one period provoked violent reaction may at another be regarded as tolerable 'cut and thrust.' The criminal aspect of libel, including sedition and obscenity, is also far from rigid. What was once subversion of a small and unrepresentative *élite* may now be regarded as fair political comment in times of universal suffrage, and outspoken literature which at one period is regarded as indecent and corrupting may at another be classified as a work of art.

Our tort of nuisance is also based on common sense. One's neighbour is not entitled to perfect peace and quiet at all hours. Land may be put to 'ordinary' and 'natural' use without fear of lawsuits. Obviously views will differ from time to time over such concepts, as society changes.

On the other hand, no one would expect every part of the law to be dealt with in the same way. The formalities of a will or of a transfer of land, and other routine matters planned in advance, are strictly regulated by law, as are situations where convenience requires some precise rule to be followed, as in procedural matters. Even here, however, there are many loopholes, *e.g.*, a bad conveyance may be cured if it was preceded by a good contract, extensions of time may be obtained for procedural steps, pleadings may be amended, even judgments set aside for adequate reason. The new Rules of the Supreme Court of 1964 stress the avoidance of undue formalism and hardship.

The gradual nature of the development of case law allows other opportunities for reflection and reconsideration. Unpopular decisions are frowned on as 'not to be extended' or are 'distinguished' on slight differences of fact, whereas generally accepted decisions tend to be followed by other judges, whether strictly binding on them or not.

No point may be treated as finally decided until it has gone to the highest court, and this is a very expensive business, although free legal aid is becoming more widely available in England. A certain strategy may be applied in deciding when or whether to take an appeal that far. A recent development may illustrate this. In the years immediately following the Second World War many wives were deserted by their husbands, who sold the matrimonial homes to third parties, since they were generally the husband's property. The courts gradually began to put obstructions in the way of such dealings, though they hesitated to interfere with normal business arrangements. In the meantime, housing conditions improved, so that wives had a better chance of finding somewhere else to live. When the problem came before the House of Lords in 1965 that body rejected any supposed property right in the wife based on her general right to have a home provided for her. However, the general outcry has led to the passing of the *Matrimonial Homes Act* of 1967, under which a wife may register her claim in such a way as to protect her right to occupy the matrimonial home against all comers.

English statute law often follows the common-law pattern by introducing a test of 'reasonableness' or giving the courts a discretion in applying the law. Where the civil-law systems, for example, fix definite shares or portions for a family which may not be taken away by the testator's will, the modern English legislation leaves the court to decide whether 'reasonable provision' has been made for dependants, and, if not, what provision to make by order. A trustee is to be relieved of liability by the court for a technical breach of trust if the trustee has acted 'reasonably' and ought in the opinion of the court to be excused. Compulsory licences may be issued if a patentee of an invention is not making reasonable use of the same in England. Under the new *Misrepresentation Act* 'reasonable belief' in the truth of a statement is a defence to an action for damages. Under housing legislation the standard of fitness for human habitation again provides for possible progress in such standards, although various details are specified.

English law is also adaptable in its interpretation of statutes and documents to achieve their desired results under changed conditions. Thus old statutes punished the furious driving of 'carriages,' *i.e.*, passenger vehicles, normally horse-drawn. The *Road Traffic Acts* were at first confined to motor vehicles. When a pedal cyclist rode dangerously he was convicted on the basis that his bicycle was a 'carriage.' Private documents receive a similar liberal interpretation. A right of way with horses and carts will justify a modern landowner using the corresponding motor vehicles, such as cars and tractors. A community which enjoys a customary right to use a green for archery may instead use it for playing football. The courts thus apply the reason behind the right rather than the right in a literal sense. In general, rights of an incorporeal nature, such as rights of grazing or watering cattle, have been supplemented by the recognition of new rights reflecting trade and industry, like the right to run an oil pipe-line or electric cable, to hang an advertising sign over a shop, or park motor vehicles.

It must be admitted, however, that this flexibility is bought at the price of considerable trouble and expense. It is much easier to apply a fixed rule which can be understood in advance than to have to apply every time to a court and pay legal experts to argue a case. An example of this may be drawn from property disputes between spouses. Many systems confer equal rights on each spouse to property acquired under various conditions during a marriage, or apply some similar simple rule. In English law the relevant statute leaves it to the court to determine the respective property rights of each couple in each particular case, which has led to a spate of costly litigation in individual instances without any broad rule for the guidance of others emerging.

Where the law was so certain that adaptation from within was not possible, lawyers resorted to three classical methods of law reform: legal fictions, equity, and legislation. It is not clear that they were used in that order, for the earlier legal fictions were used to filch jurisdiction from other courts; they only amended the law to the extent that royal courts often gave better remedies, so that reform, from the lay client's standpoint, resulted only incidentally. In fact, these three methods were used for rather different purposes: if the common law provided adequate relief to one class of claimant but not another the latter could, by a judicial fiction which was irrebuttable, be treated as if he were the former. The Romans had used such a fiction to prefer cognates to agnates as successors,[5] or *bonorum possessores* to civil-law owners. In English late medieval law similar results were achieved, *e.g.*, by pretending that a hirer of goods had accidentally found them, by pretending that a dispute between two landowners was between their respective but purely fictitious tenants, or by pretending that a man of straw had a better title than a tenant-in-tail. The effect was to prevent the hirer adopting unfair forms of defence against the owner of goods open to him under the law, to obviate the need for the landowners to resort to dilatory and expensive formal procedure to decide their titles, and to enable the tenant-in-tail to get his land reconveyed to him free of the entail, thus defeating all who could otherwise have claimed under it. The spectacle of royal judges conniving and colluding in this way was never seriously criticised,

[5] See above, p. 9.

though its constitutional authority may appear dubious. Where legal fictions were useless, equity might be applied. Thus the common-law judges decided quite irrevocably not to enforce trusts of land, and would not treat the beneficiary as the true owner, by using fictions or otherwise; the reason was the exaggerated importance still attributed to notorious and open seisin of land by its owners. Equity, proceeding against the person of the apparent owner and not the land itself, would compel him to account to the intended beneficial owner. Thus equity developed a number of parallel property rights which the Chancery court would enforce effectively in the teeth of the opposition of the common-law judges. But equity assumed the existence of some common-law rights, and could only determine relations between individuals claiming private property. It still devises new 'equities' in such property, but is generally powerless to effect broad social reforms, *e.g.*, those for which public funds will be needed. It cannot, for instance, force a man to build well on his own land, if no other person is involved; it cannot set up health services and pension schemes. Hence during the last century legislation has become the major channel of law reform, and one which is quick and direct.

The duality of strict law and equity is perhaps the leading feature of English law, if we neglect criminal law. Most legal systems have exhibited this conflict between strict generality and predictability, on the one hand, and ideas of perfect justice in the individual case, on the other. In some systems a broad equitable approach invaded the strict law, as in Roman law, or the law yielded to appeals for justice on particular, sometimes emotional, grounds, as in the law of Athens. English law is notable in the survival for centuries of separate and rival systems of law and equity on good Aristotelian principles. Strict rules were applied in all routine cases by a court of law, while resort to the Chancery, the court of equity, was open to the victim where the party relying on the strict law had been guilty of fraud or betrayal of trust. No doubt the common-law judges followed feudal notions, while the influence of philosophy and Christianity was paramount in the case of the Chancellor, a leading ecclesiastic until the sixteenth century.

This dichotomy based on personal misconduct gradually gave way to one based on the type of case appropriate for each court. Thus a man evicted from the possession of land by a stranger would sue at common law, whereas a debtor whose creditor refused to return a security after repayment of the debt would sue in equity. The qualities of judgment called for were much the same, and in fact, since the Reformation, common-law and equity judges have been drawn from the Bar, having similar training but different specialities. Equity has never lost its superiority over common law, but its possibilities of development were limited in the time of King James I (1603–1625), and it has tended to form part of property law only.

In England the High Court of Justice is still divided into separate Queen's Bench and Chancery Divisions, for administration of law and equity respectively. In Canada and the United States a single court usually administers both systems, and the differentiation into law and equity is purely historical, the same procedure also being used in all cases. By legislation in England in 1875 equitable rules were incorporated into the common law of obligations and other branches, so that there is no longer any conflict of the rules of law, the Chancery Division being assigned whole topics, like mortgages and administration of estates, and given special statutory jurisdiction over matters like partnerships and copyrights. Its specialised machinery for accounting and for easier reference to the judge as problems arise justifies the attribution of such cases to the Division. Law and equity may therefore be said to be largely, if not dogmatically, assimilated in England as well.

A notable consequence of the protracted rivalry of the courts of law and equity has been the recognition of two parallel systems of interests in land, the legal and equitable titles often being vested respectively in trustees and beneficiaries. The Romans also recognised the difference between civil-law ownership at law and bonitary ownership in equity (alluded to above), but they denied any real effect to the former and gave all remedies to the latter.[6] In England the trustee had all his legal remedies against third parties in the court of law and the beneficiary equitable remedies against the trustee in Chancery. It may be significant that when English judges introduced equitable ideas, such as the right of a beneficiary of a trust of land to legal protection, into India they deliberately abstained from introducing the added complication of two kinds of title to the same property.

The special remedies introduced by equity to supplement the common law are similar to those of Roman law and no doubt inspired by them. Specific performance of contracts rather than the payment of damages is used in English equity, but, characteristically, only where land is in question. Specific relief in Chancery may partly rest on accident, that the Court of Chancery had no executive officials to levy judgment on property and thereby raise money to satisfy a money judgment, whereas it could threaten the defendant with imprisonment until he executed the necessary legal documents to perfect his opponent's title. The Chancellors also, no doubt, felt that payment of damages was no substitute for performance and did not really absolve the defendant's conscience. The injunction, by which the Chancery judge forbids the performance of some act, *e.g.*,

[6] See above, pp. 17–18.

publication of a book, or construction of a building, is also similar to the Roman interdicts. All specifically equitable remedies are discretionary, and are sometimes refused, leaving the plaintiff to pursue any common-law remedy he may possess. In some cases, *e.g.*, where he cannot prove loss, he may have no remedy at common law either.

Of the substantive law created by equity the device of the trust, which regulates the relations of outward and beneficial owners, has been the most fruitful. It derives from medieval continental practice, though continental lawyers now profess to find it incomprehensible. The Chancery imposed extremely high standards of probity and diligence on trustees in the interests of the beneficiaries, often infants or persons as yet unborn. The trust has been extended to cover other relations, that of executor and legatee, trustee-in-bankruptcy and creditors, and even adapted for the holding of land by voluntary unincorporated bodies and by religious groups outside the Anglican Church.

A general feature of all branches of English law is its materialistic approach. It is a practical system aiming at redressing material loss. It does not directly deal with abstractions like honour, prestige, general comfort. Actions would only lie for oral defamation of character where damage could be shown, and until modern times a woman could not complain of gossips who slandered her virtue unless she had lost a suitor or suffered in pocket. Our law of libel has reached a remarkable development compared with the law of most other countries, but even here the House of Lords has recently ruled that damages must normally be limited to demonstrable loss and not used to punish the defamer. In other branches the attitude was the same: you had a perfect right to sue a trespasser for a single harmless crossing of your land, but if you did you might find you lost your costs for wasting the court's time.

The suffering of damage is generally a pre-condition of a right to sue in other cases. This can have some curious results. Thus, if a testator instructs his solicitor to include a legacy for X in his will and the solicitor fails to do so, nothing can be done. The testator's estate has suffered no loss, quite the contrary. The legatee is not the solicitor's client, and has no claim against him. The court cannot add omitted provisions to the will. In the same way a trustee who makes a hazardous investment cannot be sued if the investment turns out to be profitable, since the trust fund has suffered no loss. The court might, of course, remove a trustee who was likely to repeat the experiment. If a young child is killed by someone's neglect the parents cannot generally recover more than a fairly small sum for loss of expectation of life by the child itself—the parents are not regarded as losing anything if the child is so young as to be an expense and not a source of income. In the law of intellectual property, such as patent and copyright, relief is only given for loss of profits or royalties through infringement of the rights. Interference of a non-commercial character cannot be remedied, except, in some cases, by a libel action. After the expiration of the period of copyright there is no remedy if the work is garbled, parodied, or mis-used. The court will not usually enquire into artistic standards; it will cover with copyright protection any work, tasteful or tasteless, provided the defendant has deemed it of sufficient value to pirate it for his own profit. Occasionally our law passes value judgments, as in deciding in the law of charitable trusts that a gift is for the advancement of education and for the public benefit, *e.g.*, if it promotes the study of Shakespeare's writings or Delius's music, but here the law is conferring privileges (*e.g.*, freedom from taxation) and not merely recognising rights.

Much of the high reputation of English law rests on the quality of its criminal justice. The criminal law has reflected the changing conditions of English society. Under the Anglo-Saxons it was marked by a mixture of piety and superstition; only wrongs of particularly ill omen, such as sacrilege, treason, and witchcraft, were regarded as calling for public intervention, and most of our familiar modern crimes were treated as private wrongs, or torts. The Normans brought a group of felonies which still form the backbone of the law; they were designed to protect the individual as well as the state, and were especially concerned with the security of property. Mercenary offences, such as larceny or robbery, have always remained the typical crimes. The criminal was the enemy of the property-owning order, and his punishment was exclusion from society by banishment or death. The turbulent and rapacious feudal classes were treated more indulgently; land, to which they constantly made violent claims, was incapable of being stolen in law, and an honest claim of right was a good defence to any charge of theft.

The victim of non-violent dishonesty was regarded as something of a fool; the law being designed for the protection of the vigilant, there was great reluctance to extend the categories of capital crime to wrongs less openly defiant of society. The English pragmatic approach was then illustrated by the enactment of large numbers of statutes to provide punishment for each new offence as it became common. An inordinate importance continued to be attached to the difference between stealing by the actual removal of a chattel from the owner's possession and other types of defrauding him of it or its value, for crimes were still regarded as breaches of the peace, acts of force, of which the physical movement of the chattel remained the vestige. A new law is under consideration which will finally exorcise this old ghost and put our law of dishonest dealings with property on a sensible basis.

Except for the irreparable case of death itself, which also had superstitious overtones, the law was tolerant of injuries to the person until the nineteenth century, and sentences for such crimes were often less severe than for property offences. The death sentence was much reduced in scope in the early nineteenth century, and capital punishment for murder has recently been abolished. Imprisonment became the typical sentence for serious offences. In recent years more respect is shown to the personality and more severe sentences passed for sexual offences and offences against young people.

Although the inflexible sentence of death for murder has now gone, and was always subject to the possibility of reprieve, it has been responsible for a great elaboration of the criminal law, which now survives the abolition of capital punishment. In the case of most other crimes, it is possible for the circumstances of the case to be taken into account in fixing sentence. In murder cases there was no such possibility, and therefore such circumstances had to be considered before conviction at the trial. Hence such pleas as self-defence and provocation, and that the accused had been of unsound mind, are common in homicide cases, and have to be put to juries. These issues protract proceedings and seem often the field of the doctor rather than the lawyer.

It has become axiomatic that criminal law is properly the preserve of the legislature (*nulla poena sine lege*: the penalty for a crime must be authorised by a statute), and that judges may not create new offences. Parliament in England has always been active in creating new offences less grave than the old capital crimes. These were termed misdemeanours to distinguish them from the capital felonies. This distinction now serves no useful purpose, was abolished in Canada some years ago, and has now been abolished in England. It is still disputed whether the courts retain residuary powers to create crimes in the public interest, as the legislature cannot anticipate every possible situation. In recent years the courts have assumed the role of protectors of public morals in England, and the debate here turns on one's whole attitude to the role of law in society. A happy feature of our day is the intense interest in crime, its causes, and its treatment. There is constant discussion of possible reforms of the law, for which society feels itself responsible, *e.g.*, the question of punitive sanctions for abortion or homosexual practices. Yet even the more liberal criminal law of today abounds in technicalities, based on its long history and on our very strict interpretation of penal statutes.

English law has been said to have grown up secreted in the interstices of procedure. In medieval times procedure seemed to dominate substantive law. There is a general similarity between civil and criminal procedure. The judge preserves a neutral position between the parties and decides the case on the relevant evidence put before him by the parties on their own initiative and at their own expense. Not only does he not need to seek other proofs for himself but if he had personal knowledge of the facts of the case he would have to disqualify himself from trying it at all. The conduct of the case is largely left to advocates (barristers in the superior courts), who examine and cross-examine witnesses as to the facts and present legal authorities to the court on matters of law. The judge only occasionally intervenes to give some legal ruling necessary for the further conduct of the case or to ask for clarification of some ambiguous statement. At the close of the case the judge will 'sum up' the facts and direct the jury, if any, on the law.

It will be noted that trial is oral and not based on depositions, though recent statutes allow some evidence to be given in the form of depositions, *e.g.*, where the witness has died or gone abroad before the trial.

In criminal proceedings there are some special rules, made to favour the accused, *e.g.*, he is not compelled to testify, he need not answer incriminating questions, and there is a heavy burden of proof on the prosecution. A certain inconsistency exists in cases where guilt is admitted. If the accused denies his guilt at the trial the courts treat with some suspicion any alleged confession made before trial which is presented as evidence of guilt. Yet if the accused pleads that he is guilty at the trial he is automatically convicted without the prosecution having to make out a case against him. In practice, a high proportion of persons accused of all but the gravest crimes do plead guilty. It is also common for a person convicted after trial to admit a number of other unprosecuted offences and ask for them to be taken into account, so that his sentence will 'clear the slate' for the future.

The use of juries has already been alluded to. Our jury system has been generally acclaimed, though attempts to transplant it to countries with very different traditions have not always proved successful. Its merits lie less in its historical origins than in its somewhat accidental adaptations. It first appears as a group of accusers informing the Crown of offences (the grand jury). Then it acts as a body of impartial witnesses with existing knowledge of the facts of the case (the petty jury). The jury's 'verdict' is thus a kind of evidence, which they swear to be true. But by a happy chance judges came to use these jurors to help try other cases, accepting their opinion of the truth or falsity of an accusation after they had heard the witnesses. It may be doubted whether twelve laymen could judge facts better than a professional trained judge, but the jury represented a wider group than the judges and were often more independent of pressure from the Crown, which could dismiss a judge. The range of persons eligible for jury duty has constantly been extended but is still not universal.

Juries are widely used for serious criminal cases and in many other cases where the accused is entitled to demand it. It is little used since 1933 in England for civil cases, though more widely used in the United States. The requirement of unanimity of the jurors may date back to the days when they presented a factual report to the royal judge, and may even have a ritualistic origin—since jury trial replaced trials by ordeal or battle, and neither of these could tolerate either ambiguity or dissent. Unanimity has generally been regarded as an additional safeguard for the accused, and in capital cases is also required by military law and by many foreign systems, *e.g.*, the French. A new system has just been introduced in England which allows a verdict by a majority of ten if unanimity is impossible. This change has been precipitated by suspicions that the odd juror has been corrupted or intimidated to prevent a unanimous verdict of guilty in some cases involving master criminals.

English law has never known the distinction between public and private law characteristic of continental systems. The Crown enjoyed many advantages in its relations with private citizens, *e.g.*, it could not be sued for the misdeeds of its servants (although they were themselves personally liable), and the rules of criminal procedure—in which the Crown was generally the prosecutor—tended to be weighted against the accused (though there again the general interest of society was involved). The balance has now tilted the other way. The Crown in England is liable to be sued for civil wrongs since a statute of 1947, and accused persons have many advantages. The rules that penal and revenue legislation are construed strictly suggests, if anything, that public interests are deferred to private interests. There is no defence of 'act of state' inside England. Unless a statute is promptly passed to confer extraordinary powers, officials can only hope for eventual indemnifying legislation for their excess of zeal. Even the police are technically, if somewhat unrealistically, regarded as private citizens keeping the Queen's peace, a general duty nominally imposed on all her subjects. Just as civil and criminal procedure have a similar appearance in England, so all strictly legal matters are referred to the ordinary courts and not special administrative courts. In some specialised fields this is no longer the case, but the tribunals which operate there seldom affect the citizens as vitally as the ordinary law. In 1958 a law was passed requiring minimum judicial regularity even of these tribunals, *e.g.*, reasons must be given for all decisions, and there must be an appeal on a point of law to the regular courts.

The comparative lawyer is struck by the contrast between the relatively few general articles of modern Codes concerning torts (civil wrongs arising independently of contract) and the luxuriant growth of torts at common law. This difference has not been fully studied but would seem due, at least to some extent, to the fragmentation of land-holdings into scattered parcels, with the result that one was often incommoded or interfered with by a neighbour, boundary disputes were common, and nuisances more noxious. Our torts also grew up on the fringe of the law of real property in land; the real actions gave remedies for interference with the right to possess and the newer tort actions remedies for interference with possession itself or the proper enjoyment of land. An exaggeration of the concept of breach of the king's peace, born of the desire to increase the royal court's jurisdiction, and therefore its revenues, made assaults and other violent harm to individuals readily actionable. Courts of cities and boroughs offered many remedies based on life in close propinquity, *e.g.*, for carelessness with fire, for interference with light and air, which the jealous royal courts soon themselves adopted. Early commerce and industry led to torts based on fraud and forgery. Then the Industrial Revolution created new sources of danger, stimulating the development of the group of torts now collectively described as 'negligence.' Railways and then motor vehicles added to the risks. Deliberate torts tended to fall behind, although theoretically still important, and the subject of a whole volume of the American *Restatement of the Law of Tort*.

In order to meet possible liability in tort many persons and corporations insure against such risks, and in the case of motoring accidents such insurance is compulsory in England for all motorists. The same social evils have led to State compensation and pensions for victims of accidents, independently of the question of fault. Many accident claims are also adjusted today between insurance companies without litigation. This may foretell the disappearance of most of our law of tort, much of which is concerned with personal injuries cases, in favour of some overall insurance system. It is an open question how far such a solution is desirable. Insurance cover might reduce vigilance to prevent accidents. On the other hand, the present system imposes a heavy burden on the plaintiff, who is generally required to prove the fault of the defendant, something best known to the defendant himself, by producing witnesses, and witnesses are notoriously reluctant to get involved in litigation arising out of accidents.

In some legal systems specialised contracts are dealt with in detail in Codes, *e.g.*, sale of goods, agency. English law also recognises a number of specialised contracts of this kind, governed by special rules. The main difference is that the scope of contract is unlimited in principle, and that the terms of these specialised contracts can be varied without destroying their juridical existence. This is because of the spasmodic growth of our law of contract. Everyday dealings were formerly coped with in local customary courts, and merchants, often foreigners, had courts of their own. The royal central courts were slow and expensive and unsuited to busy business men. They would enforce solemn long-term agreements if the parties' seals were affixed to them. The test of an enforceable contract was really evidential—proof of its existence to satisfy a suspicious court. There were no type contracts (*i.e.*, legally pre-determined contracts with invariable terms), as the seal made any contract binding. Our law seems to have distinguished very little between contracts and actual conveyances of goods in this sense, both being some kind of grant, but for land a more public ceremony was required. As many people made unsealed bargains and the local courts decayed, pressure on the royal courts to enforce other contracts grew. They finally decided in the seventeenth century to enforce informal agreements, provided there was 'consideration' for them, *i.e.*, they were bilateral or reciprocal in the obligations they imposed, each party performing or promising some performance. The presence of 'consideration' made all unsealed contracts valid and, again, there was no other requirement of substance. This prevented the growth of any formal exhaustive list (*numerus clausus*) of binding contracts. Gradually the courts began to imply various obligations in special recurring cases, landlord and tenant, vendor and purchaser, principal and agent, master and servant, suitable to the nature of the relationship. The only essentials which the parties had to agree upon were things like the price of goods, the duration of service, the identity of property. Between well-known contracts others could emerge, such as hire-purchase, which is neither a hire nor a sale but has some characteristics of both.

How real is the requirement of consent in our law of contract? The decision to contract is still taken freely, but the autonomy of the will may not cover the terms of the contract, which tend to become stereotyped and uniform. Policies of insurance and mortgages of land are examples in point. Then trades and professions recommend model contracts for general use, *e.g.*, for building contracts an architect drafted form may be incorporated and the Law Society supplies model conditions of sale of land which may be accepted as they stand or varied.

Public corporations use standard forms to which consumers of their services, *e.g.*, gas or electricity, must adhere. Railways have schedules of terms for transport and carriage. Freedom of contract is limited by statute in many other cases, terms being made unalterable, not from considerations of the inner necessity of the contract but in a very practical way to protect the economically weaker party, as in the case of the liability of a landlord for certain repairs to leased property. The common law will not enforce contracts which unduly restrain freedom of trading, *e.g.*, in cases where a trainee contracts not to practise his new skills within an excessively large radius of the man or firm that has trained him. Equity, possibly influenced by canon law, will not allow penalties in contracts to be enforced, even where both parties are experienced traders, though it is slower to interpret a term as a penalty (rather than as an estimate of damage) in such cases. In the law of mortgages equity is most vigilant to relieve the borrower from oppressive terms inserted in the interests of his creditor and to secure his recovery of the mortgaged property without undue difficulty and on fair terms.

In medieval times non-traders were governed by the general law of contract, and traders by city custom or general commercial custom. As we have seen, during the sixteenth and seventeenth centuries the common-law courts accepted these customs into the common law. At first only genuine merchants could claim to benefit from the customs, *e.g.*, by enforcing a bill of exchange against an acceptor who was not a party to the contract. Eventually commercial law came to apply to certain types of transactions rather than classes of men, and it is only exceptionally now that a distinction is drawn between classes of contractors. Commercial law was largely codified in England (as alluded to earlier) by statutes on the Sale of Goods (1893), Negotiable Instruments (1882), Partnership (1890), and Merchant Shipping (1894), but in any case (as we have already noted) much of this law is of foreign origin. The widespread use of private arbitration in recent years means that few new customs come before the courts, so that our sources of commercial law are drying up. Deliberate regulation by new statutes, after full discussion among lawyers, is likely to take the place of the former more spontaneous lay development.

Industrial and labour law are Cinderellas of the common law. Master and servant relations were long dealt with by magistrates under a quasi-criminal jurisdiction and few decisions were reported. The inequality of the parties made the classical law of contract unsuitable here, yet nothing took its place. Industrial pressure and strikes are common. There has been a recent *Contracts of Employment Act* (in 1963) aiming at more formal regulation, but the process is only beginning and the machinery of enforcement is still weak.

An important adaptation of English common law has occurred in space as well as time, in the growth of the law of the United States. The settlers there kept the basic principles of common law without much alteration. After some hesitation equity was also recognised as part of American law. In view of the declaratory theory of the common law, courts in the various American states could consider decisions of English courts given after the War of Independence, even though no longer bound by them. Old statutes were generally kept in force in America unless quite inconsistent with the traditions of the New World; thus most states repealed the English statutes on entails, since America has no aristocracy or hereditary titles of honour. English post-revolutionary statutes were often re-enacted in the United States or treated as declarations of law or equity in force in such states. The differences today between the private law of any given state and the mother country are not very great; indeed, the laws of the states differ widely in detail among themselves. A greater willingness to allow a third party to enforce a contract made with that object is found in America than Britain, probably because of the influence of continental jurists. In the law of tort a distinct wrong of invasion of privacy is recognised, *e.g.*, publishing scenes of private grief without permission, whereas in England such things can only be remedied occasionally and then by varying methods, *e.g.*, defamation actions or actions for breach of copyright. Trustees in the New World may charge for their services, whereas in England they may only charge for expenses unless the trust document otherwise provides.

An important characteristic of American law is the special protection of the family home from creditors under so-called Homestead Laws, many of them enacted in the middle west and west to protect citizens from credit institutions on the eastern seaboard. Widows in many states enjoy reserve rights over their deceased husband's property. In some states, mainly because of Spanish legal origins, husband and wife enjoy community rights over each other's assets. The American law of rights attached to land is more advanced than the English, *e.g.*, profitable rights may exist as property without being attached to any land ownership in the vicinity, as in the case of trading concessions in other peoples' stores. In one respect English law is now following the American lead. The Americans refuse in general to allow a passive easement, like a right of light, to be acquired by mere enjoyment, since they see no reason why your neighbour should feel moved to interfere with such light unless he wants to build for reasons of his own. English law failed to appreciate this, following the analogy of active easements, like rights of way, which are quite different, since no one tolerates other people crossing his land without some reason, and such crossing is a wrong, whereas use of light is not. Recent English legislation and case law are beginning to recognise this.

The American legal system differs from the English more strikingly in its institutions and procedure than in its substantive law. As the fifty states are sovereign in most internal matters, the judge is not bound by out-of-state decisions, although these are examined with respect. This increases his discretion, and he may also hear arguments from opposing counsel as to the relative merits of conflicting lines of cases from other jurisdictions. Judges are elected for fixed terms in many states, though others have systems of nomination like the English, and United States Supreme Court judges are appointed by the President with the approval of the Senate. Federal courts not only deal with reserved federal topics but also with appeals on the question of the constitutionality of federal or state legislation. In 'diversity of citizenship' cases (where litigants come from different states) Federal courts apply that state's law which they think applicable. There is a system of local state and city attorneys resembling the continental system of procurator and the Scots Procurator-Fiscal, but unlike anything in English law save the Queen's Proctor in divorce cases. There is a combined legal profession in America (as generally in the Commonwealth), and clients therefore have direct access to counsel, who may also see witnesses in advance of the hearing. Challenges of jurors are frequent in America and uncommon in England. The English judge sums up on the effect of the evidence, whereas in some American states the judge may only direct the jury on points of law. The rules of evidence differ slightly from the English, *e.g.*, doctors and priests and not only lawyers often enjoy privilege from disclosing communications to them. Whereas a successful party in England recovers his costs from the opponent, this does not happen in the United States. Moreover, it is lawful in America for a lawyer to make a 'contingent fee' arrangement with a client, *i.e.*, he gets part of any sums he recovers, but receives nothing in the event of failure.

It is obviously easier for English law to maintain consistency with Commonwealth countries and the United States in legal matters, in view of their common-law background. Many uniform laws passed in American states, for example, as well as case law, resemble English rules. Even here, however, gradual changes are occurring in commercial practice, in internal American disputes. International trade between the common-law countries still rests on general similarity of law, and it would be unfortunate if the result of a case concerning a voyage from London to New York were different depending on which forum you chose for your action.

It is a different matter when we consider how far common rules might apply in English and continental European systems. The widespread reception of Roman law on the Continent swept away many ideas it once shared with feudal England. Many differences now exist in such important topics as the sale of goods. When does ownership pass, at the time of contract or of delivery? Are penalties enforceable? Great efforts have been made to unify the law of sale of goods to eliminate such differences. In the meantime express stipulations may be used in a contract to set out the rules to be applied or to incorporate the law of some named country and thus remove doubt. English legislation has accepted a number of international conventions, *e.g.*, on the formalities of wills, where wide alternatives are provided, including English traditional forms. English rules of conflict of laws give full force to rights acquired under different systems. Our courts will enforce contracts made without consideration under a law which dispenses with it. Persons entitled to succession under foreign law will be aided by grants of probate or administration in England. Proxy marriages, once possible in England, are recognised if made abroad. Foreign adoptions are being recognised. Even the polygamous marriage, once anathema to our public policy, is receiving increasing recognition. English courts come into contact with foreign law more and more often. The Judicial Committee of the Privy Council used to hear appeals on French law from the Canadian Province of Quebec, Roman-Dutch law from South Africa and Ceylon, Hindu and Muhammadan law from India. The less-frequent appeals from, for example, Cyprus, Malta, and Mauritius gave no less exercise to the juridical mind. Though the Privy Council's jurisdiction has been contracted or modified (as in the case of appeals from Malaysia), the study of comparative law is growing and English lawyers are taking an increasing part in international congresses which discuss current problems. More attention is being paid in England to Scots law, neglected for many centuries but in advance of English law in some situations. The primal differences, however, between the common law and the Roman and other systems are so great that a wholesale assimilation is unlikely. An eclectic method may be followed on isolated points, but there are difficulties in borrowing some legal solution out of context from a foreign legal system organised on different principles. Yet the ingenuity with which English law has worked in elements of law from other systems must not be underestimated, and this process may now be accelerated.

As the legal system of governments in power, the 'public law' aspects of the common law deserve some attention, including rights against the state. The question whether the individual must have some inalienable minimum of rights immune from sovereign interference is a basic problem of political science. We live in an age when great stress is laid on 'fundamental rights,' 'human' or 'civil' rights, depending on the local terminology. In medieval times there seemed to be limits on the power of the authorities, such as the insistence on 'natural rights' supposedly conferred by a 'natural law' transcending human laws, and the very real force of custom, which even rulers hesitated to offend. Ultimately, however, most states came to claim absolute legislative power, whether they consisted of a Russian tsar or a popular assembly like the English Parliament after 1688. Elaborate codes of fundamental rights are often written into foreign Constitutions in modern times, but in practice these tend to be suspended with the Constitutions themselves where emergencies arise—to use a recent phrase, the umbrella is removed as soon as it starts to rain. No formal code of this kind exists in England, and *Magna Carta* (1215) and the *Bill of Rights* (1688) declare rather than create rights, and are in any case open to repeal at any time. In the United States, on the other hand, the Bill of Rights was adapted as amendments to the Federal Constitution and forms a permanent code by which federal and state laws are judged and sometimes rejected, *e.g.*, on such aspects as due process of law and sanctity of property. This American development was helped by the traditional restrictions on the legislative powers of the former colonial legislatures and the nature of the Constitution as a treaty between independent states, in return for which they yielded up much of their freedom. Even in America emergency powers are often needed, and the Supreme Court in Washington will uphold these if really vital in the national interest, *e.g.*, in time of war, but their reaction is slow and not easily predictable. In England there is no special classification of fundamental rights and no judicial review of the validity of legislation. The electorate has its remedy at the next election if it disapproves new laws. With the growth of the welfare state and the quest for social justice, entrenched economic positions have undergone some legal limitation, *e.g.*, by the wide use of compulsory purchase powers by public bodies. Cultural and political rights, however, are preserved, such as freedom of speech (subject only to the laws of libel), freedom of worship, the right to hold public meetings of a peaceful and orderly character, and to form associations with common objectives, like trade unions. Public opinion is the only guarantee of the preservation of these rights.

Since English law as a whole is an unwritten law, gleaned from the reasoning of numerous cases, it is not surprising that the English constitution is itself unwritten and to be gathered from separate statutes and precedents. This invests it with considerable flexibility without undermining its basic stability. The precise balance of forces in the community is not specified too closely, but is nevertheless recognisable at any moment of time. The English monarch was never absolute and took as his motto 'under God and the Law.' He certainly enjoyed more privileges in the Middle Ages than now, when his powers have been whittled away by the growth of Parliamentary government. Even the Revolution of 1688 left the monarch many prerogatives, but required them to be exercised on the advice of Ministers responsible to Parliament. For the Crown is the nearest thing we have to a state, and the only incorporated part of the machinery of government. The transition from personal ruler to corporate Crown has led to curious results. Thus our antiquated treason laws still assume physical attack on the person of the sovereign, and it requires unenlightening ingenuity to postulate such an end result of a conspiracy to overthrow a political party in power, the monarch being politically neutral. Again the monarch is personally Head of the established Church of England, crowned according to its rites, and required to subscribe to its doctrines. Yet she becomes a Presbyterian on crossing into the sister kingdom of Scotland, as that Church is there the official church, and in the period when the Crown of Hanover was united with that of Great Britain the monarch became a Lutheran on arrival in that territory. The indivisibility of the Crown was more rudely shaken by the growth of the self-governing Dominions. The Crown is there represented by a Governor-General appointed by the monarch, but in fact recommended by the government of that country. The monarch thus performs executive functions in each country on the advice of locally elected Ministers. During the recent short war between India and Pakistan the monarch was technically at war with herself. The present (at time of writing) Rhodesian crisis illustrates the problem acutely. The local white government in Rhodesia wished to remain part of the dominions of the British Crown, being themselves of British birth or extraction; the British government accepts the principle of majority (*i.e.*, native African) rule. They claim that the white Rhodesians are 'compassing the death of the Queen.' As Rhodesia's own law is Roman-Dutch, not common-law based, it is also claimed that the declaration of independence by Rhodesia is treason under that system too, on the assumption that the Queen is protected by it. South Africa, however, from whence Roman-Dutch law came to Rhodesia, is no longer in the British Commonwealth.

The English House of Lords at first represented the great landowners, who insisted on a share in legislative power corresponding to their material interest. The entrenched constitutional position of the House of Lords ceased in the course of time to reflect any corresponding economic interest in the country, but the chamber retains some delaying powers over legislation of a non-financial character. Some wish to abolish the House, others to strengthen it. At present a compromise system operates, under which distinguished men and women are made life peers, and many of the hereditary peers are discouraged from attending.

The House of Commons originated in the monarch's need to raise more funds than his traditional feudal exactions could supply. The representatives of the small landowners insisted on 'redress of grievances before supply,' which gave them a delaying power of their own, and petitions or 'bills' to redress grievances came to be presented by them. Local elections of representatives were held, to be sent to Westminster to negotiate with the Crown. In modern times the electoral franchise has been widely extended to all citizens of full age. The House of Commons now meets regularly to discuss the conduct of the government and to vote the necessary public funds. It established its legislative supremacy by 1688 and its executive authority during the eighteenth century; the Crown now acts on the advice of Ministers chosen from members of Parliament, mainly from the House of Commons, by the Prime Minister, who leads the majority party in the House for the time being. He also initiates legislation. Elevation to the House of Lords is a power of the Crown exercised on the Prime Minister's advice. Judges of the Supreme Court of Judicature are also appointed by the Crown on the advice of the Prime Minister or of the Lord Chancellor in consultation with him.

In British Dominions there are written Constitutions which embody English Parliamentary institutions, in some cases with a further division into central and local authority, as in the Dominions and Provinces in Canada, the Commonwealth and States in Australia, and the Union and States in India. In the United States of America there are also separate federal and state systems, legislative, executive, and judicial. The legislatures are elective, on various bases, but the executive government is not carried on by members of the Federal Congress or state legislatures but by Presidents and Governors separately elected, choosing their executives from outside the legislatures. The President governs but cannot legislate or raise taxes, and the Supreme Court cannot enforce its own decisions without executive help. This separation of powers requires special expertise for its successful operation.

Public control of the executive is achieved in the United States, for example, by electing a President every four years, and similar arrangements exist in the individual states. The powers of the various branches of government are also laid down in Constitutions which are difficult to amend. In Britain itself Parliament cannot last for more than five years, but even this provision could presumably be repealed by Parliament and can be suspended in time of war or other emergency. The lifeblood of our constitution consists of a number of rather vague and changing 'conventions.' It is an accepted convention that the monarch appoints as Prime Minister the person approved as leader by the party with the largest number of members in the House of Commons or at least someone who can command a majority vote in that chamber. It is a convention that he must resign if his government is defeated on a vote of confidence there. It has become a modern convention that the Prime Minister should not be a member of the House of Lords; this led to a new law permitting peerages to be surrendered and to surrenders of inherited peerages by a number of aspirants to political leadership. It is a convention that the Prime Minister selects his Ministers from among members of either house, that lay peers should not participate in the judicial activities of the House of Lords, that Parliament should not discuss or interfere with a case proceeding in a court of law, and that the monarch should not appear in any court. Some conventions are now of doubtful strength; thus it used to be a convention that the Speaker of the House of Commons should not be opposed at an election, but this is no longer the case.

The British Parliament and similar legislative bodies enjoy privileges of many kinds. No action can be brought for anything said or done in Parliament, on the ground that the public interest requires frank discussion and appropriate action. Any attempt to influence Parliament improperly is a contempt, as is an attack on Parliamentary institutions or members if likely to interfere with its work. Historically these privileges originated in the concept that Parliament was a court of law. Claims to privilege sometimes lead to a collision with the courts, but Parliament is generally accepted as the sole judge of its own privileges. Imperial statutes extended the customary privileges of the House of Commons to the various Dominion legislatures. The Indian Constitution followed the example of the British in this respect. Similar provisions exist in the United States, where 'contempt of Congress' is a serious accusation. Judicial courts also enjoy similar privileges, *e.g.*, where prejudicial comment is made on pending cases or improper pressure is brought to bear on judges, juries, parties, or witnesses. The independence of the judiciary is axiomatic in the common-law system and must be kept inviolate.

In sum, English law and its daughter and companion common-law systems can be charged with several serious deficiencies in modern times, though they must be credited with considerable merits. The common-law system may be guilty of excessive technicality, much of it no longer justified by present-day conditions. The adversary system, treating a trial as a contest of parties, limits the power of the court to arrive at the objective truth of a case, and the doctrine of precedent makes us slaves of the past and not infrequently compels judges to give legal rulings of which they openly disapprove. A still graver accusation is the gulf between the objectives of our public and private law. Our society accepts, in the political and economic planes, the principle of sharing our neighbour's burdens and enshrines it in voluminous legislation, in spite of the predominantly secular character of our law. Yet it insists on a form of private litigation which is expensive and time-wasting, and continues to rely on the slow and uncertain process of law-making by decisions of judges in casual lawsuits promoted by individuals.

On the other hand, it may be claimed in favour of our legal order that, subject to the general acceptance of the principle of bearing one's neighbour's burdens, the individual's freedom from coercion and from the corrupt and dictatorial abuse of power by the state or its officials is firmly maintained under our traditions. The liberty of the Englishman sometimes obstructs the general good and may be regarded as a costly luxury in our society, but our law does ensure that that liberty remains a reality.

BIBLIOGRAPHY

THERE are few works mainly devoted to the place of the common law within the world's legal systems, although this aspect is touched on by some common-law jurists, like the late Roscoe Pound in the United States. Foreign jurists, like H. Lévy-Ullmann and René David have also taken a great interest in this subject. General aspects of the history and sources of English law may be found in:

A. K. R. Kiralfy, *The English Legal System*, 4th edn. (London, Sweet and Maxwell, 1967).

R. J. Walker and M. Walker, *The English Legal System* (London, Butterworths, 1967).

The classic account of the sources of English law is:

Sir C. K. Allen, *Law in the Making*, 7th ed. (Oxford University Press, 1964).

Histories of English law include:

H. Potter, *Historical Introduction to English Law*, 4th edn. (London, Sweet and Maxwell, 1958).

T. F. T. Plucknett, *Concise History of the Common Law*, 5th edn. (London, Butterworths, 1956).

A. Harding, *Social History of English Law* (London, Penguin, 1966).

For a synopsis of the rules of law see:

O. Hood Phillips, *A First Book of English Law*, 5th edn. (London, Sweet and Maxwell, 1965).

INDEX